SUICIDE SQUAD

SUICIDE SQUAD

The Inside Story of a Football Firm

Andrew Porter

MILO BOOKS

Published in paperback in August 2005 by Milo Books

ISBN 1 903854 46 6

Typeset by Avon DataSet Ltd,
Bidford on Avon, Warwickshire, B50 4JH

Printed and bound in Great Britain by
Cox & Wyman Ltd, Reading, Berkshire.

MILO BOOKS LTD
The Old Weighbridge
Station Road
Wrea Green
Lancs PR4 2PH
info@milobooks.com

Contents

	Prologue	vii
1	Pilgrimage to the Longside	1
2	The Big Boys	15
3	Cans and Vans	23
4	Every Mother's Son	35
5	Tooth and Nail	51
6	Local Derbies	66
7	The Suicide Squad	77
8	England Expects	99
9	Welcome to Barlinnie	122
10	Turkish Delight	137
11	Czech Mates	159
12	The Black Army	174
13	Domestic Duties	203
14	Banned for Life	216
15	Life's A Riot	239
16	Gunning for Trouble	253
17	The End of the Road	272
18	Suicide Memories	288
19	Suicide Youth Squad	310

PROLOGUE

LIKE many boys born in 1966, the year of England's one and only World Cup victory, I was keen on football and a fan of Subbuteo, the soccer board game. But our version was different. When we set up the ground and terraces, the players were very much secondary. We concentrated on the terraces. My Subbuteo ground had covered ends, an away terrace, a home terrace, segregation fences, no-man's land, perimeter fences, police, police horses, stretcher bearers and films crews. We all had hundreds of fans but most were worthless and sitting down: grandads, old women, posers and lads chanting with their arms in the air. They were not what we needed. I swelled my numbers when travelling away to other lads' houses with toy soldiers – German, American, English, Russian and Napoleonic – and placed them in the away end. It took hours to set it all up and a matter of seconds to destroy it. When the first goal went in there was a pitch invasion. It went off.

I ask you, if it wasn't supposed to happen, why did Subbuteo make policemen and horses, St. John Ambulance teams, stretcher bearers and fences?

* * *

I've read books about hooligans. Some are good, some are crap. This is my story, from being a young lad loving to watch violence to a man heavily into joining in the violence. This isn't a book where Burnley never get done, or where I never get done; this is a book of truth, of how it really was, and still is. We did this, we did that, we came unstuck. Let's face it, everyone has an off-day. Teams bringing hundreds of lads when you're expecting fuck-all, small clubs bringing most of their town to do you – it's good to take a big scalp and get a reputation. I've fought against big club firms and small club firms. The numbers usually decide who wins but sometimes it boils down to the bollocks that the people around you have. We've done bigger mobs than ours and been done by smaller mobs. No-one is invincible.

I started at the bottom, watching and wanting to be involved, always being there when trouble started. When it did it was the best feeling in the world, it was electric, the roar of people for their town or city. I had pride in my heart, for me Burnley were the best, the hardest. It wasn't long before I got noticed by the older lads and went from being a face in the crowd to a lad people wanted to talk to. Reputations quickly blossom in the hooligan business and I was soon one of the main faces. This is a journey from a time when there was no mob in Burnley through to the Suicide Squad, from England into Europe, from football to race riots and from mayhem to murder.

Perhaps, when I've done, you'll understand.

CHAPTER ONE

PILGRIMAGE TO THE LONGSIDE

THE COLD, FIZZY cider hit the back of my throat and soaked my taste buds like nothing I'd ever drunk. Four or five long swigs later and my head was already beginning to fuzz. I look at the older lads with a goofy grin. A couple more gulps from the bottle, and I was staggering. Nine years old, and I was pissed.

That's the way it was where I come from. I was born in Burnley, a Lancashire town with a population of about 80,000, and shared a terraced house with my mum, dad and brother, Ade. Burnley Wood, the area where we lived, was a close-knit community – until the smackheads took over – full of rows and rows of terraces. Everybody knew each other.

Like Ade, most of my friends were two years older than me; it seemed like all the Burnley Wood mothers had kids in the same year. At Burnley Wood Primary School, most of my friends were in the big yard while I was confined to the small yard with the kids my age. When my brother got bored I would get thrown into a circle of bodies where a bigger boy was waiting.

"Right, you've got to fight him."

No matter how big they were, I never refused. Most of the

fights were broken up by the teachers and I'd be dragged before the headmaster. It was all part of growing up. Due to the age difference, most of my friends left for secondary school and made more mates and got new ideas. They all started drinking cider, getting pissed on the recreation ground steps. It didn't take them long to start feeding me the apple juice.

As I got older, I drank cider regularly. There was a pop factory at the end of my street where lorries loaded up with soft drinks, boxes of crisps and crates of cider. The drivers would leave their vehicles unattended and it meant easy pickings for us. We found out which café they used for breakfast and would get out of bed early, go to the café and help ourselves to a couple of crates of cider. We hid them in the railway embankment, went to school to get our attendance mark, then walked back to our stash. We also knew the times of every beer drop to the pubs in our area and managed to snaffle a fair few crates of Autumn Gold.

Some of the lads started following teams like Newcastle, Derby, Liverpool, QPR, Chelsea and Wolves, but I was always Burnley, and the rest were at heart. We all fought side by side in the name of Burnley. The scene for us was punk rock, Sham, Upstarts, Sex Pistols and UK Subs. My mum used to work in the local working men's club where new up and coming punk bands would play and got me a glass collecting job so I was able to watch the bands.

My first experience of court was when I was fourteen. One of the lads had been arrested for smashing an Asian shop window. Two police cars turned up, one officer in each, but my mate wasn't going quietly so both officers had to take him in one car, leaving the other behind. Three of us smashed it to pieces in front of onlookers. It wasn't long before we were down Burnley police station with our parents. In juvenile court we got a severe bollocking and a £45 fine which I had to pay off at £1.50 a week.

The drug scene hadn't yet hit Burnley. We were only interested in beer, football and the odd bag of glue. I left school at fifteen with seven CSEs. My mate Mick Nick got me a job at a shoe factory in Waterfoot, a small village six miles out of Burnley, and my first wage was £38. I felt rich. I could give my mother board money and afford to watch Burnley away. When the older lads started drinking in pubs, I used to sneak in. They would buy me beers and the landlords got used to seeing me and turned a blind eye. In some pubs I could even buy my own beer. On Saturday mornings when Burnley were at home we would get a bottle of cider each and head into town to see if any away fans had turned up. We waited around for the battles to begin, watching lads kick the fuck out of each other. That's where I wanted to be, right in the middle of it.

I lived five minutes' walk away from Turf Moor and could see the floodlights from my house. Every match day fans walked past my front door, and I could hear the roar of the crowd and the songs when I was playing in the yard or on the back street or spare ground round the back. I could always tell when they scored. So before I ever went on the Turf, I was listening to the crowd and guessing the score from the roars. I figured if I got it wrong from the noise, the other team must have brought a lot of fans.

I cannot remember who we played the first time I went to a game and don't even know if we scored. I was very little and just stood with my mate, Kevin Waring, not seeing much but hearing a lot of noise. Then I got to the front of the Bee Hole end, up against the barrier that stopped you from falling onto the pitch, and looked in wonder at the different sections of the ground. The Cricket Field stand was straight across behind the other goal, the brand new Bob Lord stand was to my left and people were in their seats, but my eyes were always pulled to my right to the massive Longside stand. It seemed huge, with a roof on and one fence down the middle. The away fans were on the left side of the fence and on the right hand side stood the Burnley fans, packed in like refugees. You could walk from the Bee Hole stand all the way round to the fence. My eyes were always fixed on the fence and the two sets of fans on either side of it, their arms in the air pointing at each other, singing, chanting, swaying down in a wave effect. I was fascinated. The songs came out loud and clear, "You're going home in a Red Cross ambulance; you're gonna get your fucking heads kicked in."

Sometimes big gaps would open up at the top corner of the fence, you would see people running, then standing in the middle and there would be a big sway to engulf them, police would run in, helmets would go flying in the air and would usually find their way to the bottom of the terrace and be thrown onto the pitch. Then a big chant would go up, "Burnley Aggro." It was great; I knew that was where I wanted to be.

The first time I was caught in the middle I was coming back from a pie stand at half-time up at a corner of the Bee Hole where it meets the Longside. I'd just got my pie when all of a sudden I was in the middle of a big gap at the top of the terrace. Voices were shouting, "Come on you northern wankers," or something similar, people ran past, knocking into me, fists and feet were flying and I was trying to hold on to my pie. Someone pulled a knife out and I was away, head down. All I could see were people's legs, shoes and boots. Then I came to a dead stop and found myself sitting on the floor, looking at the pie in my lap. I became aware of a bubble on my head, swelling. I touched it and felt sticky blood and then men picked me up.

"You want to watch where you're going son. Are you alright? It's a nasty bump on your head."

"Yeah, I'll be alright."

With a smile on my face, I tucked into my pie (Burnley's are the best pies in the world). In my haste I had run with my head down straight into a crash barrier and ended up nearly knocked out and on my arse, but I couldn't wait to get to school and tell all my mates about it.

Gradually, I started moving away from Kev and his dad, who took us both, but still met up with them at the end of the game to walk home. I was steadily moving game by game towards the Longside. One game I had to struggle to get on was Man U; the Red Army was descending on Burnley and it took a week of getting round my mum, going shopping with her the week before to get permission. You see, Man U had been all over the news after rioting at Norwich and other places.

Shops in Burnley boarded up their windows in preparation for the invasion. Walking to the ground I couldn't believe my eyes. Red scarves were all over, there was no claret and blue except for my own woolly scarf wrapped around my wrist. I got into the Bee Hole end expecting to see the Burnley fans standing against the fence, protecting their side and annoying the opposition. But there weren't any, it was just a sea of red and white. It sickened me and I thought, I will never be like those bottleless cunts, changing teams and going with the numbers. Man U that day made Turf Moor their own ground. I didn't hear one Burnley song and I thought to myself, never again.

My mum started working Saturday afternoons for Burnley FC. She'd work in the club shop from twelve until three, then help run a pie stand at the far corner of the Bee Hole end. The time had come when I could walk to the games on my own, so that enabled me to sniff around a bit before and after the game. I would get to the club shop around one o'clock and would be allowed to go through the shop and into the ground free of charge, no queuing up. Most of the time the ground was empty and I could stand where I wanted: top, middle, bottom or the Longside up against the fence, at least until the big lads started coming in. When I got in early I used to go to the top of the Longside and walk out of the back where you could see the away fans walking down a wide path, which led from Belvedere Road past the Cricket Field and cricket club and to their turnstiles. The path from the road to the turnstiles was about 100 yards long with a concrete barrier on one side, beside a housing estate, and a wire fence on the other, looking on to the cricket pitch. I would go to the top of the Longside and sit myself on the crash barrier; it put your height up another two feet. The only trouble was, if anybody behind you pushed you off, you'd go onto the floor and your position was lost.

As it got nearer to kick-off, more and more people would congregate there, and then the songs would start from both sides of the wall, with the bricks following shortly after that. Missiles came from every direction. You'd see bricks bouncing off people's heads all around you. Then the police would show up and push you onto the terrace into the crescendo of noise and you'd be next to the fence walking to the bottom of the Longside, away fans on the other side screaming and spitting at you. Plenty of times I've walked down that fence to the bottom with a face full of green gob, but it would soon wipe off on your sleeve.

My dress for the Turf was a Wrangler jacket with Burnley badges all over it, a silk scarf on each wrist, and a woolly scarf round my neck. I looked like a claret and blue Christmas tree. I had progressed to the Longside, not to the top or the bottom but halfway along to the halfway line. It was just enough away to get caught in an occasional sway if it was a packed house but out of the way of the missiles that would be flying over the fence for ninety minutes. I saw people led onto the pitch and the St John Ambulance men run up to them and take them to the dugouts in front of the Longside. Then they would come back out with big white bandages wrapped around their heads. Some would be put on stretchers and be carried around the pitch. Others got escorted, walking always to the sound of, "Bye-bye, bye-bye." The ones who came out of the dugout back onto the terrace were heroes for the day, standing proud in the middle of the lads, big smiles on their faces, giving it the big 'un. The big white bandage on their heads might be slowly turning red but who cared about that? Nobody was making you leave your own terrace.

The missile throwing became so bad that, after an Oldham fan was hit in the head with a dart, the club put mesh on the top of the Longside from the top of the fence to the roof. The Oldham lad was pictured in the daily papers, standing in front of the Longside with a dart sticking out of his fore-head. It was the start of the introduction of "No Man's Land", plus the police had started to search everyone entering Turf Moor and taking the laces out of people's boots. As far as I know it was the first ground in the country to employ these tactics.

When a big fight occurred on the Turf you couldn't wait to go to school and tell your mates – where you were, if you were involved, who had won. We even had our own terrace fights in the playground at Burnley Wood School, just four terrace blocks away from my home. In our playground we had a shelter where you'd go if there was a bit of rain, and on the opposite side of the yard was a rockery. We would get all the lads together and split into two groups, one on the rockery, one under the shelter, and then we would go to it and try to take each other's bit of land. It was all good fun until the teachers came out to stop it.

Before long I grew out of the playground stuff and moved onto the terraces. Spurs, who seemed to have best away support of any London club in the Seventies, packed the away stand. A big gap opened up where the Longside meets the Bee Hole. I climbed up on the crash barriers but couldn't see anything so I decided to go up the terrace and have a proper look. I pushed myself through all the bodies, and then suddenly I was in the opening. Tottenham fans were in front of me, staring at me, arms outstretched, palms facing me. I couldn't go back because people were pushing each other into the gap. Then the Tottenham fans seemed to come rushing at me, just me. Then I realised that the Burnley lads further up the terrace had swayed down on them. Everyone was on me, and down I went on the floor with bodies all around. I was on my hands and knees trying to get out of the melee, looking for gaps to crawl through. I spotted one and started to crawl fast but a foot caught me straight in the stomach. I thought, I'm winded but I can't stay here. So I kept going until I was in relative safety, then rolled up in a ball and waited for my lungs to start again. That was the first (but not the last) kicking I took at a football match.

The final whistle went and I went out onto Brunshaw Road, where the Bee Hole, Longside, Bob Lord and the Cricket Field stands all empty out onto. The away fans are let out at the opposite end of the ground. I had just crossed Brunshaw Road by a wall with a fence when, in front of old people's houses, a big roar went up.

"They're here!"

I jumped up on the top of the wall, well above head height of everyone else and was able to see everything. I don't know how the Tottenham fans got round so fast. There were literally thousands of people fighting and police running everywhere. It seemed to go on for ages. Finally the police horses separated the two sets of fans; the police dogs were going mad in the middle of the road. But then the two sides ran at each other across the road. I jumped down off the wall and followed the two groups until they got to the crossroads at the Wellington Pub, where Brunshaw Road meets Belvedere Road. Police pushed the Tottenham fans up to their coaches and the train station. I walked home happy, covered in shit from the floor plus carrying bruises all over, but what a tale I had to tell at school!

As the seasons went by I progressed to the top of the Longside. I had left junior school and started at Townley High, still only five minutes away from my house. My going to and from Turf Moor took a lot longer, as I was going into Burnley town centre before and after the game, taking in the bus and train stations on my way home.

My first derby game against Blackburn, or as everyone I know calls them, Bastard Rovers, was on Boxing Day. The first thing I noticed was the sense of pure hatred. Every lunatic I knew seemed to be on the Turf and the ground was packed: 28,000 people. I was on the top of the Longside near the fence, singing, "We hate Bastards," and "My old man is a Burnley fan, Burnley fans never run away." Bricks were flying everywhere, hitting the fence, and Burnley fans were trying to entice the police into the swaying crowd. Then Blackburn scored and all eyes went to the Bee Hole end to see if any arms went up in the air or any scarves waved. Some were spotted, prompting an exodus from the Longside as lines of lads flowed into the Bee Hole end looking for away fans. Sporadic fighting broke out all over the place, and Rovers' fans soon got kicked out. Then one lad ran onto the pitch waving a Blackburn scarf. All the Blackburn fans were cheering, clapping and singing to him, but we knew who it was. Norman Jones, one of the top Burnley lads, he had taken the scarf off someone. A Blackburn player went up to him thinking he was a Rovers fan, trying to tell him in a pally way to leave the pitch, but Norman ran at him, threw the scarf on the floor and started jumping on it, goading him to fight. We all went mad. "There's only one Norman Jones," went the chorus as the police led him round the pitch. I think we got beat 3–2, but you won't see a lot of football scores in these pages. It wasn't really why I went.

My first away game, against the Bastards, was on Easter

Monday. One of my best mates, Hosker, a staunch Man City fan, said his dad would take us in his car. My mum took a bit of persuading but it was hard for her to say no in front of my mate, so off to Bastards we went. We walked the last stretch to the ground and went under the canal. There seemed to be a gang on every corner and I was scared. Lads on top of the bridge were throwing bricks, while on the other side of the bridge was a big fairground and there seemed to be fighting everywhere. Hosker and I put our heads down and walked as fast as we could, while people passed us with bust noses and bleeding heads.

We got to the ground safely and went into the away (Darwen) end. Looking to my right I could see all the Blackburn lot in the Riverside and straight across from us was another Blackburn end. Fighting soon broke out and gaps were appearing everywhere. Blackburn pushed Burnley down to the pitch, then a scuffle broke out on the Riverside but the numbers always seemed to push the Burnley fans onto the pitch. Then there was a roar behind us and a police helmet went up in the air. Police were running, truncheons drawn, to rescue their colleague. The trouble went on for the full ninety minutes.

At the end of the game I looked at the gates with apprehension, not knowing what lay on the other side. Suddenly, they opened, there was a big roar and everyone moved on. You had to go with the flow of the crowd. Out onto Blackburn Road we went with dogs, police and horses all around us, pushing us onto the pavement; Blackburn on one side, us on the other. There was singing, shouting and bricks flying. The fairground was coming up on our left, Blackburn on our right. As soon as we got to the fairground bricks were coming from both sides. There seemed to be no police on the fairground side, only in the middle of the road separating each set of fans. There was a big rush onto the fair, with people running between stalls fighting and bodies left on the ground. Lads ran to the end of the fairground, cut in front of the escort and ran across the road. That was it, the escort was broken.

Everyone went across the road. Blackburn were standing and the sides met in the middle of the road. Fists, feet, everything went. There were police horses running through people like they weren't even there, dogs biting anything that came within distance of their teeth. Shouts went up, "Come on, over here." I was scared, I was pumped up, and I was fucking loving it.

I bumped into my mate Lee Turner, whose arm was bleeding with a nasty slash.

"What the fuck happened to you?"

"A police horse just ran past, the stirrup slashed me. How've you got here?"

"Hosker's dad."

"Me and a few mates jumped on the special train for fuck all, fucking great day. Got off at Mill Hill, got escorted to the ground, and there was kicking off all over."

He was a bit younger than me and I was proper envious, but Lee and me would get into a lot of scraps in later life. Fighting was still all around us while we talked. The police dogs and horses were pushing us down to a fork in the road. We got pushed towards Mill Hill and Blackburn were pushed the other way towards their town centre. Hosker's dad had parked the car on the side street going into Mill Hill, so when the police had separated the two sets of fans and a bit of order was restored, we left the escort and got into the car.

"You alright lads?" asked Hosker's dad.

"Yeah," we said, with big smiles.

Back in Burnley we went straight up to the Rec to wait for Lee and the rest of the lads to get back on the train to fill us in on any more trouble. He said the train had been bricked on the way out of Blackburn, with a lot of windows put through, but this turned out to be a regular thing through Bastard country.

Bury is twelve miles from Burnley, just a hop and a skip on a bus. It claims to be the home of the black pudding but is not exactly famous for anything else. Who had heard of Bury fighting? Not me. So Mick Nick and I decided to get the bus, only a few bob. There were about twenty older Burnley lads, while we were only thirteen. The older lads were laughing and joking and the bus stopped at the old mill town of Rawtenstall, where a few more Burnley lads got on. They seemed to know those already on the bus, and the conversation soon got round to fighting and drinking. Mick and I just kept to ourselves. They didn't take notice of us, but they seemed to talk a good fight.

The bus stopped in Bury bus station and all the lads headed across to the nearest pub. Mick and I got in and just mooched about, keeping on the outskirts of the group. Finally we were noticed; a few lads came over and asked where in Burnley we were from. "Burnley Wood," we told them. They asked if we knew a few people and we did, we knew everyone up the Wood. "You're a bit young to be coming on the bus but you'll be alright with us," said one. Mick, being tall, got us a beer to share and we found a corner.

After an hour nothing was happening so the lads decided to walk to the ground. We walked through the bus station onto the main road. Everything seemed fine, and then the older lads started singing. Then all of a sudden a few lads appeared behind us. Then some more walked round the next corner in front of us. I heard, "Come on Burnley," then the singing stopped. The lads in front and back just ran into us: we were ambushed. The Burnley lads tried to fight but they were outnumbered and surprised and split, leaving mates behind on the ground getting a kicking. Yet we were left alone until the fighting had stopped. It was only when they had stopped kicking the unlucky ones on the floor and we started to walk that one of the Bury lads came over.

"There's two here," he shouted.

"Leave them, they're only kids," said another.

So a slap on the head was sufficient for us and off we trotted to the ground.

After the game I lost Mick, and stood outside the ground waiting to join the Burnley fans to walk to the bus station, but no one seemed to be heading that way. I decided I must have missed the ones who came by bus so started walking to the bus station mingled in with the Bury fans. When I got there, there was not a Burnley fan in sight, only loads of Bury fans, all with their eyes on the Burnley bus stop. I was in the middle of them, hearing them talk.

"Where are they? They came on the bus, fucking wankers!"

I kept my head down, not making conversation or eye contact, just waiting at any old bus stop until, finally, the Burnley bus came in. There was a shout at the end of the station, "They're here," and lads came running past me but I couldn't go to the bus yet, the doors weren't open. Lads started walking back, false alarm. The doors opened up and I started to edge a bit closer ready for a dash. Never a copper around when you want one. Another yell, "Come on, I can hear dogs barking." That was it; I dashed to the bus. Just as I was getting on there was a shout, "You Burnley cunt," and I got volleyed up the arse and sent to the top steps on the bus.

While nursing a sore arse upstairs I saw Burnley fans being escorted through the bus station, then making a run through the police dogs into the Bury fans. The Bury didn't put up much resistance. What a difference five minutes makes. I looked down from the bus to see Burnley fans talking, smiling, and walking around like they owned the bus station. Then they came on to the bus in their own time, reliving the battle that they'd had. And there was me, sore arse and pissed off, but I was on a learning curve and I was a quick learner. I had to be for the battles to come.

CHAPTER TWO

THE BIG BOYS

Newcastle, 1977

Boxing Day, and I was walking down to the Turf. You always got big crowds on Boxing Day, and I knew the Geordies would bring hordes. I was a bit early, and thought I'd have a walk around the ground. My mum was working in the club shop, so there would be no queuing up for me. At the corner of the ground is the Wellington pub, usually full of Burnley fans. It's the start of Yorkshire Street where there are two clubs and three pubs towards Burnley town centre, under the canal bridge (we call it the culvert). These pubs are usually full of Burnley fans but all I could see was black and white. As I walked past the Wellington, the window smashed and glass sprayed all over me. I heard glasses and furniture breaking. Then the front door burst open and lads in black and white tops came running out, some with cut heads. More glasses followed, crashing on the door and the side wall.

I kept walking. Newcastle were everywhere, and they all seemed like giants to me: over six feet tall, big bellies, all with Newcastle tops on. When I reached the Brickmaker's, more than sixty lads came running out. I didn't know who they were but they were all wearing pyjamas! They started to walk toward the Wellington; I could hear them saying Burnley have done this and that. They got to the Wellington only to be confronted by a line of police, who pushed them up Leyland Road towards the ground entrance.

The Newcastle end was packed. I made my way to the top of the Longside. The pyjama boys had made their way in. The usual banter was taking place and the Newcastle fans started to fight with the police. They got the upper hand, pushed the police out of the away end, and then turned to us, hurling bricks, bottles, beer cans, anything they could get their hands on over the fence. Then they started to kick and pull at the fence, pulling the bars apart so that they could squeeze through and get into no-man's land, the gap between the home and away fans. One or two ran into no-man's land but then ran back. Seeing this, the police made a line at the bottom of the Longside but they were being pelted by missiles. The Geordies were seriously damaging the fence so the police sent dogs into no-man's land and the Newcastle lads quickly tried to get back through the gaps they had made. The police line at the bottom entered the gap with truncheons drawn, whacking at the holes in the fence to close the gaps. Meanwhile, another group of police emerged from the top entrance of the Longside and charged into the Geordies with truncheons to push them down and away from the fence. After five minutes of mayhem, order was restored with a line of police either side of the away fans' fence, keeping them away from it. Little did anyone know, but this was just a warm-up for the big one.

The game finished and I made my way out onto Brunshaw Road and walked with the mob up to the Wellington. All the Burnley fans stopped at the junction of Yorkshire Street and Brunshaw Road to wait for the Geordies to make their way to the Fulledge car park. They didn't have to wait long. The roar went up and all the fans charged together. Police in the middle didn't have a chance of separating them and fighting went on for a good ten minutes. I don't know who had the best of it but a new Burnley song was started that day: "The Geordies ran away, we will fight for ever more because of Boxing Day."

Their hated rivals, Sunderland, visited us for an FA Cup tie. I got in the ground early, on my usual spot in the Longside, and saw the Turf fill up fast. The Sunderland end was packed with an hour to kick-off. All of the stands were full but I noticed the Bee Hole end had an unusual red and white tint at the edges. Burnley's team came on to the roar of their fans but there was a second roar at the corner of the Longside and Bee Hole end. Thousands of Sunderland supporters in the Bee Hole end were trying to force their way onto the Longside but the Burnley were pushing them back. It was going to be a long ninety minutes. All the lads from the top corner of the fence where I was were needed to stem the tide. "You'll never take the Longside" was heard again and again as sway after sway was repeated into the Bee Hole end. We were fighting for our stand. The police moved in to form a line between the two sets of fans but it was broken on numerous occasions. Sunderland tried different tactics, sneaking round the police line, coming from above us, below us and straight through the middle, but we held firm. They weren't taking our end. For me, at the age of twelve, the Longside was my pride and joy.

Yet both this and the Newcastle game were merely warm-ups for the main event.

Celtic, Anglo-Scottish Cup, 1978

This was the Big One or, at least, the first Big One. It was the holidays and I had just come back from camping with my mates, Mick Nick and Hosker. We got some food together and sleeping bags and tents and went up to Hurstwood Reservoir. It pissed down non-stop but we still had a laugh. Mick Nick nearly killed us putting the burner on in the tent; he fell asleep and knocked it over and set his sleeping bag on fire but, as it was raining heavily, no real harm was done. Our parents came to check on us in the middle of the night and I still don't know how they found us, it was pitch black and still raining. They wanted us to go home with them but we were having none of it. "We will be back for the match on Tuesday, OK?" was our response. We couldn't have gone home with our mums just because it was raining.

We stuck it out till Tuesday morning and then set off early to Burnley. It was about five miles away, so I got home about ten o'clock, had some breakfast and a bath, then set off to Hosker's and Mick's. Walking out of my house, I was amazed to see Celtic fans already arriving in cars, even though the match was an evening fixture. I went to Hosker's and we saw some Celtic fans on the Rec kicking a football about with loads of beer around them on the floor. We then went to Mick's house, near the Butterfly pub, where there were loads more Celtic – and it was only midday. All the pubs were packed with Celtic fans, even in the town centre. Green and white shirts were everywhere and every Scot carried booze of some description. Some clutched bottles of sherry and were already pissed out of their heads and flat out on the pavement. All the windows of the Swan pub went through before Celtic fans staggered out. There didn't seem to be any Burnley fans around but it was only early.

Four o'clock came and as I walked up Todmorden Road back to Burnley Wood, coach after coach went past, each with Celtic fans holding cans or bottles. There were coaches from all over, Leeds, Newcastle, Sheffield and Derby. I was looking forward to this game. Mick, Hosker and I tried to get to our usual spot on the Longside but there was no way, it was heaving, so we made do with standing at the bottom next to the fence, where there was no mesh roof to protect from missiles. Fighting had already started and Celtic fans were getting kicked out of the Longside. The Bee Hole end looked all green and white, while it seemed the Longside and the seated stands were a sea of claret and blue shirts.

Before the teams came out, the cans and bottles filled with piss started flying over the fence. I remember the cans had pictures of girls on them, they were Tennants lager cans, the first time I had seen one of those tins. The teams came on and there was a big surge from the Bee Hole end into the Longside. The battle cries began. We couldn't watch the game because of all the missiles so I decided to climb up a drainpipe. It had square boxing round it so it was easy to climb. When I was about ten feet up I had a great view of the ground and the game. I could see everything. Cans were hitting the drainpipe, but lower down; I was safe for now.

A big gap opened up in the fence between the Bee Hole and Longside ends and Celtic fans ran across the gap in numbers. Fists and feet flew and the police were so outnumbered they could do nothing but stand and watch. The song would go up every now and again, "You'll never take the Longside," then battle would commence again. Burnley fans tried to push into the Bee Hole, where they were met and pushed back into the Longside. Even though there must have been well over 10,000 Celtic fans in the ground, at least half of them were in the Bee Hole end. Burnley were fighting all the way top to bottom of the Longside. Half time came and went. No-one noticed the teams leaving and returning to the pitch. "Argentina, Argentina," went the chant – a taunt about the crap World Cup campaign Scotland had just had in Argentina.

Now the Celtic fans behind the fence were going mental trying to get over again and the outnumbered police had to retreat down the terrace. Everything was coming over the fence; the air was full of glass and piss. Celtic fans started climbing the fence pulling the bars apart and actually snapping them off. Police retreated to the pitch. They couldn't send dogs this time as the floor was covered in glass. The Celtic fans poured through their fence and ran up to ours, throwing kicks and punches through it. It was time for me to get down from my vantage point. Then, when I thought it couldn't get any worse the Celtic fans started using the snapped-off railings as spears, pushing through our fence and stabbing at anyone and everyone. Burnley fans were trying to move away from the fence but they were moving into the battle at the Bee Hole end. All hell broke loose then as the railings started flying through the air. One lad, just up from where I was, was struck on the ankle by a railing that came from nowhere and he hit the floor straight away. He tried to get up but couldn't, so some others gave him a hand. The railing went back over the fence only to be thrown straight back again.

The fighting in the Bee Hole end intensified. We were making progress but not enough and finally the pressure building up from both sides of the Longside gave and everyone went on to the pitch. Fighting carried on in the centre circle and penalty areas and people were jumping into the stands to get out of the way. Mick and Hosker managed to get into the Bob Lord stand. As for me I couldn't get off the pitch. The problem was that all Burnley's ends were raised about six feet above the pitch and me only being a short twelve-year-old stood no chance. There were people all around me fighting. Police horses were galloping around pushing fans back onto the terraces. I ran and jumped to try to get hold of the barrier on the Bee Hole end but there was no way, I was just getting squashed against the wall as the horses were pushing everybody off the pitch. Suddenly two pairs of arms and hands were grabbing at my ears and shoulders. I was being lifted, it felt like I was a cork in a bottle, fans were still trying to use me as a stepping stool. Finally I could see around me again. I could see tops of heads and police horses still pushing people off the pitch. I looked and saw the two who had lifted me, a man and a woman, both wearing Glasgow Rangers scarves. "You alright little 'un? We thought you were a gonner." I told them I was OK but I needed to stand and catch my breath.

The pitch was finally cleared and the police made their way back into no man's land, so I left my saviours and went back to my beloved Longside. I walked against the perimeter fence all the way. The battle of the Bee Hole end had subsided a bit and I managed to get through, through people's legs. And there I was, back in the Longside. The floor was covered in glass and hundreds upon hundreds of cans with women on them. Police must have brought in reinforcements because there were two lines now in front of the Burnley fans and one in front of the Celtic fans in the Bee Hole end. The game finished and Burnley won one-nil. Steve Kindon scored, I think, but no-one was bothered about the game. A defiant, "You'll never take the Longside," went up. I was proud, Burnley fought that night like nothing I'd ever seen before or since on a football ground.

Afterwards, all the Burnley lads moved as one down Brunshaw Road. Most of the Celtic fans didn't want to know, they were off to get their coaches home but Burnley had unfinished business. Past the Wellington they went, meeting Celtic walking towards the Fulledge car park but the police had large numbers and kept both sets of supporters apart. There is a large roundabout at the other side of the culvert and all the Burnley fans went over the roundabout rather than using the subway that leads to the bus station. The Celtic fans had used the subway and as they walked up the ramp out of the subway, singing and shouting, the Burnley fans pounced. There was fierce fighting and Burnley repaid some debts. The police arrived and I had seen enough. I walked up to the canal, then another 200 yards and I was home.

Liverpool, 1978

My first trip to Liverpool in 1978 was a cup game and a night match, and I went with my brother, Ade, and our uncle. We left our car on the Stanley Park car park and walked towards the ground. Loads of Burnley fans appeared, all singing, smiles on their faces – then heads started popping up between cars, not just one or two but thirty or forty. You knew they were Liverpool fans by the way they were dressed and their hairstyles. The Burnley fans grew silent but the scousers had their targets in sight and moved in. They gave the Burnley a proper kicking, nicking all their scarves. I felt sorry for the Burnley lads and I was glad we were kids and that we were with our uncle. We got to the ground safely and watched our fellow fans come on with bust noses and no scarves, some even without shoes. I overheard stories of how they'd been ambushed and battered.

We had to go back through the dreaded Stanley Park. As we got to Anfield Road, scousers mingled with us and you could hear fists hitting heads in the dark. We had to walk through some trees to get to the car park. I couldn't believe it but the scousers were actually dropping out of trees into the Burnley fans and taking whatever they wanted. It was a joy to get back to the safety of the car unscathed.

The following day I talked to mates who went back on the coaches; they had bad stories of how the scousers had even walked onto the coaches and started fighting. Everyone said the police didn't give a fuck, saying, "Don't come to Liverpool again," and turning a blind eye. Burnley lads had been battered, robbed and given a lesson.

Over the next couple of years my devotion to Burnley FC continued to grow. It was exceeded, however, by my love of football violence. The excitement and challenge of mass disorder were utterly compelling, and by my mid-teens I was ready to get involved in earnest.

CHAPTER THREE

CANS AND VANS

Wimbledon, 1981

At five o'clock in the morning, I climbed into the back of the Transit van with Mick Nick, Bridgy, Dave Pick and Buzby, and several carrier bags full of beer cans. None of us was looking forward to the long journey. We'd been to a few games in the van that year but this was the furthest so far. Rough as fuck and still half pissed from the night before, I had opened my first while walking to the pick-up point outside the Turf pub. I was still only fifteen years old.

There were already seven lads in the back of the van when we clambered in and three in the front.

"Fucking hell Pot, watch my legs."

"Sorry lads. Just move up a bit and let me get in the corner."

Everyone shuffled a bit but the ones with the comfiest places didn't want to move. Once settled, and with the van fuelled, we were off to Plough Lane, the home of the club that had memorably knocked us out of the FA Cup when we were a First Division side and they were non-league. Most of the lads tried to sleep but that was useless until we reached the smooth, straight motorway. The roads in Burnley were bendy and being in the back of the van was like being on the Wild Mouse at Blackpool Pleasure Beach.

For breakfast time a few lads went lifting at the motorway services and climbed back into the van with every pocket full of sausage rolls, sandwiches, scotch eggs and pork pies. On all of my journeys, I've never seen anyone caught. We got into London early but there were already loads of people around. We went past Fulham's ground over the Thames and parked up. It was the day of the Boat Race so we thought we'd stretch our legs. We walked towards the river, all with cans in our hands and went past a big boozer on the corner; opposite Fulham's ground on the other bank of the river.

Outside the boozer was a good mob of Carlisle, who were playing Fulham. They asked who we were and we told them Burnley. They had a lot of big lads with them but they were sound. We joined them for a few beers and both wished each other well, then it was back in the van and on to Wimbledon. We parked up near the ground before midday and all wanted more beer. After finding out where the away end was, we headed in the opposite direction towards the home fans. There was no-one around but there was an off-licence on the corner. We piled in, keeping the shopkeeper busy as a few of the lads passed trays of cans through the door. We had a good chain going and stacked them round the corner. The shopkeeper didn't have a clue.

We were sitting on a wall, drinking free beer, when the Burnley coaches started to arrive. Driving past, some thought we were Wimbledon and gave us the Vs and wanker signs. The rest acknowledged us as Burnley fans; we were getting to be known faces. The coaches pulled up and a few of our mates came over demanding a beer. We explained about the offy and told them not to bother buying any as we had plenty over the wall.

A lot of Burnley had made their way to a pub called the Plough by Wimbledon's ground. Outside were a few wooden tables and benches, the weather was fine and sunny so we all sat on the tables drinking our cans. Why pay for a pint when you've got free beer? Plus I didn't even look old enough to drink. The trouble was, every time the landlady caught me she took my can off me. I moved with some others across the road to drink them in peace. The pub was packed with Burnley fans both inside and out and we had not seen any Wimbledon lads all day, but that meant nothing. Every team and every town you go to has lads that are willing to fight and you can come badly unstuck taking things for granted, it's one thing I never do. I respect every place I go.

Around twenty of us had decided to go into the Wimbledon end, and ten minutes before kick-off we paid to get into the terrace behind the goal. I went through the juveniles' turnstile. I was apprehensive, feeling butterflies, pissed, the sun cracking the flags. We waited for everyone to come through and then walked into the end together, taking a position near the corner flag. The end was only little, possibly fifty steps up with a roof on, half full with the main body of people gathered directly behind the goal. I was buzzing. We must have stuck out like sore thumbs.

"Fuck it," said one of the lads. "We're going right behind the goals and then let's see what happens. Everyone up for it or what?"

We nodded our heads and started to move into the middle. As soon as we got to the edge of the main body of the crowd, I heard a smack and Buzby's glasses flew past my face. Bridgy caught them. Me and Bridgy looked at each other, then looked at Buzby, who was wide-eyed with his nose and cheeks covered in blood. Well, that was it; Bridgy and I cracked up laughing. One of the lads at the side of me punched the lad who had hit Buzby and more came bouncing down the terrace. Our lads flew straight into them, no backing off. Bridgy and I were still pissing ourselves at Buzby's glasses and how Bridgy had caught them while the battle went on around us.

The police moved in and we went to one side, out of the way. The police got all the Burnley lads together and began to lead them round to the away end, and they were all looking at me and Bridgy, still laughing.

"Get on the pitch and into our end," said someone.

"No, we're staying here," I replied. "See you later."

The lads were marched around the pitch and when they reached the away end you could hear clapping and singing, "Burnley Aggro." Heroes' welcomes. Bridgy and I remained behind the nets most of the first half before we noticed some lads with beer in the paddock, so we made our way over to them. There was a bar but we couldn't get served. I didn't even look fifteen.

Half-time came and I said, "Come Bridgy, we're going on the pitch. Just follow me." I walked to the perimeter wall, hopped over it and ran into the centre circle. I turned to look at all the Burnley fans behind the goals and, to my surprise, they all came running on to the pitch, as the police looked on in amazement. The lads ran up to me and carried on towards the Wimbledon end. "Come on, Pot, it's round two." With that I joined the rest of the lads and the Wimbledon end started to evaporate. We were on the perimeter wall and went straight up the back of the stand. A few game lads stood their ground, fair play to them. They didn't last long, but they didn't give up their end without a fight. Most of the Wimbledon fans filtered into the side terrace or out of the ground and we left the ones who didn't want to fight. Job done, I was making my way back onto the pitch and had just jumped on the perimeter wall when my arm was shoved up my back and another arm was around my neck. I was lifted back on to the terraces. I thought, who the fuck is this? Then the words came out, the ones that I would be hearing a lot in life: "You're nicked."

I was taken behind one of the stands but I struggled all the way. "You're fucking strangling me," I told him. He dragged me to a Portakabin where I saw my mate Mick Nick standing in front of a desk trying to keep a straight face while he gave a copper his details. Once they were done he was cautioned and ejected from the ground. As he passed me he said he would wait outside. I went in front of the copper at the desk, my details were taken and I was cautioned and ejected, right beside the pub we had been using before the game. I asked Mick what he had been smirking at and he said, "Fuck me, Pot, I nearly pissed myself. All I could hear was, 'Fuck off you're strangling me,' and you going mad, and then you pop through the door, arm up your back and the copper's arm round your neck. It was well funny." We both started laughing.

As we walked behind the Wimbledon end, approaching us was a biggish lad with a couple of birds. We thought nothing of it until suddenly he got to the side of us and shouted, "Come on then, northern wankers." I jumped back, taken by surprise, but Mick said, "Come on then, you fucker." The lad started to spit at Mick, all the time backing off. Mick was still going forward when the lad then grabbed hold of one of the birds and started shouting, "Fuck off, you northern wankers." Then the bird started shouting it too, so Mick just told him to fuck off and we both walked towards the away end. Once there, we made sure there was no-one about, jumped a few fences and we were back in the ground.

The lads thought we'd been locked up. They shook our hands and patted us on the backs as we went through everything that had happened. Bridgy and Buzby with his bloody face were there. Bridgy had given him his glasses back. I started talking about the glasses incident and everyone started laughing at him again. No-one was bothered about the game. The feeling of all the lads being back together and safe was fucking brilliant. I knew from that point I wanted this again and again, I was hooked.

Walking back to the van afterwards, a Millwall fan walking

in the opposite direction through all the Burnley fans declared himself and shouted, "Come on then, who wants it?" Most of the lads just walked past him but Simon Massey walked up to him and knocked him clean out. Simon and me would become best friends and partners in crime at future games. As soon as the lad hit the floor the police had hold of Simon and he was later charged and fined.

The journey home is a big comedown after the battle, the adrenalin has run dry and you don't look forward to the long trip in the back of a Transit. The van stopped outside our favourite off-licence but his time all eyes were on us and there was no chance of any freebies. We got our cans, got back in the van and settled down for the journey. Once the beer had run out it was time to try and get our heads down and sleep it off. The following day's match report said Burnley fans marred the game. "Before the game they attacked Wimbledon fans and then at half time they ran the full length of the pitch to get at them again." I thought, what a good day, plus we made the papers. Perfect.

1982–83

Burnley FC were back in the First Division. I had a job and money in my pocket. Travelling was no problem. I was fifteen. Bring it on.

The first game of the season, Middlesbrough away, was an eye-opener. I went up on a coach which was mostly lads, a few of my brother's mates, and Simon, a guy I had been drinking with but wasn't yet on mate terms with. The journey up was full of stories plus plenty of beer. We got to Boro at eleven o'clock, the first coach to land, and stopped right outside the ground. The coach driver said, "Right, this is it, the police will show you where the coach is after the game."

Everyone got off and seemed to go in different directions

and I stood there wondering where they'd all gone. There was me left with Simon and four of our Ade's mates. We walked all the way round the ground and my brother's mates went into a pub. Simon and I tried to get in but they wouldn't let us, so we decided to wait outside the away end. There was no Old Bill about as we made our way there. We had just got to the end when eight lads came walking towards us. I quickly crossed the road but Simon didn't bother. As soon as the lads got to him, bang, he was on the floor with loads of lads giving him a kicking. Then, as quickly as it had started, it finished and the lads walked off. Simon had covered himself up well, the usual ball on the floor; head wrapped in his arms waiting for the kicking to stop. It was strange, not a word spoken.

I watched the lads walking down the road slapping each other on the back, one of them showing the others the punch that had knocked Simon to the floor. Simon's head then popped out from under his arms as he checked to see if there was anyone else lined up to give him a swift boot to the body. I dashed over to help him up and ask him if he was OK, saying what cunts they were, and that was it; Simon and I ended up great friends and went to every game together. He got up and dusted himself off and we realised he didn't have a mark on him. We sat outside the away end waiting for the rest of the Burnley fans to arrive and nothing more happened outside.

Once inside the ground the Boro lads in the stand at the side of us were giving it the big 'un but we had managed to fill the away end. By half time the Boro lads were well up for it. I don't know how they got in but suddenly they came running up the steps right into the middle of us. I had already stood and watched Simon get a kicking and I wasn't standing back from this one. Even though they were well outnumbered up they came, straight into us. They had some bottle but we pushed them down by sheer numbers. One lad in a yellow jumper kept flying into us. Down on the floor he would go but he'd bounce straight back up. The police soon moved them out of the away end but one Boro lad had managed to get through all of us and made his way to the front of the terrace where he was faced with the perimeter fence. He tried to climb it but some of the Burnley fans were on his heels. He got halfway up then was pulled back into the crowd and disappeared under swinging arms, and that was the entertainment over for the day. Burnley won the game 4–1.

We were now having fights week in and week out at home and away. It's funny how people get to hear about your exploits and come to join you in your escapades. Simon and I were joined by Phil Feebie and Dave Devassy, who was the only coloured lad to travel with us at this time and would sadly lose his life to drugs, a waste of another good lad.

Lads were starting to fill the coaches. They all seemed to travel on the same buses so that was a bonus for us. Around fifteen of us would board the coach at Burnley bus station and a bigger number would get on at Accrington. Soon we were up to fifty solid lads. It was the foundation of things to come.

Burnley v Bolton 1982–1983

I went down to the town centre early with Ade and a few of his mates for Burnley's first league game of the season. Bolton were already everywhere, mobs roaming round the centre waiting for the pubs to open. We made our way to the Wonderland amusement arcade for a few games of Space Invaders. A mob of Bolton ran past and bricks and dustbins came through the windows. They didn't try to enter the place, they just moved on to the next target.

We bought a few bottles of cider from the supermarket and went to a little park. A lot of tramps drink there in the summer, so no-one bothered us. After knocking back the apple juice, we made our way back into the shopping precinct. Bolton were now smashing up pubs and the police couldn't handle their numbers. We headed towards the White Lion, usually a Burnley pub, but not today. A small mob of Burnley was on the street but didn't last long. Bolton came from everywhere. Innocent people were running into shop doorways, mothers and children were trying to run to safety. A few Burnley were at the bus station when a bus full of Bolton pulled in and ran straight off the bus and into everyone, punching and kicking anyone that was in their space. They ran into the Concorde pub, and seconds later was the sound of glasses smashing, then they came out and moved on to the next pub. On the way to the ground Bolton were doing anyone in their path with so many mobs the police seemed powerless to stop them.

I was expecting to see Bolton all over the Longside and Bee Hole end, but they weren't. The Longside was packed with Burnley. Why weren't they in the town centre defending it? Maybe after the game, I thought. When the match finished, we headed towards the town centre. Thousands of Burnley walked this way to catch buses home. We got to the crossroads where the home and away fans meet and police lined across the street up to the away end stopping Bolton fans getting through. The lines didn't hold for long. This time Burnley put up some resistance and police dogs and horses were brought in to separate the fighting fans. Bricks and bottles were flying over the road. Bolton kept trying to get through the police lines and Burnley charged to meet them. Finally we got to the bus station. Police held Bolton back giving Burnley fans time to catch their buses home. A lot of Bolton had broken free and casually walked onto the bus station. When they reached the middle of the station they all started chanting, "Bolton," and then attacked everyone, slapping young lads who were school age, they were taking liberties. Burnley bus station was now Bolton's. I made my way home along the canal bank. What a mob Bolton had brought, hundreds of them. Burnley couldn't touch them. If this was a taste of what was to come then God help us when we needed a mob and quick.

Fulham, 1983

An early start, travelling down by coach. I bought my fifteen or so cans of beer the night before. Getting on the coach I could see the familiar faces: Simon, Phil Feebie, Finney, Kelvin and Fagan. I would be greeted with, "Alright, Pot," a nickname given to me at an early age as I always seemed to have a broken arm, with a plaster cast or "pot" on it.

As soon as the coach moved away the first ring pulls were separated from the tins. The long journeys would always fly past with the beer flowing and the odd play fight on the way, "You'll never take the back seat," then everyone would steam the back seat. We got to Fulham well watered and decided we were all going into the ground, mainly because it had a bar and once you got the taste you wanted more. I can't remember much about the game but we all sat in the main stand. Twenty minutes before the final whistle we decided it was time to see if they had any lads. We marched out of the stand, walked behind the away end and saw the doors were open under the paddock. Everything was sound, no-one had sussed us, fifty lads going to have a good do at seeing who's who.

We got halfway along the stand when we saw a set of big double doors; these were open with two Old Bill on them, one a woman. The Fulham lads must have seen us leave the stand and knew what we were up to because they were now on the other side of the doors in the middle of the road. We both saw each other at the same time and the two Old Bill didn't know what to do other than draw their truncheons and make a lot of noise. Simon picked up a dustbin and threw it at the Fulham lads and we all followed the bin into the crowd. The WPC made a beeline for Simon and kicked him in the bollocks.

Down he went. A few of us cracked up laughing, but then there was business to sort out.

We piled out of the ground, onto the street and into the Fulham. They were backing away and we charged and scattered them. Some stood their ground but were soon dealt with; we were pushing them into their own end when the cavalry arrived. I fucking hate police horses. The Fulham fans in their own end could see what was going on and were coming out of the ground to give the others a hand. The horses quickly separated us but one of the mounted Old Bill had his sights set on Devassy, probably because he stuck out like a black thumb. Up and down the road he chased him but he couldn't catch him. Finally an Old Bill on foot caught him and gave him a bit of a slapping and a kick up the arse and told him to fuck off back to the coaches.

The police took us back to the coaches and made sure we got back on them. Everyone was buzzing like fuck. Did you see this? Did you see that? All reliving the row again. Someone shouted out, "Did you see Simon get kicked in the bollocks?" and the coach burst into laughter. The laughter would just start to die down when someone mentioned Devassy getting chased all over the place and get a slapping off the Old Bill and the giggles would start up again. The Old Bill stood at the door of the coach to make sure none of us got off again. It had been thirsty work and we set about looking for any spare cans. It was a great result for us to come down to London and have the best of it, even if it was only Fulham. We felt we were getting it together.

As the coaches were being escorted away a lad on a moped gave us the V's and the wanker signs and we gave it back. The coach stopped and he went to overtake us but we opened the emergency exit door and the lad went straight into it! His moped kept going but he flew onto the other side of the road. A car coming the other way just managed to swerve and miss his head. The traffic came to a stop and the police pulled the coach over. The other coaches were allowed to carry on home but we were told to park in a side street outside a pub, surrounded by Old Bill. A lorry pulled up with a police Portakabin on the back, which was then lifted off and the police came on the coach saying this was a case of attempted murder.

Nobody said anything. They took us off one by one for interview in the Portakabin. Some of the lads came back sweating, saying if someone admitted opening the door it would be a shitty charge. Everybody looked at each other, "Yeah, right, sit down." After an hour we noticed a few lads creeping around at the end of the street. Ten minutes went by and more lads gathered. A brick came over and everyone jumped up with shouts of, "Come on," and we headed for the door of the coach. The police tried to get us to sit down but we were having none of it. As another brick landed on the roof the Old Bill chased the lads away. It was thanks to those lads that the police realised that they didn't want our coachload hanging round so they gave us a severe bollocking and sent us on our way. There was a loud cheer.

CHAPTER FOUR

EVERY MOTHER'S SON

Cup Runs, 1982-3

We had done alright in the Milk Cup. Our next game would be a Tuesday night match against Birmingham City. The Zulus were coming to town, and the prospect of a big firm coming certainly got the juices going.

I finished work at five o'clock and got home by twenty past. My mate Bridgy was knocking on the door five minutes later and I was throwing my tea down my neck. I couldn't wait to get down to the White Lion in town which was getting to be our regular boozer. I remember thinking it would be packed with Burnley lads. We were out of the house by half past five and walked down the canal to the bus station. It was pretty quiet with nobody about. The White Lion was just around the corner when five lads appeared and walked past us, then turned around and asked Bridgy, "Have you got the time, mate?" Before he could respond, smack, the lad punched him. Bridgy was quick and was straight on his toes. I was right behind him.

"Get into the White Lion."

We both fell through the doors expecting it to be full of Burnley lads but I didn't recognise one face. We looked at each other; he had a cut above his eye and blood rolling down his cheek. "Fuck it, I need a drink," I said. The landlady served us and gave Bridgy a tissue for his eye. She was sound. I used to drink with her son and she probably knew I was underage. When we got our drinks a few lads with Brummie accents came up asking what had happened. "One of your lads has just banged me," Bridgy explained. The pub was packed with Birmingham fans. They asked if the lads that had done it had come back in, but they hadn't, and they said that they weren't impressed with them. I couldn't believe *our* boozer was full of Birmingham fans but it turned out that they were top-notch. They were all talking to us and we didn't have to buy another drink, they wouldn't let us go to the bar. As kick-off approached they even said, "Come on lads, walk up to the ground with us, you'll be alright, there's loads of us about." So we did. There must have been 100, plus they were right, there were loads of mobs of Birmingham on their way to the ground. I couldn't believe there were no Burnley fans.

As we left Turf Moor, outside the cricket ground a couple of lines of police blocked the away fans' exit and behind the lines the road was packed with Brummies. We'd passed the police lines and the Wellington pub and there was a separation of bodies in the middle of the road. Then suddenly, feet and fists were flying, Burnley fans on one side, Birmingham on the other. Before we could look round and gauge the situation they were into us. It seemed every one of them was a big fucker. They had us backed up against the railings of the church and the people in the front were dropping down. Adrenalin took over. "Come on!" The next thing I knew we were in the middle of the road. Birmingham seemed to have the best of it, then, all of a sudden, Burnley's older and bigger lads came steaming through like a tidal wave, lads we hadn't seen for years. This time it was Birmingham on their toes, the older lads taking no prisoners. The Birmingham went quiet, trying to regroup but Burnley were still into them, giving all us young ones a lesson on how it's done. It gave us the confidence to carry the momentum on. We were under the culvert now, going towards the bus station, pockets of fighting here and there, Burnley flushing away fans out. We were in the bus station and people were running from one side to the other. "They're down here," someone would shout and everyone would go charging to where the shout had come from. "They're up here," and again everyone would follow the direction of the shouts in the defence of the bus station.

A big Rasta walked onto the station. A few ran up to challenge him. He walked towards us with his arms outstretched, but I couldn't make out what he was saying. Dave Pick ran forward, punched and kicked him and I followed, but he reached inside his coat and pulled out a machete. Everyone scattered but he only had eyes for Dave. Dave was away, he was fast, but the Rasta was behind him. I've never seen Dave caught by anyone, he was one of the fastest lads I knew, which was fortunate for him. Three minutes later he was back in the bus station with a big smile on his face. "Fuck me, Pot, he wasn't giving up easily, he chased me all the way up Centenary Way." With that we burst out laughing.

Police were filtering through the crowds now. People were getting into queues to catch the last bus home. Me, Dave and a few more lads decided to go back under the culvert towards the Turf and the away fans' car park to see if we could sniff out any more Birmingham fans. We didn't have to catch any buses as we all lived on the doorstep of Turf Moor. The streets were quiet, just Burnley lads walking about doing the same as us. Each group exchanged information about where they had been and if there were any away fans and what the police situation was like. There was nothing happening so it was back to Burnley Wood for us, a few drinks and home.

The day after the match the local TV and newspapers were full of reports about the violence. Birmingham had snatched a lot of money from the turnstiles and there had been a full-scale pub brawl in the Rose and Crown after the game. Ade's mates were all regulars there and a number of people had needed hospital treatment after weapons were used. A Birmingham fan had supposedly had his throat slashed, but the more interesting news was that we were going to Tottenham for the quarter-final.

Spurs v Burnley – Milk Cup quarter-final, 1983

This was one of the best games ever from a footballing point of view. Norman Jones had organised a coach for the older lads. At sixteen I felt privileged to be allowed on, travelling with all the old heads. I felt I was part of something. My mate Mick Nick, two years older than me (of course), had also got a seat on the coach which was good as he could buy the beers from the supermarket. I didn't even look sixteen, never mind eighteen. We boarded the coach at eleven o'clock and everyone had carrier bags full of cans. In those days the coach drivers didn't give a fuck about drinking during the journey.

As soon as we sat down we opened our first beers. We had twenty cans to go at. I've been on trips where the young ones got the piss taken out of them, lads telling them to move seats because they wanted to sit there and other lads bullying beers out of them, but there was none of that on this coach. I wouldn't have given my beer up for any fucker anyway. A few piss-takes were going on between the lads that lived outside the town and the Burnley lads and as the beers went down the piss-taking got a little more heated. The journey was going well until the coach pulled off the motorway and stopped at a roundabout off the slip road. He explained that we had a puncture and would have to wait until it was sorted, though how long that would take no-one knew.

Everyone took the opportunity to have a piss and stretch their legs. Mick and I took our beers and sat outside getting a bit of fresh air. A few Burnley and Colne (a small East Lancashire town near Burnley) lads came marching off the coach not too happy with each other. Obviously the piss-taking had gone too far. A fight soon started, one lad from each group. I couldn't see what was happening as the other lads had made a circle around them. Fight over, the lads shook hands and walked back on to the coach. A few of the lads had started throwing empty cans onto the motorway below and the police soon turned up and told everyone to get back on the coach. The puncture was sorted and we started back on the road. We were all still having a crack and the piss-taking had ceased. Mick and I started talking about what would be waiting for us. Spurs had a good reputation on the hooligan front, I had seen them in action years before at Turf Moor but all the older lads just talked about doing the cockney wankers. They didn't seem to give a fuck what was waiting and this made us feel a bit better.

As soon as we hit London the police were waiting to direct us to the ground. We parked with the rest of the coaches on a road nearby. Hundreds of Burnley walked towards the ground with no escort. All the fans seemed to be in a party mood, Spurs fans wishing us well. After all, everybody expected Burnley to get a good beating on the field. Spurs had their all-star team, with Ricky Villa, Ossie Ardiles, Glen Hoddle, Gary Mabbutt and Steve Archibald. Inside the ground the atmosphere was brilliant. Around 4,000 Burnley had made the trip.

Spurs went one up and everyone was expecting more to follow before half time but it didn't come. Burnley equalised in the second half and we all jumped on the perimeter fence going fucking mad, hoping to hold on for a draw. We scored again and back up the fence we went. We couldn't hear the Spurs fans singing anymore. Another goal, we were 3-1 up, this couldn't be happening, fuck the draw, we want to win. The

Spurs fans went silent and the Burnley fans went mad as we scored another to make it 4–1. I couldn't believe what I was witnessing, the mighty Spurs getting well and truly beaten at White Hart Lane by a team struggling in the Second Division. The final whistle went and you'd have thought we'd won the Cup. People were climbing the fence, the Burnley players came over to salute the fans, it was fucking brilliant and we were in the semi-final.

We walked out of the ground singing "Burnley, Burnley" in our thousands. This time the police escorted us and everyone was expecting pissed-off Spurs fans to attack us and send us back up north nursing a few bruises. The attack came as we passed some blocks of flats and a Spurs mob came running out of an underpass. Burnley surged forward but police horses charged the Spurs mob and chased them back where they had come from. When we got back to the coaches there were no more surprises waiting. I was proud to have been at such a game. It will go down as one of my all-time great games – and no violence.

Leicester City, 1983

This started badly and got worse. We'd organised two Transit vans to take forty of us down but they didn't turn up until twelve o'clock. Everyone was pissed off, as we should have been in Leicester by then. The journey was terrible and we got stuck in loads of traffic jams. We arrived in Leicester just after three, parked the vans up the side of a river and walked to the ground. There was no-one about. We got to the away end and it was sold out. We walked right round the ground and found every turnstile locked. It was a complete sellout. Leicester were on the verge of promotion and we needed points to avoid relegation. We listened to the game sitting outside the away end with no beer or fuck all.

Ten minutes before the end the gates opened to let out fans who wanted to go home early and we managed to catch the last few minutes. The final whistle went and Leicester had won. They were promoted. The Leicester fans were jumping around while some of the Burnley fans had tears in their eyes. We had lasted one season in Division Two. We made our way out, where the police were waiting to escort us back to our coaches and vans. As we approached our vans we could see a small mob of Leicester waiting for us. We charged. Some of them fucked off straight away, some were game and wouldn't move, but we had overwhelming numbers. One of the Leicester fans was knocked over some railings running alongside the river. A spike went right through his leg. He was hanging upside down and lads were still kicking him in the head. Another Burnley lad snapped off a car aerial, ran up to a Leicester lad and whipped him round the throat with it. It looked like his throat had been cut. Police and ambulances were soon on the scene. We jumped into the vans knowing something serious had happened and we weren't hanging around. Police surrounded us and another van from Crosshills and told us they were escorting us out of Leicester.

Everyone breathed a sigh of relief. It was premature. The police took us straight to Leicester police station. We pulled into a courtyard with the gates shut behind us and cops waiting. The doors of the van opened and we all lined up outside while the vehicles were searched for weapons. None were found, only empty bottles of cider and beer. The Leicester fans were brought in to ID us through the windows of the police station. Statements were taken from us about who we were with, what we had seen and where we had been when the incident took place.

"I saw fuck all," I insisted. "I was sat in the back of the van on my own."

Then the guilt trip came. "The lad's in a bad way, he may lose his leg, are you sure you didn't see anything?"

"I've told you," I insisted, "I was sat in the back of the van on my own."

The interview was over and after a few hours the police decided to keep the van from Crosshills and all the lads wearing yellow tops. This meant we had to leave Dave Pick and Dave Devassy. No-one liked leaving their mates but everyone was happy to be out of there.

We would never get back to Burnley in time for a drink so we decided to go to the nearest town or village to catch a couple of hours' drinking. I don't know the name of the place where we stopped, it was only small with four boozers at most and they were packed with locals. We got a few funny looks but no-one bothered us. We got a few beers in and watched Derby v. Fulham on *Match of the Day*. All the Derby fans were on the touchlines before the final whistle, the players were unable to take their throw-ins. Last orders went and we went back to the van. A tasty mob of local youth walked out of a side street.

"Do you fucking want it lads?" I asked.

You just know when people aren't up for it. We charged at them and they fucked off. Not one punch thrown. This happens so many times in football. You can claim a victory without throwing a punch. We got back to the vans, which were still in one piece. I climbed in and fell asleep. I hate travelling back home after the game. I was woken up as we pulled into Burnley bus station. Dave Pick and Dave Devassy got released without charge. The Crosshills lads gave them a lift back to Burnley, but some of them were later jailed for the attack on the Leicester lads.

Liverpool v Burnley, semi-final, Milk Cup, 1983
We had drawn Liverpool, the one we didn't want; we had all fancied another day in London playing Arsenal. It would be

hard getting a result at Anfield on the pitch, let alone off it. Norman Jones collected names and deposits for the coach and all the talk was about Stanley Park and the last time we'd played there. A lot of lads had bad memories. At least if we were all on the same coach we could stick together. A lot of lads had the same idea because it wasn't long before Norman had enough names and deposits to fill two coaches, all lads, a mixture of old and young. Maybe it was time to show the old 'uns what the youth could do.

A few lads took half a day off work the day of the game and met up at our local pub. There were around fifteen of us, a few mates from school, my brother and his mates and Simon. We knew we could get a drink after lunchtime closing. The general talk was about how many we'd get beat by and if we could keep it at 1–0 we would have a chance back at Turf Moor. I discussed other things with Simon, like how many scousers would be waiting? Would they be tooled up? How many Burnley would be tooled up? Would the rest of the lads be up for it?

There was a real mob waiting at the coach station, most had cans in their hands and were singing, "We hate scousers, we hate scousers." All seemed eager to get to Liverpool and this time, with this mob, it wouldn't be a walkover. Some of the lads were even flashing blades about saying what they were going to do to a scouser. A lot said they had scores to settle; maybe they wanted their trainers and coats back.

We arrived in Liverpool and lads were banging on the windows, then the skylights got punched through. Lads climbed out and sat on top of the coach as it pulled up at the side of Stanley Park. It was dark and there were no police. We got off and headed into the park.

"Everyone together, no fucking off."

Halfway across, we started to see silhouettes in the distance walking towards us.

"They're here."

Everyone charged, most not knowing why we were running. They hadn't seen the scousers. The silhouettes were on their toes. I kept to the back of the mob in case they tried to infiltrate. We were nearly out of the park when there was a lot of shouting at the front of the mob, so we started to make our way forwards. Burnley started running past us.

"Fucking stand, don't fucking run," I shouted, grabbing hold of them.

Finally, we were at the front of the mob with scousers running towards us. We took no backward steps. One tried to give me a flying kick but I hit him first; it was toe to toe all around with no-one backing off. The lads who were leading the mob back into the park realised we were giving as good as we were getting and came back. There was a rush of bodies behind us and the scousers were on their toes. As they hit the street we were close behind and they kept running. The police charged us back using batons and horses. They were nicking people for fun. Finally, order was restored and we were escorted to the turnstiles.

Burnley's huge following had most of Anfield Road plus the Kemlyn Road stand all the way to the Kop. The game wasn't that bad, though Burnley missed loads of chances and lost 3–0. Back on the streets, most of the mob stayed together. We made our way back to our coaches and there was no sign of any scousers. We got across the car park, still no sign and the coaches lined the streets leading to Goodison Park. Someone spotted a mob of scousers gathered on an old petrol station forecourt, with a graveyard at the side. We made our way between the coaches, no shouting, nothing, then charged them. A few stood and took a beating but most bolted across the graveyard with Burnley giving chase. Police and ambulances turned up as people still lay on the floor.

The police ordered us onto the coaches, then proceeded to take us off one by one for a body search. Once everyone was off they checked every seat on the coach. Apparently someone had been stabbed but no weapon was found. The rest of the coaches started to drive past us but we weren't going anywhere. Eventually, police boarded with two scouse lads. They had no coats on. They were told to walk down the aisle and take a good look at us. I don't know how they felt as some of the lads took the piss under their breath.

"Lost your coat, lad?"

"Want to buy a coat, lad?"

"Is it cold out there?"

Fair do's to them, they didn't point anyone out, but what a difference a few years makes. On our previous visit the police had let the Liverpool fans do what they wanted, and if you complained you were told to fuck off home. Obviously they didn't like it happening to their own. Anyway, with the ID parade out of the way and no-one arrested we were allowed to leave under police escort.

Everyone seemed deflated that we had been so close to Wembley. We knew we wouldn't score three in the second leg. Then one of the lads told me that my brother Ade and his mate had been nicked before the game. What was I going to tell Mum when I got home?

I walked into the house and Mum asked, "Was it a good game?"

"Yes, it was alright."

"Any trouble?"

"No, not really."

"Where's your brother?"

"I don't know, I haven't seen him." Problem solved.

The next day, Ade's friend's mum came round to our house and told my mum that they'd both been arrested and locked up all night. It didn't go down too well.

Ade walked into the house around teatime with a smile on his face as if nothing had happened.

"Do you want some tea?" asked Mum.

"No, I'm just going to jump in the bath."

Mum waited for Ade to get into the bath. She was only a little woman, was Mum. She brought mine and Dad's tea, went back into the kitchen and picked up a big saucepan. Then she ran upstairs and twatted Ade over the head with it. All I could hear was Mum shouting, "You've been arrested, I've had Hodge's mum down today." This was followed by two loud bangs as she hit him again. I was laughing my head off, so I left my tea and fucked off out before Mum came back downstairs.

Burnley v Liverpool, Milk Cup second leg, 1983

We arranged to meet in the White Lion in Burnley centre. My mate's mum ran it, so getting served wouldn't be a problem. I decided to go early and have a scout. A few little mobs of scousers were doing a bit of shoplifting. I was outside the pub waiting when a few came over and asked, "What time does the boozer open, lad?"

"About five minutes."

"Alright lad."

Then they were off to another shop. When the pub opened I was first in, followed by five scousers, who got their drinks and started to play pool. A few more Burnley came in and most stood at the bar. I think the scousers were waiting for this. While the barmaid was busy, one of them pulled out a big screwdriver, drove it into the pool table, got the money out and put the screwdriver back. It took literally seconds. One of them came over to me and gave me a handful of coins. "Get yourself a drink, lad," he said and they were away.

One of the Burnley lads came over to me and asked if I'd seen any scousers.

"You what?" I said. "They've just been in here and robbed the pool table."

He thought I was taking the piss but he checked out the table, came back and asked where they went. We had a look but they'd gone.

The pub was filling up and all the main lads came in. I told them about the pool table. Mick M and Simon weren't too happy.

"Did no-one say anything to them?"

"No, they were sound, after they did the pool table they gave me a bit of money and fucked off."

Then one of the lads came in and announced, "There's fucking loads off them drinking near the ground, they're in the Oxford."

"They will still be there after this beer," said someone but most took a different view.

"Fuck off, we're going, we're keen as fuck, there are fifty of us."

A handful of us walked into the Oxford and it was full of them. We headed for the bar but didn't make it. Glasses started coming from everywhere and tables and chairs soon followed. They had us pinned at the corner of the bar and we had to pick up the tables and chairs to use them as shields. Most of the other lads were still outside and started throwing bricks through the windows and doorway. We had a choice to make; stay and get glassed to fuck, or get to the door and hope the lads recognised us so they wouldn't brick us. We chose the second option. When we got out of the doorway there were a lot of lads with head wounds. A lot more Burnley fans came to join the fracas and the pub was surrounded. We tried to charge in again but were beaten back by missiles.

Then Liverpool made the mistake of trying to steam out. As soon as they came out of the doorway we were into them. There were no glasses to throw. One of our lads had a bottle of paraffin and splashed it onto them followed by burning matches but it didn't light. Apparently paraffin is a slow-burn and difficult to spark outside, unlike, say, petrol, which explodes. Liverpool retreated back into the pub, the doorway a mass of battling bodies. The scousers were trying to close the doors and then sirens were heard and caused a lot of our mob to depart, enabling Liverpool to close the doors. Police soon turned up with horses and dogs and sealed off the pub.

We made our way to the ground, most of us with tickets for the Bee Hole end. A rumour was going round that the scousers had got tickets for this end too but none were found. Burnley won 1–0 but, of course, it wasn't enough.

Back on the street, 100 of us, we made our way along Brunshaw Road towards the town centre. Most Burnley fans walk this way and usually anyone walking the opposite way are away support. There was a mob on the opposite side of the road and we all steamed in. It was dark and there were thousands of fans on the road as well as Liverpool fans trying to mingle in with Burnley. Pockets of fighting broke out everywhere, sometimes Burnley against Burnley. Horses and dogs were soon on the scene pushing everyone onto the opposite side of the road.

A few of us headed back to the Oxford. Chances were if Liverpool used the pub before the game they would probably use it afterwards. Plus they had probably parked their cars and vans near the pub. It was boarded up and shut. We scouted round the side streets but found nothing and made our way to the Turf as we knew the rest of the lads would be there. It was packed and there was no way of getting served so we checked out the bus station again but no joy, so we finished the night off where we began, at the White Lion.

Burnley v Chelsea, 1983

A lovely sunny day saw us all outside the White Lion: Simon, Mick M, Kelvin, Adam and Mad Kelly (who was on day release from hospital), a good mob of us. Some of the older lads were telling us to be careful today, Chelsea were well up for it.

"So fucking what," I said. "We're up for it, we're not here just to make up the numbers."

Thirty Chelsea were escorted past on the other side of the road. People lobbed glasses over the police vans and horses but Chelsea made no attempt to break out. The police charged us back into the pub with their truncheons out and Chelsea were marched to the ground. Some of the lads were shouting, "Is that it? Is that all you've got?"

Mad Kelly, Kelvin and Adam decided that they were going into the Chelsea end. Chelsea hadn't brought that many, 500 at the most. Then one of the lads saw a well-known face; it was Norman Jones singing and chanting with the Chelsea lads. A song went up, "Norman Jones you're a wanker, you're a wanker." Norman disappeared from the fence. Then Mad Kelly, Kelvin and Adam appeared next to the fence in the middle of the Chelsea lads. They started to sing Burnley songs and a gap appeared around them. Knuckles and boots quickly crashed into them. The three Burnley lads were getting pushed along the fence but they were fighting all the way, while "Burnley aggro" was sung all around. The police grabbed the three, dragged them out of the Chelsea end and marched them onto the pitch, heading for the cells, while the Longside applauded.

With ten minutes of the game left, Chelsea fans started to leave. We knew where they were going. We made our way round to the Bee Hole end by squeezing through or climbing the railings that separated the two ends to the exit point in the middle of the terrace. We didn't have long to wait. There were about thirty Chelsea fans and we met them halfway but we had the high ground and the numbers. Chelsea fucked off back out of the ground and we quickly made our way to the side exit. Chelsea were there first coming back into the ground but we steamed right into them, driving them back onto the street. We had them in retreat. Police started to appear and Chelsea were on their toes. We gave chase and the Chelsea lads stopped and turned. There was no time to back off and the street was soon full of battling lads. The police weren't having much luck trying to separate the two mobs, then Chelsea were on their toes again. A Burnley lad was lying in the middle of the road with police around him and people were saying he'd been stabbed but I couldn't see any blood.

The Chelsea lads weren't for stopping this time, they ran back to the away end and the police blocked the road. We couldn't get through. Ten of us headed for the bus station and Chelsea appeared in equal numbers. No police, everyone bouncing around in the middle of the road, no-one wanting to make the first move. I ran in and started battling with a lad, other lads flew in, yet some from both sides just stood and watched. There were a few Chelsea on the floor and the rest of them started to bottle it. I ran and banged another lad who got straight on his toes and the rest were soon running in different directions. Some of the Burnley lads gave chase. I couldn't be arsed chasing, I had done my bit. They'd backed off, not me. Chelsea never reappeared that day.

CHAPTER FIVE

TOOTH AND NAIL

Blackburn v Burnley, 1983

This was the one we'd been waiting for. The town was at fever pitch. All the lads arranged to meet at Burnley Central Railway Station to catch the mid-morning train into Blackburn. The platform was packed, 300 lads eager to do Blackburn. The train pulled in and we squeezed into the two carriages. You couldn't move. Hector the collector wouldn't be checking any tickets on this journey.

The train pulled into Accrington and around 200 got off, mostly young lads. Accrington is about halfway between Burnley and Blackburn and they had decided to walk the four miles there because they thought the police would be waiting at Blackburn station in numbers and no-one wanted to see them at this time in the morning. Plus they would be in Blackburn half an hour before the pubs opened. The 100 left on the train were mostly older lads from Accrington Road, and then there was me and Simon. We had a different plan.

The train pulled in at Blackburn but no-one got off. Next stop Mill Hill. This was supposed to be the roughest part of Blackburn, where most of their lads lived. We got off the train, not one policeman in sight. Our next objective was to find a pub. It was still well before opening time but we found one at the side of the canal and one of the lads banged on the door. The landlord appeared and someone shouted, "Is there any chance of an early drink, there's a few of us?" The landlord opened the door and looked round.

"Yes, as long as you behave yourselves."

"We will."

You could see the pound signs in his eyes. A hundred pints before opening time plus the beers when it was official, who was going to throw away trade like that? There was no singing, no shouting, we were off the streets, drinking in Blackburn and the police didn't have a clue.

We left the pub around noon and made our way to another boozer where the police would usually escort the away fans past. Blackburn would always be mouthing off through the windows. We went in but it was empty. We all got a beer, some of the lads started to get a bit noisy and the landlord looked a bit worried. He disappeared for a while and came back with a smile on his face. Five minutes later six policemen came through the door, with more outside. They had a word with the landlord then came back over to us. It was one o'clock. "Right lads, we are keeping you here until the train comes then we will escort you to the ground together." No-one was impressed with this. The police surrounded the entrance of the pub and some of the lads were getting restless. We needed a plan.

The Burnley train pulled in and we could see them through the windows being escorted towards us. The lads in the pub started to sing and a pool ball was thrown through the window towards the Burnley escort. Burnley fans thought it was Blackburn in the pub and tried to break the escort. The pool table and the bandit went over and more windows started to go through but the police on the door were more concerned about the escort. The bandit was picked up and thrown straight through a window, bouncing on the pavement, and about twenty of us followed it outside. We put a bit of distance between us and the escort and stopped. No police were chasing us. They had their hands full controlling the escort. We headed towards the ground.

A few Blackburn stood on the corner. One of the lads ran straight into them on his own. They didn't put up much of a fight even against one lad and were quickly on their toes. We turned off the main road on to the street leading to Blackburn's end. As we approached the turnstiles there were Blackburn fans all over. They thought we were locals until we threw a punch. "Come on, we're fucking Burnley!" Blackburn didn't know what to do, they were getting slapped all over and started to run towards the turnstiles and the police.

Finally, some Blackburn ran towards us. There were traffic cones all down the street and we all got one. Heads were still bouncing down the road towards us. We ran into them smacking them with the cones, they outnumbered us but we had bigger bollocks. They ran. Even fans queuing at the turnstiles were on their toes. The police appeared and we used the cones as missiles against them. They charged us and we ran. Blackburn fans walking towards the ground tried to trip us up so that the police could catch us, the wankers.

We were back on the main road, the escort was behind us and Burnley were everywhere. We headed for the Nuttall Street paddock next to the away end. Every time I had been to Blackburn there were always a few of them in there. We got on the terrace and kept quiet. It wasn't packed but there were a few Blackburn lads around. The away end was jammed. There was sporadic fighting in Blackburn's end where some Burnley fans had infiltrated but police soon moved in to drag them out. We made our move on a bit of a mob near the halfway line and walked along the back of the terrace until we were right behind them. Simon was the first in. We steamed down the terrace into them. They turned to fight but we had the momentum and they were quickly pushed on to the pitch to a chorus of "Burnley aggro".

Back in the away end, a wellington boot was tossed in the air. The police took offence to this and made their way towards the centre of the terrace. They grabbed a lad and tried to drag him out but Burnley fans swayed down onto the police. Punches were thrown and they let go of the lad. Police helmets then started flying through the air. Truncheons were drawn, a gap appeared and the police were totally surrounded, getting attacked from every direction. Loads of other police charged out from the concourse where they sold pies and drinks on to the terrace. They were hitting everyone and eventually they got to their colleagues. Burnley fans countercharged, fighting toe to toe, pushing the police back to their entry point on the terrace. Burnley's confidence was growing with every backward step by the police. They charged the police who were on their toes and off the terrace and out of the ground.

The pie stand was trashed. Lads start punching the asbestos sheets on the roof. Holes soon appeared and bits of roof were thrown onto the pitch. Police watched from their control room and one lad ran up to it with a three foot length of roofing. He tried smashing it through the window but it was Perspex and the length of roof asbestos just kept breaking. Finally he was left with a small piece in his hand which he threw at the window before vanishing back into the crowd. Various people went onto the pitch to calm the fans but none of the efforts worked. Then Norman Jones went on and stood in front of the Burnley end, telling the lads to calm down. This sent the lads mad and they started singing, "Fuck of Norman, fuck off Norman." Lads were trying to rip the perimeter fence down. Norman was trying to dodge missiles being thrown at him and then he was away, running back to where he came from.

Whilst everyone's mind was set on trying to pull the fence down, the police had regrouped. They charged on to the terrace again, this time in greater numbers and backed up by dogs. They weren't taking any chances. They beat the Burnley fans across the terrace, restoring order. The players eventually came back on and Burnley lost 2-1. We left the ground, police were everywhere but we thought Blackburn would be up for it. We were wrong. They were a waste of time and wouldn't even come out of their own ground. Some Blackburn lads said that the police stopped them, but the police were there to stop us getting at them.

As they escorted us back to Mill Hill station, the police were well up for it, and took any chance to nick you or smash you with a truncheon. Reinforcements had been shipped in from other Lancashire towns. The pub that was smashed up before the game was boarded up and shut and we were put on trains back to Burnley. Police were at every station to make sure no-one got off until we reached our destination. Once there we all headed to the town centre for a night on the piss. Everyone was buzzing about what had happened. We had made national headlines. What happened to the 200 that got off at Accrington, someone else will have to tell you. I wasn't there.

Carlisle v Burnley – FA Cup, 1983

We had been to Carlisle earlier in the season for a League game and didn't get much opposition. Maybe Carlisle couldn't get to us. For the FA Cup match, about seventy of us decided to catch the train north and I dressed appropriately in a donkey jacket, white jeans and Doc Martens. Carlisle was sunny and hot so I was boiling. We had a good mob and expected it to be a walkover.

We had a few beers in a pub across from the station and moved into the centre. As soon as we got there, Carlisle arrived down a side street. We charged, some stood, and some ran. I ended up with a few others chasing one lad; he stopped on some steps and stood his ground, bouncing up and down.

There were four of us around him each waiting for someone to make the first move. I ran straight at him, he didn't move and we both exchanged punches. The other lads ran in. The Carlisle lad was on his toes but I thought he was game as fuck.

The rest of the lads were battling down the street. The police arrived and Simon picked up a dustbin and threw it through the police car windscreen. He was nicked straight away. The police were now there in force. Three of us decided to fuck off, found an off licence and got a few bottles of cider. We sat down near the courthouses and didn't get any hassle. Eventually we headed off towards the ground. We were on a road that seemed to go on forever, walked past a junction and a mob of Carlisle came steaming into us. The other two lads were a lot bigger than me and they were holding their own but all eyes seemed to be fixed on me. I was away on my toes.

I seemed to be running forever. Every time I looked over my shoulder it looked like the full street was chasing me. I was knackered and sweating cobs with my big donkey jacket on. Then I was tripped up and hit the ground. I saw a big foot and looked up to see a policeman extending a helping hand.

"You alright, son?"

I tried to say yes, but as soon as I spoke it felt funny, my tongue wasn't hitting any top teeth. "Where've my fucking teeth gone?" The top middle three were no longer there, which was disappointing for a lad of sixteen. The copper, however, remained unmoved and just shrugged his shoulders.

I walked to the ground and paid to get in. All the lads were laughing at me. "Fuck me, Pot. You've got a boot print right down your face, you can see every nail he's ever stood on." The players came out but I couldn't make out who was who. All I could see were shapes on the pitch. My vision was blurred and my head was banging. One of the lads asked, "You OK Pot, you don't look too well, you might have concussion."

I was taken to Carlisle hospital and advised to stay overnight after they had done their checks but I signed myself out that evening so I could catch the train home. I got a taxi to the station and just managed to catch the train. The lads were saying Carlisle attacked them all the way to the station. During the journey home they all took the piss out of me saying I looked a cunt with no teeth. I replied to one lad, "I'd rather look like Bugs Bunny," which upset another lad who jumped up from the seat in front and turned and asked me if I was taking the piss because he had false teeth. He proceeded to punch me a few times. I just sat there and took it. I had never seen him before. I was sixteen and he was in his late twenties. I got up and fucked off into the next carriage.

The train pulled into Preston and we all got off. Someone came up and told me the lad who had punched me was fast asleep and they'd left him on the train. When we got back to Burnley I wasn't in the mood for a drink, I was aching from head to toe so I went home and got straight into bed. The lad we left on the train woke up in London. I waited two years for my revenge and after that he became one of my best friends. Sadly, he died recently. RIP Steve Ward.

Burnley v Leeds, 1983

We sat in the White Lion waiting for the famous Leeds Service Crew. Spotters sent to the train stations had reported that a mob of more than forty had arrived and was walking down Manchester Road into Burnley centre. The word went round we would ambush them when they got onto the main street. We all moved towards the Swan and the Red Lion pubs, both on the corner of the main street and Manchester Road, and waited silently round the corner. They approached without a care in the world, thinking they were bossing the place.

Finally they were close enough and we charged round the

corner, taking them by surprise. Pool balls went flying and individual skirmishes broke out in the middle of the road. We had the numbers and they started to back off. This gave everyone more confidence. We all charged together and Leeds were running now towards the train station. Inevitably the police arrived and pushed us back towards the White Lion. Back inside, everyone was patting each other on the back. We had matched and run off the mighty Leeds. So what if we had the numbers?

On the way to the ground, more little pockets of Leeds were getting slapped. Did they think they could walk over every town without any opposition? The atmosphere inside the ground was frenzied. Leeds had packed the away end but none had infiltrated the home ends. The police were keeping the Leeds fans in after the game until the streets had been cleared so most of the lads headed back to the centre.

Around fifty of us went into the Centre Spot, a pub underneath the Bob Lord stand. We knew some of the Leeds fans would walk this way and there were no police around, they were busy escorting the visitors back to the station and their coaches. We were after the lads in vans and cars. Leeds fans walked past the pub and we steamed out, they didn't have any police to protect them. Burnley took the piss, slapping everyone, chasing them everywhere, making sure they knew they had been to Burnley. We found out later that a few Leeds had broken the escort and done a few Burnley, slashing one down the face and putting a few windows through.

Burnley v Sheffield Wednesday, FA Cup quarter-final, 1983

This was another big game. Wednesday would bring thousands and it was rumoured that their lads had been over buying tickets for the Bee Hole. I had volunteered to work overtime on Saturday morning but as soon as I had clocked in at eight o'clock, my mind was on the game. Seven hours before kick-off. As every hour passed the buzz inside me grew. The longest hours of your life are when you are clock watching. At ten o'clock I told the boss I didn't feel well and half an hour later I was on the bus back to Burnley. I would be in the White Lion shortly after eleven. I couldn't wait and didn't even bother getting changed out of my work clothes.

The normal faces were in the boozer: Simon, Mick Moore, Phil Holmes, Feeby and Fuse. The pub soon filled up and some of us stood outside as it was sunny and it gave us an advantage, we could pinpoint any Sheffield fans walking through the centre. As time went by lads started to get impatient, Sheffield were nowhere to be seen. Lads went out scouting all the pubs in the centre but found nothing, so ten of us decided to look round the pubs near the ground.

We had just left the Coach and Horses and walked past a multi-storey car park when we heard the Wednesday fans behind us. They were ten big lads.

"Come on then," we said. "We're Burnley."

All of us were on our toes towards them, bouncing about and running into them. Some of them wanted to exchange punches but their mates weren't backing them up, they just watched as two of us ran into a lad and put him on the floor. We turned our attention to the static lads who were watching, and they bolted. One jumped over a wall only to realise too late that there was a ten-foot drop into a river on the other side. He was flat out on the riverbank and one of the lads decided to throw bricks at him. Fortunately for the faller, they missed.

We moved to the pubs near the ground, packed with Burnley, had a few beers and moved to the ground. While walking to the Bee Hole end a Sheffield mob approached us on the other side of the road. Police stood around, watching as insults were exchanged. I lost it. I ran straight into one mouthy cunt and kicked and punched him. I noticed a police horse running towards us, left the lad and was on my toes. I had my head down running through the crowd. The police horse was on my tail and then a Burnley wanker tripped me up. I got back on my feet but the mounted policeman was on me and gripped my collar. I couldn't get away. A copper on foot soon had my left arm up my back and walked me to a detention room in the ground. With every step he took he tried to get my arm further up my back to cause as much pain as possible. I thought to myself, I've had enough of this fucker, he's got my left arm up my back but I'm right-handed. I punched him straight in the head and knocked him to the floor. I tried to run but there was another copper nearby and I was soon on the floor with a few of them on top of me.

I was handcuffed behind my back, bundled into a van and taken to Burnley police station. Due to my age they had to get a reasonable adult (my father) before they could interview me. My dad didn't look too impressed with me during the interview, probably because they had to drag him out of the boozer. At the end of the interview I was told to go home and not return to Turf Moor. I didn't have a charge sheet or fuck all. I thought I had got away with it, and on the way home told my dad what really happened. He didn't seem to mind, just told me to watch myself in the future. Fighting at football seemed to be acceptable to him.

We got to our house and I told my dad that I was going to my mate's.

"DON'T go near the football ground," he said, sternly.

"I won't," I lied.

The game was still being played and I ran back to the Turf. I knew the gates would be open to let people out early and I walked onto the Bee Hole end. Police had a small mob of Sheffield surrounded; there had been fighting and the game had been held up for fifteen minutes. Sheffield were led onto the pitch and taken around to the away end, but some stayed in, willing to trade punches with the Burnley lads.

The game finished a draw after Trevor Steven had missed a penalty. I made my way to Burnley centre and there was sporadic fighting all the way. I was well out of the way when all of a sudden a lad ran past with a Sheffield scarf hanging out of his pocket. Loads were chasing him and I followed. They caught him quickly and gave him a proper kicking. He was curled up in a ball. I pushed my way to the front and said, "Fucking leave him, he's had enough." The kicking stopped and I helped the lad up.

"Where you going, mate?" I asked.

"Train station."

"Right, come on, I'll show you."

I walked the lad up to the train station and no-one else bothered him. He shook my hand and thanked me then went onto the platform. I'd seen and had enough for one day, plus Mum would probably want a few words with me, so I headed off home.

I was expecting Mum to go mad, after all, she had battered my brother with a pan when he was in the bath after he got nicked at Liverpool. But when I got home she didn't even give me a lecture. Maybe the difference between me and Ade was that he stopped at school to do his A levels, he had good prospects of getting a good job and she didn't want him to waste what he had achieved. Me? I was working full-time and didn't give a fuck about qualifications and school. My mum always knew I would be a hooligan.

The replay at Hillsborough is hardly worth mentioning. We got the special train, got escorted to the ground, got beat five-nil and were escorted back to the train station.

I thought I had got away with punching that copper but, on my seventeenth birthday, a letter came through the post. I had been charged with threatening behaviour and police assault.

The local paper reported the case.

> Policemen watching two rival groups of supporters outside the Bob Lord stand at Burnley Football Club saw a young Clarets fan hit out at another youth with a clenched fist and kick him about the body.
>
> When the Pc tried to arrest the youth and take him to the detention room at the ground the youth refused to go and, while being pulled along by the arm, punched the Pc in the face and knocked him to the ground.
>
> The youth was taken to Burnley police station where he said he was provoked. Andrew Porter, seventeen, a shoe operative of Burnley, admitted using threatening behaviour and assaulting a police officer and was fined £150 by the magistrates.
>
> His solicitor said the youth was only sixteen when the offences were committed. Porter, he explained, was walking with the Burnley fans, was provoked by something said by one of the opposing fans and a fight started.
>
> His solicitor claimed the policeman had Porter's arm up his back causing him considerable pain. Porter asked the Pc to release his grip and then started to struggle to free his arm.
>
> Porter was fined £50 for threatening behaviour, £100 for assault and ordered to pay £6 costs.

Hull City v Burnley 1983

For the first league game of the season we travelled east in two Transit vans, packed in like sardines. We parked near Hull's ground and headed for the nearest pub, the Silver Cod. Forty of us were in the boozer by about noon. There were a few Hull fans in there but no-one took any notice of them. The weather was nice and we went outside to drink our beers. All the talk was about what firms we would meet this season after some good results off the pitch the previous season. We had the makings of a good firm, we had dropped down a division, we knew we could get numbers, so hopefully we would be one of the top firms in this division.

Nobody noticed Hull fans going into the boozer one at a time. By the time I went in to get a beer the Hull lads probably outnumbered us but nothing was said between the two sets of fans. Soon the Hull lads moved outside and started drinking at the side of us. More and more joined them. Everything was quiet, you could have cut the atmosphere with a knife. Everyone was waiting for the spark that would kick it off, but it never came. Hull well outnumbered us now but still there was silence. A couple of police vans pulled up and then Hull started throwing glasses at us, prompting us to throw ours at them. We had to back off due to the amount of glass smashing around us, but the glasses were running out. We charged the boozer but the police charged us back towards the ground. Hull made no attempt to follow.

We were marched to the turnstiles with police dogs up our arses snapping at us every chance they got. The game was shit, we were getting well and truly beaten and it was nearly time for the final whistle. Everyone was up for it after the game. I decided to go for a piss, you didn't want to be dying for the bog in the middle of a battle, plus you never knew how long you would be stuck in the back of a police van if you got nicked. By the time I got back the lads had fucked off. I went on to the car park outside the ground to see if I could see them but all I saw were little mobs of Hull. I stood around and was clocked straight away; my claret and blue Fred Perry top hardly blended in. I went back into the away end, as it was better to walk out in numbers. The game finished and most of Burnley made their way under a bridge with Hull fans all around us, along with plenty of police.

We had got just under the bridge when the first punches and kicks were thrown at one of the lads, to shouts of, "Come on you Burnley bastards." One Burnley lad went up to a copper and asked for a police escort to the car park. He was quickly told to fuck off. We got to the corner of the street leading to the car park and Hull were waiting. As we got to what looked like an old garage forecourt, Hull came steaming into us. We had to back off, our backs were now against the walls of the building and we were surrounded. A shout went up, "Down here," where there was a little alleyway at the side of the building. Hull charged. We ran down the alley, climbed a fence onto an embankment and found ourselves on train tracks. We now had loads of bricks to throw at the Hull mob who were charging down the alleyway. They didn't try to climb the fence, the police were behind them dragging them back.

We moved along the train tracks down the embankment and onto the car park. There was no Hull mob here but there was no van waiting for me either. The lads I was with were happy, they had a car to get into, but I didn't know what I was going to do. I asked the lads if I could squeeze into their car until we were away from the ground but they said no. I told them I'd jump into the boot but again they refused, saying the suspension was fucked (wankers). They all jumped into the car and fucked off. I started asking around for a lift home but everyone seemed to be from Hull.

There was only one thing for it, I would have to walk back to the ground through all the Hull fans, wearing a claret and blue top, and hope to jump on a coach. I was shitting myself. I walked down the centre of the road, Hull fans on either side of me, walking towards the car park. A copper was in front of me and I quickly caught him up. He was listening to his radio, then he was off, running in the opposite direction to where I wanted to go. I stood there in the middle of the road thinking, what the fuck do I do now? I was frozen to the spot, it felt like I had been there ages and that everyone was staring at me.

A shout snapped me out of it. "You Burnley bastard." I was on my toes, running for my life towards the bridge with both sides of the road closing in on me. People were trying to trip me up, I didn't look back, the coaches were in front of me. I didn't know if I was still being chased. A mob of Hull was attacking the coaches. I ran past them and up to the police lines, explained that I was Burnley and they let me through. The coaches were pulling away. I saw Norman Jones on one and banged on the door. It opened and I jumped on. I found a seat and spewed my guts up. I couldn't stop shaking. I just kept thinking how lucky I had been. When I got back to Burnley I went straight home to do some serious thinking.

CHAPTER SIX

LOCAL DERBIES

Burnley v Bolton, 1984

We met in the White Lion early doors. One of the lads looked out of the window and saw a big mob of Bolton walking past without any police escort. They carried on walking through the centre. As official opening time arrived, the police and fans started to arrive in numbers. We had a decent mob. At around one-thirty we were told a mob of Bolton were coming through the centre. We emptied the pub and walked down towards the Swan. Bolton met us on the corner. After hurling a volley of pool balls at us, Bolton charged. There were a few scuffles but soon Burnley were on their toes.

The police escorted Bolton out of the centre and we all went back to the White Lion. We moved up to the ground at two-thirty and stopped at the Princess Royal for a drink. Dave Pick told me that he and around fifteen others had been sat in a pub when a mob of Bolton went in, bolted the doors and battered everyone in there. Dave said it was mad. Mobs of Bolton were everywhere near the ground but there were also loads of police.

We all went into the Longside and the game got underway. One of the lads noticed that there was a mob of Blackburn in with the Bolton. The lads then started shouting at the Bolton fans, telling them that they were wankers for teaming up with Blackburn. The Bolton lads didn't seem to find this funny and steamed into Blackburn. All the Burnley lads were now chanting, "Get into 'em!" We were laughing our bollocks off at the Blackburn fans' demise.

The final whistle was blown; we didn't head back to the centre but walked round the side looking for easy pickings. We found no-one. At the station Bolton once again steamed across and did Burnley. The police later blamed the Bolton fans, saying gangs of Bolton arrived before noon and, despite a considerable police presence, a number of fights occurred causing damage to pubs and shops.

It was another lesson learned from Bolton.

Blackburn v Burnley, 1984 – Norman Bell's Testimonial

A Tuesday night game. Two hundred of us took the service train from Burnley Central. As the train approached Blackburn, someone pulled the emergency stop cord as the train entered a long tunnel. We all jumped out on to the lines and ran out of the tunnel, up the embankment and over the fence at the top. We were on Blackburn's turf – and there were no police to be seen. Everyone was buzzing. We marched straight into the centre and as we got nearer saw the police vans coming out of the boulevard (Blackburn's train and bus station). Loads of police followed on foot, and we were surrounded before any damage was done.

The police started to escort everyone to the ground but ten of us managed to slip away. We mobbed up on the opposite side of the road and carried on walking, keeping just behind the escort. There were no Blackburn about. As we got nearer to the ground loads more police joined the escort and the ten of us fucked off into the side streets, ending up on a grass bank behind the Riverside, Blackburn's home end that ran the length of the pitch. We came off the banking and into a street outside Blackburn's end behind the goal. Blackburn fans were queuing up at the turnstiles. We spread across the road and walked towards them.

"Come on Blackburn, do you fucking want it?"

The Blackburn fans looked at us in disbelief and tried desperately to get through the turnstiles. Some of them went to the police complaining and pointing at us and the police soon got onto their radios. More appeared and we were on our toes. The Burnley escort was getting marched past on the main road and we mingled in with it, losing the police who had been after us. There was no trouble at the game and we were escorted back to Blackburn's main train station afterwards. In the end nothing happened, a complete waste of time. What can you say about Bastards? It was supposed to be a derby game.

Burnley v Bolton, 1984

Another night game in a poxy cup, and none of the lads were out. No-one expected any Bolton fans but I wasn't so sure. I went down to have a look. There were none in the town centre before the game, it was deserted, and in the ground you could see why: Bolton had brought only about 100 fans. After the game, I made my way back into town and had just passed the Wellington pub when some Burnley lads I knew came running down a side street being chased.

"Why are you running from these cunts?" I asked.

Eight Bolton boys were bouncing up and down in the side street. There were a few police about but, fuck it, I hate Bolton. I ran straight into them, taking on a number of lads. I was probably giving more than I was getting when the other Burnley lads steamed in too. Bolton backed off but I wasn't finished, I flew into another lad and as soon as I did a policeman grabbed hold of me, "You're nicked." I started to struggle and managed to slip out of my coat. I was running through the crowd when, bang, I was on top of another policeman. I'd only run straight into him. I tried to get off him but he just kept dragging me back down. Soon more arrived and I was handcuffed and thrown into the back of a van, taken to the station and charged with police assault and threatening behaviour.

This was how the prosecution put it in court, "A policeman saw Andrew Porter, aged seventeen, punch and kick a Bolton supporter. He attempted to arrest him but Porter slipped out of his jacket and ran away. He collided with another officer as he fled and then fell to the floor. He continued to struggle and the officer was punched in the face. Eventually Porter was handcuffed and arrested." The prosecutor added that I had convictions for similar offences and the bench said that they had no alternative but to send me to a detention centre for one month. "Mr Porter has promised never to go to a football match again," claimed my defence solicitor in mitigation. "He has been working at the same place since he left school and a custodial sentence would mean that he would lose his job. Incidents at football were often a case of six of one and half a dozen of the other, where the person who appears before the court is not entirely to blame. The policeman who was punched was not badly hurt. The problem was that, at seventeen years of age, one is showing off to the group of people that one is with."

The speech didn't do a lot of good. But the detention centre was alright, really. I got a job in the kitchen and was due out on my eighteenth birthday. My girlfriend was waiting outside for me with my son and her dad. No-one had bothered to tell them that I was up in front of the Board of Governors on that day and got an extra nine days for fighting. But I made sure I walked out of the gate on the next date.

York City v Burnley, 1984

The transport for the Boxing Day match was a Burnley and Pendle double-decker bus. Talk about travelling in style. Half of us were still pissed from the night before and the other half were rough as bears. We had a problem, the bus was full but we were meant to be picking up twenty lads from Crosshills, about fifteen miles away. We pulled up at half nine in the morning outside the pub in Crosshills where the lads were drinking. We walked into the bar via the back door to find a good forty lads there. I burst out laughing.

"How the fuck are you going to squeeze this lot on?" I asked the bus organiser.

"Right," he replied, "I'll go and see the driver."

He came back with a smile on his face having managed to get another bus, a single-decker, which would take an hour to arrive. This brought a smile to everyone's face; you could sink a few beers in an hour.

The bus arrived and we were back on the road. Burnley had a good mob of around 110 and we knew York wouldn't have the lads to bother us. We arrived just after midday and spotted little mobs of Burnley everywhere while York were nowhere to be seen. We drank in the centre until kick-off. Burnley had brought thousands and York were no match.

We went into the away end behind the goals and packed the terrace. Everyone seemed up for a fight – they always do on Boxing Day. We noticed York fans mobbing up in the seats to our left. Part of the stand was being used for segregation, empty seats then a fence splitting the stand into two. The York fans were on the other side of the fence and Lee, Fuzzy and I decided to go into their seats. There was an open door at the side of the stand with just one bloke preventing anyone going through. We went up to the guy and filled him with loads of shit, telling him we weren't Burnley fans and that we had come into the wrong end. He must have believed us because he let us through the door. We walked under the stand to where the York fans accessed their seats by the fence. They had a tidy little mob together. Seeing this, the Burnley fans in the away end came onto the pitch and went into the empty seats.

The police were unable to stop them, they didn't have the numbers and the seats were soon filled with lads. A few police lined up along the fence, preventing them from getting over, and York fans started mouthing, singing, "Fuck off Burnley, fuck off Burnley." Burnley fans replied with a few seats. The three of us decided we'd had enough, jumped up and turned round to face the York fans.

"Come on York, we're fucking Burnley."

They looked shocked, even more so when we flew into them, sparking panic. We were punching them for fun and dragging them over their seats, while the Burnley fans went mad, ripping out seats and throwing them into the York fans. The police lost control and lads climbed over the fences to join our battle. I was chasing a York fan over the seats and had almost got him when this big arm appeared round my neck.

"You're nicked, mate."

As I was marched around the pitch, I could see the Burnley fans still going mad, seats flying everywhere. I looked back wishing I was still involved, sick I was missing it. They put me in a detention room and it wasn't long before I had company. It was always good to see your mates when you'd been nicked. You knew you were in the same situation, plus you had more of a chance of a lift home. Fuzzy, Phil H and a few others were also nicked and we were all taken to York police station and charged with threatening behaviour.

They started to let us out after midnight. A couple of lads waited for me, as they'd organised a lift home. This was the following day's newspaper report:

Burnley soccer fans ran riot during yesterday's match at York's Bootham Crescent ground and thirteen are to appear in court in the New Year.

York police said there was a small element among the Burnley fans who were determined to cause trouble and things got out of hand. They added that after discussions between the two clubs they had been expecting a small good-humoured crowd ready for a holiday match.

The information proved to be totally wrong. There was a larger turnout and some of them certainly were not in a holiday mood.

Ten minutes before kick-off a fight broke out in York's popular stand. More than sixty seats were ripped out and used as missiles, fans climbed over barriers as disturbances broke out in various parks of the ground.

Police reinforcements were brought in but the trouble was not brought under control until ten minutes into the match. There were two pitch invasions as Burnley fans went to join the fighting in the stands.

I was fined £150.

Wigan Athletic v Burnley, 1984

We had heard Wigan had been mouthing about what they were going to do to Burnley, so we decided to show the dickheads who had the hardest crew in Lancashire. A leaflet was passed out a week before the game.

Wigan Athletic v Burnley
18th February 1984
Springfield Park, Wigan

Meet at Burnley Central train station to catch the 9.50am service train. We have heard Wigan have been mouthing about what they are going to do to Burnley so let's show these dickheads who's got the hardest crew in Lancashire

Everybody remembers "Ewood 83"
Welcome to "Springfield 84"

The Friday night before the game, I was invited to a work friend's stag do and took Simon with me. We were heading for the Bier Keller in Manchester. Around thirty lads made the journey by coach and stopped off at a few pubs on the way. It soon became clear that most of the lads were keeping well away from me and Simon. Maybe it was because we were jumping on tables singing and letting everyone know where we came from. The lads we were with weren't into football, just a quiet drink. In Manchester we got into the first pub and Simon and I went to the bar to get a beer. When we turned round, the rest of the lads had gone. Fuck it, they weren't on our wavelength anyway.

After a few hours of going from pub to pub, we decided to find the Bier Keller. It was packed with mobs from all over Lancashire and people were throwing beer all over each other. A little battle broke out and the bouncers came running in. The lads we had come with were sat in the corner, quiet as mice. Simon and I stayed away from them; we had tomorrow's game in our minds. We scouted round trying to see if there were any Wigan lads but found none. When we boarded the coach home one lad went round with a hat and everyone threw in their loose change for the driver. The lads all got dropped off at various points until there was only Simon and I left on the coach. We were just coming to the outskirts of Burnley when the driver pulled over and stopped. He told us that this was the end of the journey and that we had to get off.

"What are you on about? We are in the middle of nowhere and it is a five-mile walk up country roads over the moors to Burnley."

"There's a telephone just down the road, you'll have to call a taxi."

There were no taxis around and besides, they weren't just going to pick us up off a country road. We tried to blag the driver to take us home, offered a fiver each, which was good money as Burnley wasn't that far. But he refused and asked for a tenner each, cheeky fucker. We'd had a collection for him and offered him a tenner and the cunt wanted more money. "Fuck you, we aren't leaving your coach," I said. The driver then got the hump and jumped off, saying he was going to call the police. Simon jumped into his seat while I followed the driver on foot to the phone box. I opened the door to speak to him and he said that he was on the phone to the police. He got a bit mouthy so he got a slap and I walked back to the coach. Simon couldn't get the brakes off so we got off the coach and jumped over a wall and onto the moors.

It wasn't long before the police arrived. There were spot lamps all over the place and we were crawling on our hands and knees, trying not to laugh out loud. It took us four hours to get home. I got back in the house for seven, knackered, and had to be at the train station in two and a half hours. My clothes, face and hands were covered in sheep shit, so I had a quick bath and put on some clean clothes. I tried to get a couple of hours on the settee but there was no chance. The anticipation of things to come was buzzing in my head.

The train station was packed with around 200 lads, all the familiar faces. I laughed with Simon about the night before but all the talk on the journey was about what we were going to do to Wigan. Loads of police were waiting for us and penned us in under the station. We were told that we would all be searched and then escorted to the ground. All the lads started to ditch their tools, dropping things onto the floor at the back and then moving well away from whatever it was they had dropped. The escort was massive and though we kept trying to break away, the police were well on top. At the ground they put us straight in, and when some managed to climb out again they were soon on the scene. They pushed us back with their truncheons drawn, hitting anyone that got too close.

The game began. Burnley fans had infiltrated the Wigan end behind the goal and we watched them walk round to the side terrace where the Wigan lads had congregated. They spotted the Burnley fans and fighting soon erupted in the Wigan end as the two mobs came together. The Burnley fans in the away end were going mad. We tried to get onto the pitch but police horses and dogs blocked our path. A few lads got through and ran straight into the Wigan end as missiles started to rain down on the police. We tried climbing the segregation fence separating the two ends but the police charged us back. Fighting was still going on in the Wigan end and Burnley were getting pushed out. A few Burnley jumped out of the end and tried to return to our section, halfway across the pitch.

John Bond, the Burnley manager, grabbed one fan and the police were soon there to back him up. More also came into our away end and restored order. The lad Bond apprehended was being escorted round the pitch – and we saw it was Dev, one of our top lads.

"Fucking hell, Dev, you got nicked off John Bond!"

After the game, we crossed the car park and forty of us broke the escort. We saw an equal number of Wigan on a side street, charged into them, and they backed off and ran around the corner. We followed – and there was loads of them. They steamed straight into us. Fighting went on all around but we had to back off. Then other Burnley fans came to join us and our numbers swelled. We charged into their mob, who again would not back off. The road was now full of lads fighting. You just didn't know who was who; you just punched the nearest person and hoped that it was a Wigan lad. If it wasn't, you just moved on to the next person. The police steamed in and were also hitting anyone. They finally pushed us back into the escort and charged Wigan down the road. We never encountered another Wigan mob on the way back to the station, but fair play to them, it was a good little battle.

The police later dragged me out of work and arrested me concerning the coach driver. That pleased my boss, but who cares? I was fined £45 for threatening behaviour.

CHAPTER SEVEN

THE SUICIDE SQUAD

Burnley v Hull City/Sheffield United, 1984

Tuesday night, last game of the season and Hull had to beat us by three clear goals to get promotion, otherwise Sheffield United would go up on goal difference. We expected a lot of Hull – but were unprepared for the additional arrival of a Sheffield contingent, who had decided to come along to (hopefully) celebrate.

We met, as usual in the White Lion. Everyone was expecting Hull to be in the centre. They would be bringing thousands. We waited and waited, lads were going round pubs looking for Hull supporters, but they came back saying there were none around. Hull must have been drinking nearer to the ground. We made our way there, taking in the various pubs, but again there were no Hull around. We settled down in the Turf pub, everyone disappointed about the no-show, and had a few beers before heading up late to the ground.

Just after kick-off, fifteen of us were still walking when we saw a big mob surrounded by police. We thought they were Hull but, after a few words were exchanged, we found out they were Sheffield, who had decided to attend the game that could see them promoted. We quickly got onto the Bee Hole end, found the lads and told them the police were putting Sheffield in with us. We congregated in the centre of the terrace, close to the entry point.

Sheffield seemed to come through the turnstiles all at once. They charged up the steps, straight into us. We weren't backing off, we had the high ground. More and more Sheffield came in and we fought like madmen to keep them off the terrace, but their numbers were pushing us back. All of a sudden, another mob of Sheffield came steaming across the terrace – they had come in a side entrance – and ran straight into us. We were battling on two sides. Sheffield kept coming, hundreds of them, and we couldn't hold our own ground. We were outnumbered and the lads in the Longside weren't coming to join us. Finally the police steamed, ignored the Sheffield fans and pushed us into the Longside. Sheffield had taken the terrace.

United had brought around 500, while Hull had packed their end with well over 4,000. When Hull went 2-0 up, all the Sheffield lads began singing for Burnley alongside the shirters in the Bee Hole end. The game finished 2-0 and Sheffield had won promotion. No-one was interested in fighting, they shook the Burnley lads' hands. An hour and a half before we'd been kicking the crap out of each other, now they were patting us on the back, wishing us well for next season. We headed back to the town centre expecting to see pissed-off Hull fans but none came. The only fun we had was with Sheffield.

Scunthorpe v Burnley, 1984

Fifteen of us, squashed up as usual, travelled in a Transit van. We arrived in Scunthorpe shortly before midday, headed straight for the centre and went into the first boozer we found. Scunny were an unknown quantity and no-one knew what to expect. Did they have a good mob? How many numbers? More and more Burnley were coming into the pub and soon our numbers were around fifty. Lads went scouting the centre looking for mobs but most came back with nothing to report. Finally we got some good news, some Scunthorpe were heading our way. We decided to hit them before they got to the pub, and everyone downed their pints.

We saw Scunthorpe down the street and we charged straight at them. They didn't stand, they were well away, and we couldn't be arsed chasing them. They knew where we were, it was up to them to come to us. We went back to the pub and it wasn't long before the police turned up, came in and checked everyone out. Scunthorpe never tried to return to the boozer, and we made our way to the ground.

Twelve of us went into the Scunthorpe end and waited for the game to start. Despite our earlier success on the street, going into your opponent's end is always nerve-wracking. My heart was racing, my mouth was dry and I felt sick. We went through the turnstiles one by one and made our way onto the terrace near to the corner flag. The Scunthorpe end was packed behind the goals and they spotted us straight away. We could see lines of them walking towards us and we stood our ground, waiting. They stopped a few yards away and started mouthing and asking what we were doing in their end. "It's up to you to get us out lads," we said. "Come on." But they still wouldn't come into us. Instead, they started spitting. Police were soon on the scene, pushed us off the terrace and walked us round to the Burnley end. It was up to the Scunthorpe lads to get us out of their end, not the police.

After the game we made our way back round to the Scunthorpe end, this time in greater numbers. Scunthorpe had gathered on the car park but most of them were on their toes. The few that stood got a bit of a beating. Police came from every direction, nicking lads for fun and pushed us back to the away end. We explained that our van was parked in the car park and they escorted us to it and told us to fuck off out of Scunthorpe.

We stopped for a piss on the way home and a lad brought back a dead cat, as flat as cardboard and stiff as a board. Its claws were sticking out and, of course, everyone got scratched. We stopped for a drink in Todmorden, just seven miles from Burnley, and found a pub where people were eating. The lad with the cat went from table to table asking, "Excuse me, can you spare any food for my cat, it's a bit hungry." The look on their faces was priceless but the owner of the pub wasn't pleased and was straight on the phone to the police.

Bristol Rovers v Burnley, 1984

We stopped outside Bristol and found a pub that sold Scrumpy Jack cider. The landlord said we could only have three pints of it each, as it was so strong. Everyone went on it and the landlord quickly lost count of how many times we'd been to the bar. By the time we got back onto the coach we had polished off a barrel and everyone was off their heads. The coach driver didn't have a clue where the ground was and we didn't get there until quarter past three. The coach pulled up on a bit of a hill above the ground and we made our way to the nearest turnstile. Bristol fans came out of the stadium and we charged them back in. We had to fight our way into the ground.

Finally, we were all in, behind the goals. The end was segregated with Burnley on one side and Bristol on the other. We were in the Bristol side. The lads who had tried to stop us getting in seemed to have disappeared. We made our way over to the segregation fence, and laughed and joked with the Burnley fans in the away end. We thought we had taken the end no problems and we stood there like lords of the manor. Everyone was buzzing.

Suddenly, Bristol came from behind, straight into us,

knocking us down the terrace. Burnley fans jumped over the fences into the away end. We weren't moving. We steamed into them, pushing them back up the terrace. The police moved in separating us, opened the gates and pushed us into the away end. All the Burnley fans cheered us, it felt brilliant. We'd got into their end and the police had to get us out. For us, that was a good result. Bristol was known to be a rough place but we had stood our ground and held our own.

Plymouth v Burnley, 1984

Unusually, Simon and I took our birds out on a Friday night round Burnley Wood – unusual because Friday night, followed by all day Saturday and Sunday, was for the lads. I had gone to the off-licence before we went out and loaded up with more cans than usual for the Plymouth journey the following morning. The evening was boring, really. Simon and I played pool and talked about the trip to Plymouth, about possibilities, if they had a good mob, would we get a result or would we be the ones defeated? The girls were stuck in a corner chatting away. I couldn't wait for ten o'clock when the birds got dropped off home and we picked up our beer and went to Burnley bus station.

After quite a few games of pool and more than a few beers, the birds were home, cans picked up and we were at the bus station with over 100 pissed up lads. We had a real mob, every one a top lad. Go out on the piss Friday, straight to the bus station to get on a coach with loads of cans, good music, blue films on the video and packs of cards – what could be better? The coaches had bogs so it was drink till you dropped and woke up in Plymouth.

Somehow the police got wind of the commotion at the bus station. I don't know what they were thinking but a few vans soon turned up and the dogs were out. They had us surrounded and you could see the glee on their faces, knowing they would probably have a quiet weekend. We climbed on the coaches, the ring pulls were unzipped and soon we were all having a crack. We got a game of cards going and it was like being in a nightclub on wheels. After the cards it was time to circulate up and down the aisle and always the conversation turned to violence. What would be waiting? Would they be up for it? But we all knew we had a top mob together, two coaches of lads who would not run. As the night wore on people got their heads down, me included. Tomorrow would be a long day.

I woke up to Simon saying, "Come on Pot we're nearly there." It was six-thirty and we were on the outskirts of Plymouth. Some were still asleep, others were well into the swing, open cans in hand. I got loads of stick for falling asleep but the ones who had gone straight through with no sleep were completely off their heads, staggering up and down the aisle, trying to get to the bog before they spewed up. Both coaches pulled up together in Plymouth centre. It was a case of getting your cans together as it was a long time before the pubs would open. The coach drivers said they would see us after the game near the ground and they drove off.

We walked around aimlessly. There was an indoor market setting up for the day and some lads came back with loads of fruit. We were trying to plan what to do when Bob chirped up, "I want to see a battleship." He set off and we followed. No-one knew where we were going, we just followed Bob. We passed a milk float, which was quickly a few crates lighter. The driver left not too impressed. We seemed to be walking for hours but everyone was having a laugh and most of us still had cans. Finally, we came to a spot where we could see the sea stretched out in front of us and there, in the distance, was a battleship. Everyone cheered.

"Right, that's it, I've seen a ship, let's go back," declared a satisfied Bob.

"Fucking hell, Bob is that it, a glimpse and then fuck off?"

"Well, I can't fucking swim out to it, can I?"

We had passed a pub down the road. One of the lads went back, knocked on the door, and returned saying it would open in half an hour after it had been cleaned up. Everyone was happy; Bob's trip to see a battleship had not been in vain. We were about to be drinking in a pub at nine-thirty in the morning so, all in all, it was a result.

We sat outside the boozer finishing off our cans and, true to his word, the landlord opened the doors and we piled in. He asked us to keep it down and we all agreed; you don't fuck up a good result. He would make a few quid and we'd be having an early drink. We stopped in the pub until official opening time arrived at eleven bells, when a lot of the lads with itchy feet felt we should get into the town centre. We hadn't come all this way to sit in a pub out of the way.

We moved as one into the centre. There were no Plymouth fans; it was too early. We made our way through the centre, taking in pub after pub. The police had their eyes on us now, time was getting on and still no show from the Plymouth lads. Spotters kept coming back saying the only action we were going to get was up near the ground, so we decided to head there, up a dual carriageway to a pub on the corner.

The pub had two doors, each leading into its own room with its own bar. As we entered the Burnley side of the pub you could see there were a lot of shirties in. Some of the lads stopped outside, keeping an eye on the Plymouth side of the pub, and a few went into the Plymouth side to ask where the lads were. As time went and it got nearer to kick-off, songs started to come out of the Plymouth bar. We thought, let's have some, and ran into the Plymouth side. I think they were expecting us because they all seemed to have acquired a few glasses apiece and as soon as we entered the room they came flying our way.

You are in the room, glasses bouncing off everything, shattering on the walls and hitting every part of the doorway. Tables and chairs are bouncing in front of you, some bouncing off you. You don't notice or feel these things. Time seems to slow down but the sound of glasses smashing, furniture hitting walls and bodies, people's shouts, the sound of a battle in a pub, is unique. It's like the rumble of a train before you see it. All the sounds blend into one. Once the furniture and glasses have stopped coming your way and have littered the floor all around you, you pick up a chair and back it goes in the direction from which it came. People are pushing you into the room from the doorway behind you; too many lads are trying to get through to a small place that is already full, some falling over at the side of you, quickly getting to their feet looking round to see if anyone has seen their entry. With people pushing you forward the distance between you quickly narrows. It's funny how such a packed room a minute ago seems rather empty as bodies push up again the bar and into the corners, you see people trying and struggling to get as far into the corner as possible, pulling people aside then putting their arms over their heads.

All of a sudden tables and chairs come flying past you from behind and into the people in front of you, then someone grabs hold of you. "Come on, Old Bill are on their way." You're pulled out of the doorway as police are running towards the pub, the road is full of blue flashing lights and the sound of sirens, you calmly walk past the police and head towards the ground you think, all that in a matter of minutes, if that. Then a smile appears on your face, yes, this is what we came for. The adrenalin is still pumping round your body at a million miles an hour. You scan the horizon in front of you looking for groups of lads, seeing if you can make eye contact with them, but no takers.

We approached the ground, walking over a car park with bushes and trees down one side, up to the turnstiles. Someone decided we were going in the stand, and a large police presence didn't stop us. Once inside, sitting in the stand, I scanned the crowd looking for lads. There was a terrace beneath us but no-one there. Time to sit back and watch twenty-two men kicking a ball about.

When the game had finished, a few of us decided to jump down onto the terrace. The others went out the normal exit but we walked with Plymouth, back onto the car park where we had entered the ground. We spread out, the adrenalin surging back. The Plymouth lads should be waiting for our fans coming out of the away exit. We were in among them but none of their lads was around. Then came a shout, and a gap opened. We ran towards it, only to come face to face with our mates. There was another surge towards the corner of the car park, where it met the road, and the sound of fists hitting heads. We saw heads moving fast away from us, going at a line of police until the police pushed them back. The Old Bill quickly rounded us up, pushed us back on to the car park and escorted us back to our coaches. There was nobody around, everything was quiet. The police seemed pleased with the job they'd done and we were now more interested in looking for stray cans than fans.

I sat down, deflated. We'd done a twenty-four-hour shift, and once the adrenalin stops pumping, fatigue takes over. I was asleep before the coach left Plymouth and was woken by Simon saying, "Come on, we're home. We're all going down the Circ." It was time to start on the piss again.

Burnley v Plymouth, 1984

I was on my way to the town centre with Burnley Wood lads Ade and Dave Pick. We walked towards the Culvert, a street packed with pubs – the Princess Royal, the Turf, the Brickmakers, the 110 Club, the Wellington – that runs into Burnley town centre. It's a good place to go drinking. We were walking down a little later than usual, about one o'clock, because no-one thought that Plymouth would turn up. As we came down

Plumbe Street and onto Yorkshire Street, we noticed a few Burnley lads in the middle of the road, near the Brickmakers. We were about thirty yards away when, suddenly, the Brickmakers emptied and lads steamed right into us, leaving bodies all over the road.

We ran towards the Brickies and the lads went back inside. I saw Dave Devassy on the floor outside the Turf. He had a bit of a bloody nose but was OK.

"Fucking Plymouth, Pot," he said. "There's loads of them in the Brickies."

All the Plymouth lads had got back in the boozer. The Burnley dusted themselves off and walked over to us. "There were too many of them, Pot." We surveyed the situation; there weren't many good lads around. One of us went into the Princess Royal to see who was in there. "Give it twenty minutes, the Plymouth aren't going anywhere yet," said someone inside. We went in the Turf and got a beer apiece while one lad kept checking what was happening outside. Ade and Dave Pick decided to go to the bookies across the road from the Brickies as a bit of a Burnley mob started gathering outside the Turf and the Princess Royal. I was looking through the window when someone banged it and said, "Right Pot, come on."

I headed for the door but it was slammed shut in my face.

"If you go out you don't come back in," warned a doorman.

"Just open the fucking door will you," I told him, and that was me outside.

The Plymouth lads were out of the Brickies and glasses came flying from everywhere. They were well up for it and didn't give a fuck about the police, who were doing nothing anyway. They came straight at us. I took a few bangs to the head and body but I didn't go down and repaid some bastard with a few slaps of my own. The police then separated us, pushing the Plymouth fans back into the Brickies and us towards the ground. I bumped into Ade and Dave Pick. They had been battling in the bookies. Some had gone in to place a bet and started giving it the big 'un, a few punches were exchanged and then the entire place emptied.

One Burnley lad said that he heard Plymouth saying that they are going into our end. The police kept pushing us towards the ground. They had cordoned off the Brickies but a few of us doubled back and went back into the Princess Royal. We got a beer but there was nothing else happening, the police had sorted it. We were all gutted and not a lot was said. We just hoped that they could get into our end.

The match started and we waited in the Bee Hole end for them to arrive. All that happened was that one of their lads arrived with the landlady's daughter. He was well pissed and no-one touched him, we stood and had a chat. Apparently Plymouth lads were on a weekend trip taking in the game, then moving on to Blackpool. I shook his hand and said, "Fair play, you got the result today." Then we fucked off.

Suicide Squad

For years we had a firm but no name. Most firms had names by the early Eighties: West Ham's ICF, Chelsea's Headhunters, the Leeds Service Crew and so on. We were just the Burnley crew, and even tried that out as a name, but it didn't sound right. We wanted a tag that everyone would remember.

It was 1985 when suicide bombers started operating in the Middle East that one of the lads came up with the one. We were walking from the Broadswords pub to the White Lion when it suddenly came to him. One of the lads had it printed on cards and we all knew straight away that it was exactly what we wanted: "Burnley FC Suicide Squad." It sounded catchy, it sounded good. In a moment the Suicide Squad had been formed. The name just rolled off the tongue and it gave us our anthem, "Su, su, Suicide."

I had begun as just a face in the crowd but now I was one of *the* faces in the main crowd. Some said Norman Jones was our leader but, while Norman had his day, a new generation had come through, more intent on violence. We didn't have leaders, we all led ourselves. Game lads got respect from other game lads. I respected one lad in particular: for me Mick Moore was our top lad. No-one will tell me any different.

Bolton v Burnley, 1985

A service bus took a small but good mob of forty to the edge of Bolton centre, and we were in the nearest pub for eleven-thirty. Half an hour later, one of the lads came in and told us that Bolton were outside. We left through the back door, which led up to a small car park. The pub must have just had some work done to it, as there were loads of scaffolding bars on the floor. We ran out of the car park and onto the street but there were no Bolton, just a line of police stood across the road. Everyone rushed back into the car park, dropping the scaffolding on the floor, and ran back into the pub. The police followed and said that they were escorting us to the ground.

They took us past a pub called the Bradford Arms and the lads managed to push inside before the police could stop them. The police didn't bother dragging them out. A few young lads carried on towards the ground, and I went with them. The police left us and we headed over to a big white pub at the side of the ground. A big bloke on the door was allowing people in and out. There were loads of Bolton lads looking out of the windows. We tried to get in but the bloke said it was Bolton only. The lads looking out of the windows started to sing, "Let 'em in," laughing at us. After all we were only bits of kids. At eighteen, I was probably the oldest of the eight.

Fuzzy told the Bolton fans that we were drinking in the Bradford Arms and we made our way back there. I got a beer and stood outside. The lads inside were told to expect a visit from Bolton. Then they arrived, emerging over the brow of a hill. It was like a scene from *Zulu*. They had one of the biggest mobs I'd seen, and charged towards us. We ran back into the pub and locked all the doors. All the windows soon came smashing through and bricks were thrown through the broken windows. Lads were picking tables up and using them as shields, while others dived over the bar. The Bolton fans started to back off, and I thought that the police must have turned up, but they were merely regrouping on a petrol station forecourt. One policeman turned up on his motorbike and parked in the middle of the road, but Bolton charged past him and started to climb through the broken windows. Some were trying to kick the doors in, while Burnley lads fought to keep them out. Tables and chairs were used to keep the Bolton away from the windows.

Eventually sirens signalled the end and the Bolton cleared off. The police arrived in numbers and sealed off the pub. In truth they saved us that day. We were escorted to the ground without further incident.

As the game approached half time, I went under the terrace for a piss. A wooden door separated the two sets of fans. This was quickly kicked open and Burnley and Bolton ran into each other in another major ruck. Some of the lads had iron bars. A policeman went down, loads of other police rushed in to his assistance, battering anyone in their path, and quickly restored order.

After the game, a massive escort led us to the station and we were put on the train for Burnley. When it pulled into Darwen, all the windows were put through. We saw Blackburn fans were on the platform with baseball bats and we tried to get off, but the police travelling with us stood at the doors. Someone punched the copper guarding our door and he was pushed to one side, then we were onto the platform, but the Blackburn lads hadn't hung around, they were nowhere to be seen. More police soon put us back on the train.

The next station was Blackburn and there were loads of police and no chance of getting off. The train pulled out of the station into a tunnel and someone pulled the emergency cord. Everyone got off the train and walked back to the station but the police were still on the platform. We were told they didn't know how long it would take to sort the train out, but we managed to persuade them to let us get a taxi. We were back in Burnley in time for a night on the piss.

Burnley v Bolton, FA Cup 1987

Payback time. More than 200 of us met up in the General Havelock, a pub on the outskirts of Burnley town centre. Everyone was up for it, especially me. I class Bolton as my main rivals. I hate them because I respect them; they have turned us over so many times.

When all the main lads had turned up we made our way into the town centre, checking every pub on the way for Bolton fans. None could be found, which was very unusual. The White Lion was packed with Burnley lads, some we hadn't seen for years. All the old faces were out for this game. The police were out in force too, with dogs and horses everywhere. We moved towards the ground but our mob was too big to fit into one pub so most of the lads went into the Princess Royal and a few of us went next door into the Turf. As soon as we walked in, we spotted a mob of Bolton in the corner. They looked sick when they saw us. There was no way out for them, they had to walk through us to leave.

I went to the bar and bought a drink and the pub went quiet. They stood up to leave and I turned round and said, "You're going fucking nowhere lads," threw my beer over them and then ran into the group. I punched the first lad I reached and glasses and bottles started to fly into the Bolton and me. They were backed into a corner and covering themselves up against the flying glass. I ran into them again and started battling. I dragged one lad to the floor and the others took over, giving him a kicking. I went into another lad with Dave Pick at my side, picked up a table and smacked him with that. The top of the table came off and I went to pick it up but Dave had the same idea and we started wrestling over the tabletop, with bottles and glasses still smashing all around us. Dave got it off me and used it to batter the Bolton lads, while I used my hands and feet. Someone shouted that the police were outside and we were out of the pub fast, leaving the Bolton lads in tatters.

I was banned from the ground but walked there anyway with some Crosshills lads to scout around. The game had started and there were few police about. We had just walked past the Brickmakers pub when some Bolton lads appeared behind us and said, "Come on then, Burnley."

"Come on then, Bolton," we replied.

We were straight into them. We were game lads, they weren't. A police car sped up the road towards us with the sirens and lights going mad. Everyone separated, the Bolton lads picked up their mates from the floor. A taxi pulled up and one of our lads, Phil Holmes, jumped out and asked, "What's going on, Pot?"

"We've just had it with these cunts here."

The policeman was out of his car and talking to the Bolton lads, who then started pointing at us, the wankers. They brought it on, they came unstuck, then they start complaining to the police. We got on our toes towards the ground. The Crosshills lads went on while Phil and I walked round towards the away end, only to be sent back by police. We chose another way to go and walked into ten Bolton coming up the road with a few police. We walked past them and snarled, "Do you fucking want it, Bolton?" They looked surprised and backed off and looked at the police, who came up to me and Phil and started pushing us away. Watching this, a few of the Bolton started bouncing about, realising they were ten and we only two. The police got on their radios, a police van came down the road and we were on our toes again, the van close behind with the siren going.

We shot past the Wellington. I ran left, Phil ran right, and they followed Phil. He was soon in custody and the Bolton lads outside the Brickmakers identified him as the one who attacked them. Phil never threw a punch but he received a custodial sentence. There were no police on my case, so I hung around a side street waiting for the match to finish, and when it was nearly time I made my way to the Bob Lord stand. Burnley fans were walking past looking pissed off; we were losing. I heard a loud cheer from inside the ground. The final whistle had gone and Burnley fans streamed out of the ground.

I saw Ade walking up the road. Bolton fans had gone on the pitch and there were loads in the Bob Lord stand so we ran straight through the exit points up into the stand. The first thing I saw was Bolton on the pitch. Burnley fans were climbing over the fences in front of the Bee Hole end to get to them, and police horses were also on the pitch, while other Bolton fans were trying to get back into the away stand. I turned to the side to see Bolton fans in front of me and Ade. We steamed into them but suddenly I found myself on my back, stuck between some seats with a fat bastard on top of me. I looked up and saw Ade battling with a few of them and more Burnley joined the fight. They saw me under Fatso and pulled him off. Back on my feet, I had to run as the police closed in. We were out of the ground with our heads down trying to fade into the crowd, and walked past the Wellington towards the centre.

Now I had the taste. I wanted more. A good mob of us managed to bypass the police and make our way to the away end, where Bolton were still coming out of the ground. Police were everywhere but they hadn't noticed us. We waited, there were no lads coming out, only families. Finally, they appeared.

"Su, su, Suicide."

It sounded like there were more of us. We charged in and Bolton scattered. They were on their toes back in towards the away end and we were smacking them for fun. The police came streaming in and we all melted into the crowd, to meet up on another side street. Someone shouted, "They're here." Bolton were walking up the street towards us. "Su, su, Suicide." We charged again and they ran. As I gave chase, I was slammed into a wall. "You're nicked." I struggled to get away but more police arrived and I was handcuffed and literally thrown in the back of a van. I was taken to the station and charged with threatening behaviour.

Burnley ran Bolton ragged that day, and they've never been the same since, thank fuck. Full respect to you, lads. You were the top team in Lancashire – until this day.

I was described in court as a screaming fan who punched a police officer. This is how the prosecution put it: "Innocent people were left shaken after a large group of football supporters bore down on them while chasing a smaller group. Porter was among a group of thirty fans running towards the smaller group. Police noticed Porter howling as he ran down the road. One of the officers had earlier turned him away from a Turf Moor turnstile for being drunk. He still appeared to be intoxicated and was only arrested after a struggle in which he punched the officer." My solicitor said in my defence that my involvement was only minimal and nowhere near as serious as other offences on the same day. I was, he said, responding well to my present community service order, which I still had to complete. They gave me another eighty-two hours to do and I was again banned from football until May 31, 1989.

Burnley v Bolton, 1987, League match
It was the week after the Cup game and they didn't turn up. Enough said.

Burnley v Carlisle, 1987
"Carlisle are outside!"

As if in proof, a golf ball crashed through the window of the White Lion. None of the few lads in there had expected Carlisle to show up, so the warning shout came as a big surprise. We all ran out, some grabbing mops and brushes from a nearby shop. The forty Carlisle outnumbered us and charged us back into the pub doorway, where we battled to keep them out. The police soon turned up, pushed us back into the pub and surrounded the Carlisle lads who were then escorted out of the town centre. We sat in the White Lion, pissed off. Carlisle had come down and taken the piss. We weren't having that.

The rest of the lads started to arrive. They couldn't believe it when we had told them what had happened. Everyone was narked. We all headed up to the pubs around the ground seeking some revenge but there were no Carlisle about. Lads went looking round the streets for vans and it didn't take long to find them. There were two Transits parked on a side street behind the Wellington near to Turf Moor. With this information in mind my beer started to taste better. Fuck all happened during the game and I couldn't wait for it to finish. We all mobbed up behind the Wellington next to their vans. I was proper up for it. Carlisle had given me a good kicking up there a few seasons ago. We spotted them walking down the road with a police escort and waited round the corner, everyone quiet. Carlisle had just passed the Wellington when we all charged out. It was a good mob, about 200-strong. Fuck the escort. I ran straight through it and into the Carlisle fans. Fists and feet were flying and Carlisle were trying to drag me into the middle of them. One cunt pulled a blade out. My mates saw it and came charging in to rescue me. I was dragged back out. Lads were saying I had been cut. They had a look at my back, but the blade had just sliced through my coat and missed my skin.

The Carlisle fans were going nowhere, they were trapped. Police tried to keep us back, swinging their truncheons wildly. I charged back into the Carlisle fans. I didn't give a fuck that they had blades. I was battling with five or six of them. They couldn't get me down and another mate, Steve Smith, came running in to help me. Steve was a big lad; he just grabbed hold of me, picked me up and took me back to the Burnley fans but my head had gone and as soon as he put me down I was straight back into them. I think they were getting a bit pissed off with me by this time. All I could hear was, "Su, su, Suicide." Again, I was fighting with a number of lads and this time I got put on the floor but not by the Carlisle fans, by the police. I was handcuffed and put into a van. I could still hear the sound of the battle going on but my entertainment was over for the day.

I was charged with using threatening words and behaviour. The court was later told, "Porter was seen lashing out wildly with his feet and fists. He had lost self control and was inciting a large group of Carlisle fans." My solicitor put my version, that I had had not been to the match but had visited a friend's house after playing soccer for a local team and, as I walked home, was surrounded by Carlisle fans and fighting broke out. I was not in the group of Burnley fans and was not a member of the Suicide Squad.

For some reason the court didn't believe my story and I was given a 200-hour community service order plus a six-month banning order.

Bolton v Burnley, 1988

This game was worth the risk of breaking my ban. After the FA cup and league games at Turf Moor, we had to put on a good show at Bolton. Two coaches were organised, one-way only for the short trip. A good 120 lads were on Bolton's streets shortly after eleven in the morning with not a policeman in sight. We headed straight towards the centre. I was at the front, looked back at all the lads and I felt proud to be part of this mob. Everyone was well up for it.

We went into a pub straight across from Yates's. There was no singing or shouting, it was up to Bolton to come to us now. We had done our job. We had got there unnoticed and we were drinking in their centre. We waited and waited, Bolton weren't showing and some of the lads were getting impatient. Small groups left the pub to have a scout round but soon came back with smiles on their faces, telling us they'd had it with Bolton and had chased them off. The trouble now was that the police had followed them back to the pub and turned up in force. Once we'd been sussed the singing started, glasses started to smash, a window went through and we spilled out onto the street and walked back towards Yates's. The police pushed us back and the dogs were soon out of their vans barking like fuck. We were surrounded by police. "Su, su, Suicide", echoed all around the streets and shoppers were stopping to have a look.

The police started to move us towards the ground. We walked past a pub with the curtains closed and someone inside decided to have a peek at our mob walking past. This was a bad mistake. The window soon went through and to the call of, "Come on Bolton," missiles flew into the pub. The police came in with dogs and pushed us away from the windows. "Su, su, Suicide," we charged forward and more riot vans turned up. Police poured out, batons already drawn, and lads were wrestled to the floor, handcuffed and arrested. Order was restored and we were escorted to the ground.

As Burnden Park came into sight, the police started to jump back into their vans and about forty of us left the escort in ones and twos. We walked to a big pub outside the ground, usually packed with Bolton, and found a small mob outside. They didn't notice us until it was too late and the first punch had landed. Under a rain of blows and kicks, Bolton scattered. We walked into the pub expecting a hostile reception but there were already a few Burnley in and the Bolton lads didn't want to know.

I was buzzing like fuck. How many times had I seen Bolton turn Burnley over? Now the shoe was on the other foot. I hope they felt the way I did when Bolton took the piss. We stayed in the pub until kick-off. I hadn't definitely decided to go due to my ban but I thought, fuck it, if I get sussed I get nicked and if I don't then it's a bonus. I kept my head down on the way to the turnstiles, mingling with the Burnley shirties and got through, no problem. All the lads were already on the terrace and I made my way over to them and stood in the middle of the mob, keeping my head down. Burnley had brought thousands, which was good for me as it's harder to spot someone on a packed terrace.

We all thought Bolton would want revenge after the game, and as we walked out together, I couldn't wait. Everyone was itching to get at the Bolton lads. We walked across a grass wasteland and saw Bolton in front of us. "Su, su, Suicide," everyone started to charge towards Bolton. There weren't just 120 of us, there were thousands, all chanting "Suicide". Bolton saw us running at them and just melted. Then the horses charged through us, knocking people to the floor. Dog handlers chased people round and the dogs were trying to savage anyone in reach. Riot police went steaming in, not caring who they hit, and pushed people back towards their coaches.

Our mob headed back towards the centre but the police soon rounded us all up. They had laid on a special train so that we would get out of town and we were escorted to the station. No Bolton tried to attack. I felt good. I had waited so long for this, my main rivals put to sleep. We bossed the day. It was a long time coming but we eventually did turn up and we turned them over on their own patch.

CHAPTER EIGHT

ENGLAND EXPECTS

Euro 88

This would be my first away trip following the national side. I had heard all the stories about battles on foreign soil and I wanted a bit of it. I had missed the game against Germany in Düsseldorf months before; all the lads came back with good tales to tell, saying the Germans were up for it, so I wasn't going to miss the Championships.

My wife hadn't been too pleased about the previous year's events, and in an effort to save my marriage, I had decided to move to Luton with her, our two lovely children and her parents, who were sound. They were originally from London and had family in Luton. My wife's uncle rented us a large house on Trinity Road, near the town centre. The area looked alright and I quickly found a job making double-glazed windows, but it didn't take long for me to start missing my mates and the football violence. I used to phone Simon up to find out what the Squad had been up to, and he'd tell me about the battles. I was buzzing just listening to them but was also sick I was missing out.

With a third kid on the way, money was tight, so the only thing for me to do was to sell the car. I had lost my licence six months previously for drink driving but I was sorry to see my first car go. I was hoping to save money weekly to finance my trip, but things don't happen like that when you have bills to pay. I still hadn't enough money, so the car had to go. The problem was that I had to sell it quick and the lad buying it knew that, so I sold it for £700 less than I had bought it for, but fuck it, I was going to Germany.

I met up with Simon and we went down to the travel agents and got a month's inter-rail apiece, giving us unlimited train travel for a month. That was it, our holiday had been paid for. I still had money in my pocket, so the only thing for it was an all-day session on the piss. Out of the travel agents and into Yates's, we were downing our first pint by twelve bells. Then it was off to the Butterfly, our local at the time, to meet up with my brother and a few of the lads. Simon and I were on a high, asking everyone if they were going to Germany. When they said no, we would reply, "Oh well, it must be us then!"

The beers went down fast. We left the Butterfly and went on a pub crawl around Burnley Wood, taking in six pubs on our route, and made our way to the Corporation pub for the Friday afternoon strippers. It was absolutely packed on Fridays; all the lads were in there and Simon and I were getting louder after each pint. At around six o'clock the lads started disappearing for some tea or to get ready for a night out. Me, Simon and my brother Ade went way back to the Butterfly where more beers were downed, then the three of us staggered to the town centre. We took in the Sidewalk, Yates's, Swan, White Lion, Red Lion, Big Window and Smacks, then made our way back to the Sidewalk. On our way back we had a small argument with some lads, nothing major, or so I thought.

Once in the Sidewalk, I went to the bogs and by the time I got back a major gap had appeared. I pushed through the crowd, saw plenty of police outside and my brother being put into the back of a cop van. Then Simon came past with his arm up his back with a copper behind him.

Simon said, "Thought you were Suicide?"

"I am," I replied, walked up to the copper holding Simon and punched him to the floor.

The police came steaming in, tables and chairs were flying everywhere and the bandits went over. The coppers dragged me to the floor and then hauled me out of the pub by my legs, with one of them on top of me trying to get handcuffs on. They managed to throw me and Simon into the back of the van that already contained my brother. The police station was only 100 metres from the Sidewalk pub but it took nearly ten minutes to get there. Three of us in the middle of the van, three policemen either side of us. We weren't for keeping peaceful and neither were they. All I can say is, I hold no grudges. I think we had the best of it and I think the police were glad to get us to the station.

Once there, the van was reversed to the doors, the back was opened and we were faced with a line of police up both sides of the steps leading into the station. It was like being in a rugby scrum all the way up the steps to the charge desk and then they put us into separate cells, still handcuffed. After that it was a case of getting your head down and waiting till morning to see what charges had been brought and if we were getting bail. We all did. I was charged with threatening behaviour, police assault and police obstruction. Ade got charged with police assault and threatening behaviour, and Simon was charged with threatening behaviour. We were all back in the Butterfly for one o'clock, starting another all-day session and having a laugh.

(After we were sentenced, the local paper said, "Three football hooligans singing 'Suicide invasion of Germany' have been jailed.")

So, Simon, Mick and I were off to Germany. Needless to say, we started off with plenty of beers on the train down to London and the banter was good. In London we made our way to the Lancaster Gate headquarters of the English FA to try to get some tickets. We had heard you could get them from there. We filled out some sheets of questions, showed our passports and waited. I don't know what they thought of three pissed-up lads, two of them convicted football hooligans, sitting in their lobby waiting for tickets. Anyway, out popped a woman who asked what semi-final tickets we wanted. She advised us to buy both but we were not shelling out for a ticket we weren't going to use, so we decided to buy tickets for just one semi and try and use them wherever we ended up playing. The woman never said a word, but just sat and listened to our conversation. We opted for the Hamburg semi and the three group games. She looked at us, walked through a door and a couple of minutes later came out with our tickets. We handed over £78 each.

Tickets in hand, we walked out of the door and into the nearest boozer, bought two beers and laughed our bollocks off at how easy it was to get the tickets. We finished our drinks and headed for the off-licence to get beers for the train journey to Dover and then the ferry to Ostend. The train journey was again filled with stories of battles and the time flew by. I had downed all of my beer and was feeling a little worse for wear, but we hit a few pubs in Dover for good measure before boarding the ferry. This was turning out to be a really good session; we were just priming the pump. We boarded the ferry no problem. Now I knew my journey had begun, this was it.

We were leaving friendly shores towards uncharted territory. I had been involved in numerous battles at home but this was unknown to me. The rush was well on its way, the sick feeling, the "fuck 'em" attitude and the knowledge that what will be will be. We hit the bar, then went to the duty free shop. I bought a few bottles of wine instead of queuing at the bar and these would come in handy while we were waiting for the next round to arrive. We also all purchased a litre bottle of Blue Label Smirnoff vodka each for the train journey into Germany.

When we arrived in Ostend, I was well and truly pissed, staggering through Passport Control. I barely realised that we hadn't seen another England fan on our journey; we were the only ones. But, I thought, sod it, whatever comes at us we will deal with one way or another. Mick took control of finding out about the trains and where and when we had to change. I didn't have a clue. We boarded the train and got our own little compartment with six seats in it and a table near the window, which was soon filled with three pints which had come off the ferry, three bottles of vodka, three bottles of orange juice and a bottle of Coke. That was our bar sorted.

Hector the collector came in once to check the tickets. We didn't have a clue what he was saying and he started waving his arms about muttering "English this" and "English that". The reply was, "Here are our tickets, now fuck off." He never popped in to see us again. The vodka was flowing and the next thing I knew I was being woken up.

"Fuck me, Pot. Wake up, we're here." We were pulling into Stuttgart station. "We've had to carry you from train to train, we even put you on a luggage trolley, now sort your fucking head out."

I staggered out of the station and into the sunlight. I was rough, and Simon and Mick looked well pissed. We wandered through the town and finally arrived in the main square. It looked like there was a town hall with steps and squares of grass and bushes here and there. Simon and Mick made their way to the grass and said, "Right Pot, it's our turn to get some sleep, you watch over the bags." Around the square were little kiosks selling fags and beers, so the only thing for it was to get a few liveners down my neck. By the time the lads had woken up I had a good collection of empty cans round me. We headed back to the station where we put our heads under a tap for a quick wash, brushed our teeth, changed our clothes and went to left luggage to leave our bags under lock and key.

Off the square were side streets full of bars. We hit the first and got a light beer apiece. The glasses were massive. We had started to see a few England fans about but there were more Irish, our first opponents in the competition. We were making our way from bar to bar when we heard someone shouting, "Pot, Mick, Simon – up here." We looked up to see Dev hanging over the balcony of a bar.

"Fuck me, Dev, how did you get here?" I asked.

"Well, I heard you had set off so I just got a flight out of Manchester. I've only been here a couple of hours."

I couldn't believe it, all that way and we bump into Dev, one of our top lads. Three became four and we heard that the place for the English to be was a pub called the Ascot bar. There we met a few Palace fans who'd been up to Burnley a few times so the banter started straight away. One Forest fan, sitting between me and Simon, told how he'd got into Germany using a false passport. His name was Paul Scarrott and, according to the papers, he was England's Number One hooligan. I've read stories about the lad, but I thought he was sound, just one of us but with a bit of press coverage. The papers later ran a story claiming that Scarrott had been seen in Ascot bar with his two "generals", plotting trouble. Well I was no general and I was plotting fuck all. We were just chatting and singing, "Su, su, Suicide." That was the chant for the day and even Scarrott was singing it.

After a few hours in the Ascot bar some German punk rockers came in and started singing, trying to shake everyone's hands. They might have been friendly but it always felt like they were trying to take the piss out of you. As time went on, we all got louder. The Germans had a dwarf with them and everyone was saying he was their main man. Then the dwarf was caught trying to pick Fat Stan's pockets. Stan, a Palace fan, went mad and shouted, "You little cunt, you've just tried to rob me, fuck off," and gave him a back hander. The lads were pissing themselves and Stan was getting hold of the dwarf when one of the other Germans took a swing at him and then the dwarf threw a glass at us. So that was it, over the table we went, straight into them. They stood for a moment, but only a moment. My main concern was getting hit on the back of the head with a glass thrown by one of the English lads. The dwarf and his mates were kicked out of the door and down the street and the Ascot bar closed for the rest of the day, so it was time to find another watering hole.

We walked around the corner and outside McDonalds were a mob of German skinheads. We walked up the road, no singing, no shouting, getting closer. All of a sudden the dwarf came bouncing out of the crowd followed by plastic glasses of beer. We just kept on walking and they seemed to be getting braver. The distance between us closed and, bang, we were in the middle of them. The floor started to fill up with green flying jackets and camouflage jackets as we split them up and picked our targets. Then the bouncers from a club across the road came over to join in the party but it was a bit too rough for them and they scattered, picking their mates off the floor as they ran. We couldn't help thinking, was that it?

We made our way to the club where the bouncers had come from. The entrance was at street level and there was a flight of stairs down to the bar room. More bouncers came running up the stairs but we were thirsty so they were put to one side. The bartender had already pulled a few beers when we got to the bar and we started to drink. Then a few bouncers came downstairs with a few big lads. Round two, we figured. As there was only one way out. We approached the group at the bottom of the stairs ready, but then one of the Germans pulled out his wallet and flashed his police ID.

They took us out of the bar and onto the street where the other Germans had gathered again. Minibuses of police had arrived, blue lights flashing, but we went through them and into the Germans again. The cops were surprised and so were the Germans, who scattered once more. I saw Mick, Dev and Scarrott getting put into one of the vans. It would be the last time I would see Mick for a few months; he was locked up for the rest of the championships. So was Scarrott. When I returned to England I couldn't believe the press coverage about him, how he'd organised the battle in the Ascot bar, how he had led the charge around the corner on that day. I never saw him throw a punch, let alone organise anything.

Once we saw Mick and Dev locked up, Simon and I headed for another bar away from the street and quickly got back into the swing of things. A few of the Palace lads came in and we got talking about what happened and what would happen to Mick and Dev. Simon and I had no accommodation but the Palace lads invited us to their campsite. They had no spare tent but they had plenty of beer. Besides, I could get a fire started at night for a bit of warmth.

Next morning when we woke, the first thing we did was start drinking. A caravan was next to the tents and I asked if anyone had been using it. They said that they hadn't seen anyone. One of the lads said that the caravans were often left during the week and used only at weekends. So that was it, our accommodation was sorted for our stay in Stuttgart. Simon and I then set off to the train station for a wash and to brush our teeth. Outside was a big mob of English and a lot of police. After our clean-up we went back to the town square for another session and were in the first bar when we saw Dev. He came over with a big grin on his face. No matter what shit he was in, he always wore a smile. He had been held for a few hours, then released, but said he thought Mick was getting charged.

We moved on to another pub and bumped into two more Burnley lads, Bern, a good solid lad, and Ian Makey, who was a few years younger than me and keen (sadly he got his head blown off a few years later in an argument). I still couldn't believe that I had come all this way to bump into people I knew. In years to come it would be a regular occurrence. The day passed off quietly. There were a lot of England supporters about but we seemed well outnumbered by the Irish and we made our way back to the camp. I don't know how you find your way around foreign soil but I seemed to get it right most of the time, even though I was well out of my head. We had already decided we were sleeping indoors that night and lifted Ian on to the top of the caravan so that he could pull the skylight off, jump in and open the door. I don't think the Palace lads were too impressed. They asked us what we were doing and we replied, "Getting our heads down in here for the night." The caravan door popped open and in we piled, straight on to the beds.

I woke up the next morning with the sound of frying and the smell of food in my nostrils. Dev had got up early and got a load of beers in. "Alright Pot, I've put the beers in the fridge, the Germans have left us a load of food, it would be rude not to eat it. I'm the chef today, cheese omelette and a can of beer is on the menu." It was the first food I had eaten since leaving English soil and I got breakfast in bed.

It was the day of the game. In town, as usual, there were a load of Irish still outnumbering us, but they weren't after trouble and the England fans seemed the same. We went to the train station to see if any more Burnley lads had made their way over. There the atmosphere was a total contrast. All the England fans seemed up for it. There were a lot of police around, most of them in a line across the street, separating the English and a large mob of Germans. The Germans seemed up for it as well, not the same type of lads we had encountered a few nights before.

We made our way through the England fans into the station, checked the bags, had a wash and loaded up with a few cans of beer. The mood outside was getting more volatile and we joined the mob. It was only a matter of time before it all went off. We made a charge at the police lines, but they and the German mob stood firm. We charged again and a barrage of missiles followed behind us. The police had had enough. They drew their truncheons, brought in the dogs and steamed right in to us, splitting us and pushing us away from the Germans. Snatch squads were pulling people out and there was tear gas in the air. It's funny how the mood of a crowd can change in a matter of minutes.

We made our way to the ground, nothing to report, shit game, we got beat, the Irish didn't want to know, so it was back to the square to drown our sorrows. We cleared a few bars when we thought the Irish were taking the piss, the police came in but we pushed them back with a barrage of missiles. They steamed back into us with the big stick so tables got dismantled to use as weapons. We had them on the run to the extent that some of them drew their guns. Most of the English dispersed so it was back to the campsite for us to get a good night's kip.

The next day was all about sorting our heads out. One of the lads wanted to fire the caravan but it was too near to the tents, so that idea went out of the window. We were depressed about the result but we had Düsseldorf and the Dutch to think of. Plus the Germans down there were well up for it. England had played there in a friendly and the Germans had turned out big style.

Düsseldorf – England v Holland

The stage was set, the Dutch and the Germans were supposed to be turning up and we were already there waiting for them. The atmosphere in Düsseldorf was a complete contrast to Stuttgart. As soon as we got off the train you could feel the tension. Firstly, there were more English lads, everyone in their own little mobs. A lot had missed the first game against the Irish but this was the game to be at. The station was well policed and there was heavy press presence, with film crews everywhere. A few Germans stood around in their flying jackets, some trying to talk to us, but all they got back was, "Fuck off." The police were always watching and you got the feeling the Germans were put there by the police to start something. If it did start you knew it was the English that would be nicked.

We met a few lads from Colne, Nelson and Brierfield and moved away from the train station. We had heard that one part of town was wall-to-wall bars, so made our way there. There were English mobs everywhere. Tales kept filtering through about Germans roaming about, picking off the English. As we made our way from bar to bar the tales got taller but we encountered no opposition. The word was that the Dutch wouldn't arrive until the day of the game, as Düsseldorf was on the border of Holland, bottle-less bastards. A few of the lads decided to go into a sex shop so we all followed. Everyone was looking at big dildos and wank magazines. At least ten lads squeezed into a wank booth. The coins went in, the numbers were programmed, and then this old bloke pops up on the screen wanking over a pig. Well, that was it, one of the lads shouted out, "Your dirty German fucker," and all the other lads burst out laughing. The old bloke could have been any nationality, even English, but today he was German.

Someone decided to kick the TV screen through and we all left the booth. The shopkeeper ran from behind the counter only to see his wank booth being turned over. He went mad, shouting his head off, so one of the lads hit him on the head with a dildo. I couldn't stop laughing. We stumbled out of the shop and most of the lads had dildos or vibrators in their hands and proceeded to smack everyone on the head with them, including Germans walking down the street. They didn't seem to find it funny; mind you, neither did I. The dildos were OK, they were soft and bent around your head, but the vibrators were a different story, they were hard as steel. One of the lads ran up behind me and smacked me on the back of the head. I thought it was a truncheon. I looked round and the cunt is pissing himself running up the road. What could I do except laugh. A German lad got smacked with a dildo and it took the shape of his head from ear to ear. He shouted a few obscenities in German but we didn't give a fuck.

The lads soon got bored with this. We had worked up a thirst so it was back to finding the bars. We found the Old Town, which was a street full of bars, a drinker's paradise and we planned to have a drink in every bar before the night was over. We all settled down with a beer apiece laughing about what happened in the sex shop. We were moving from bar to bar, well from table to table. A different waiter would come out each time for our order. It was great when you didn't have to waste time queuing at the bar. The street was full of English lads, everyone asking what team you supported.

In every bar we heard different stories about the Germans and Dutch and most of it was bullshit. About thirty yards down the street it opened into a large square with loads of different streets sprawling off it. The time was getting on and it was going dark. I think the Italians were playing someone. You'd hear shouts from inside the bar where lads were crowding round a TV but I wasn't interested in other teams so we just carried on drinking. There were English in every bar, the streets full of lads singing songs and a few standing on tables. It was getting quite boisterous. The TV game finished, I think the Italians won.

A few carloads of victorious fans started going past the square with flags out of the window, pipping their horns. One was surrounded by English spilling out of a bar and was overturned. You could hear smashing glasses down the street. We were just finishing our beers when a Man U lad came running up.

"There's a big mob of Germans across the square."

The beers were downed quickly. "Come on, let's have it." English lads spilled out of the bars across and down the street. We had a good mob together and ran across the square. The Man U lad was right. In front of us, coming out of a street was a large mob of Germans. They came bouncing along, well armed with baseball bats and pieces of wood. The Burnley lads were all together and we went straight into them, throwing punches and kicks everywhere. English lads were being knocked down and sometimes it was necessary to go in to rescue them if they had a few Germans kicking them. In we'd fly, backing them off, picking up the lad and getting back into the English lines. There was a lot of running in followed by backing off.

The Germans seemed to be getting round the sides of us, and Burnley and a mob of Bolton found themselves together. The Germans were pushing us back, so the cry went up, "Come on, stand and fight." But when I looked, to my amazement there was only us and Bolton left. We couldn't just turn and run, somebody could easily be left that way, so we still fronted the Germans, running forward exchanging a few punches, then dropping back. We couldn't let them get around us; we would be surrounded if they did. We had created enough space between us to let everyone know we were going to run. Everyone knew the score; we worked out where we were running.

We ran into the Germans one last time to put them on the back foot, then we were off, with them on our arses. We ran down a street with chairs stacked in piles outside the bars. I was running past when this cunt started pulling them all over as he's running past them, so I had to hurdle these chairs. I tripped over one and went arse over tit. I was on the floor looking at a German standing over me, bat in hand, swinging it at my head. There was fuck all I could do except wait for the thud and the stars to appear but, all of a sudden, there was a hand on my collar dragging me up. I felt the draught of the bat as it passed my face. I was up and running with Simon at my side.

He'd seen me flying over the chairs and came back for me. He'd saved my life for all I knew. We kept running down different streets until they had given up chasing. I burst out laughing, thanking Simon, maybe it was nerves but soon the laughing stopped and the anger rose. Where did all the rest of the England fans go, leaving us and the Bolton at the front getting fucking run by the Germans? I didn't come to this country to run. We made our way back towards the square to see a large mob marching towards us. I was in the middle of the road. Someone shouted out, "Who the fuck are you?" I replied, "I'm fucking English, where the fuck were you when the Germans turned up, on your toes?" Another lad then said, "We run from no-one." So then it was back to the square and as we walked past the bars other English came out to join us. Now we were building a top mob. Still more came out. We got to the square where there were loads of police about, particularly on one street. Through the police we could see the Germans drinking outside the bars all with smiles on their faces. They thought they'd had a result.

The police saw us coming but they weren't going to stop us and the German smiles vanished as they all tried to get into the bars at once, pushing each other out of the way. We broke through the police and went into them. They were the same cunts who'd chased us but now it was equal numbers. Tables and chairs went flying into doorways and through windows. Germans were climbing over the bars but they weren't for coming out, so we had to go in for them. We went through the hail of glasses and in, dragging them out of the doors, some by the legs, some by the arms. Their mates could only throw glasses and they soon ran out.

Then someone had a grip on my collar again, only this time it wasn't Simon, it was a policeman. He dragged me and another lad into the square, which by this time resembled Blackpool Illuminations with lights flashing everywhere. We were bundled into the back of a van and Simon and Dev soon followed. Our drinking was over for the night. Dev said he'd got into a bar when they ran us at first. He'd had a beer then seen us walking past and came out to join us but everything kicked off. There were probably ten lads in the van by this time. It started moving and all you could hear was the sound of sirens. The van stopped, the door opened, we were told to get out and we were in the yard of a police station or jail. We went up some steps and through a door one by one. Our details were taken and then we were put into a cell. The cells were for one person but the door of mine kept opening and more lads kept coming in, including Simon and Dev. There must have been twenty of us in there and you could hear lads going into other cells on either side of you.

Inside the cell there was a bog in the corner and a bench. Everyone was squashed against each other. They tried to get their heads down but there was not much chance of that because if someone wanted a piss, everyone had to move. It was a case of getting to know each other by asking questions like where are you from, what do you think will happen, will we get out for the game? Everyone seemed to think we would miss the match.

"My stomach is killing me," said Simon. It was going to be a long night. After a couple of hours Simon announced, "I've got to go for a shit. I have to shit now." I was so glad I wasn't near the bog. Everyone seemed to be asleep as he tried to get to the bog without bumping into people or moving them. It was like going through a minefield. He got there and the lad next to it had to move. Simon dropped his pants and, splat, out it all came. Dev and I roared with laughter but now it was a case of trying to find some bog roll to wipe his arse and we got the pleasure of waking everyone up looking for it. Simon wasn't too impressed, but in the end, so to speak, you need to wipe your arse and eventually we found some. The whole thing was funny and definitely worth the stink (and it did stink!).

By the time the day came around the cell was hot so we were banging on the door for some cups of water. Most of the lads felt the same as me, rough as fuck off beer. As time went on we were taken out to another room where we were put in front of a desk one by one. There was an interpreter and a German sat behind the desk. I didn't know who he was, he might have been a judge, head of police, anyone, I didn't have a clue. The interpreter told me but it went in one ear and straight out of the other. They asked what we were doing when we got arrested then said they were keeping us until after the game.

We got out after ten o'clock, set free in little groups. Simon and I went straight into a bar across the road for a few liveners and waited for Dev but he never showed. After a while, with a few others, we made our way over to the train station and, as we turned the corner, there was a big mob of Germans out front, with a line of police stopping them going into the station or the English coming out. We had no alternative but to go into the station; our bags were in the left luggage lockers. There was only one thing for it, we had to go through the German mob.

As we approached them nothing was said. I remember thinking, fuck me, what a day, straight out of the cell and into another battle. The Germans watched us approach and did nothing. We quickened our pace and still nothing was said. It was weird. Then, when we were about ten yards from them, they separated and let us through. I couldn't believe it. This couldn't be happening but it was and we walked through the Germans and up to the police line. They wouldn't let us into the station and pushed us back into the German mob. "Look we're English, do we look German?" I argued. After a few minutes arguing, pushing and showing our documents from the cells, they allowed us into the station.

Inside were English in little mobs all over the place, some trying to get their heads down, some drinking. I made my way over to the lads that were drinking where I acquired some cans of beer and listened to the tales they had to tell about the Dutch and Germans. Apparently it went off after the game with the Dutch outside the ground. Plus it went off in the train station between the Dutch and the Germans with the English caught in the middle. Some German had tried to drive his car through the front of the station and the police had arrested another German for carrying a gun. These are the tales you usually hear at England games. I don't know if it was a load of bollocks because I wasn't there.

Anyway, I soon got fed up with tales of what I had missed and decided to check on the bags, get a wash, change my clothes and brush my teeth. We got a few cans out of the bags and bumped into the Palace fans again. Most were asleep on the floor in their sleeping bags. Fat Stan was awake, plus he always had plenty of beer. So we sat around, chatting with Stan for a few hours. He told us a group of English lads were taxing other English lads and to be aware of it. Simon and I had decided to make our way home in the morning; money was short and England had lost again and couldn't qualify. We couldn't see anything happening with the Russians so we went to the train destination board to find out how to get to Ostend. The next train was at nine o'clock the next morning so it was time to get some sleep. We decided to get our heads down next to Stan, considering what he had said about the taxing situation. I slept for a couple of hours then woke up to find Simon missing so I went back to sleep only to wake a few hours later and still no Simon. I wondered where he had gone but decided he couldn't have gone far so returned to the land of nod.

I woke up in the morning as the police were rousing everyone and the trains had started running. I went to the kiosk for a few cans of beer and Simon came past.

"Where the fuck have you been all night?" I asked. "I thought the Germans had sneaked in and kidnapped you."

"No," he said. "I was watching your back all fucking night. I went for a piss and heard some lads talking. They were on about taxing you and Stan so I just kept watch."

This pissed me off. "Right, where are these lads now?"

"They fucked off on an early train; they were Man City and Northampton fans."

"Fucking wankers," I replied, and then forgot about it.

We got our bags and a load of cans for the train then boarded for our destination. We got ourselves a compartment to ourselves so we could have a stretch and get our head down. Once the journey was underway we saw an English lad dodging Hector the collector all the time. He kept passing our compartment so I told him to come in for a beer. He was a West Ham fan who had jumped the train over with his mates but lost them in Düsseldorf. He had only come out for one game. The beer was flowing and we soon ran out so I went to the buffet car and bought more. We told the guy to stop worrying about Hector as we had Mick's train and ferry ticket in his bag. It would be pointless wasting them, so the problem was solved and a good session started.

Once we had boarded the ferry at Ostend, we grabbed a few beers and then Simon suddenly jumped up and gripped this English lad.

"This is one of the lads that was after taxing us."

One of the lad's mates came along and asked, "What's going on, who the fuck are you?"

"We're Burnley," I replied. "Who the fuck are you?"

"Northampton."

With that the West Ham lad jumped up shouting, "Do you want it, ICF?" The Northampton lads bottled it, you could see the fear.

"Let's have 'em over the ferry," suggested the Hammer, at which some of Northampton's mates disappeared behind other passengers. The lad Simon had hold of was as white as a sheet. Simon gave him a clip round the ear and fucked him off and the three sat back down with our beers and had a laugh.

Minutes later, this guy came over to us and asked, "Were you nicked in Düsseldorf?" Puzzled, we admitted we had been but asked how he knew. "Your picture is in the centre pages of the *Daily Mirror*."

"Fuck off!"

He showed me the paper with my photo and the caption, "Nicked, Millwall fan and mate." I pissed myself laughing. We got back to London on the train and wished the West Ham lad all the best. I can't remember his name but he was sound.

Back in Burnley we headed up to the Butterfly to tell the lads our tales of foreign soil. They had my *Daily Mirror* picture pinned up on the wall, all expecting not to see me for a while. Mick followed us home six weeks later.

Blackpool v Burnley – pre-season, 1988

Blackpool was always a good day out and everyone seemed to go. On this occasion most took the train, but I travelled over by car with three other lads. The driver was going to do a bit of fishing off one of the piers. It didn't take long to find the rest of the lads and the crack was good. We moved from pub to pub towards the ground, but I was banned and it wasn't worth the risk for a game like this.

Around forty of us walked round Blackpool's end. They were queuing up outside the turnstiles and we charged towards them chanting, "Su, su, Suicide." The Blackpool lads jumped the turnstiles to get into their end. None of them would come back out. Police horses came up the road towards us, so we all made our way to the big car park beside the ground. We spotted a Blackpool mob going down a side street, charged down and flew straight into them. They stood and soon the whole street was fighting. A few of the Burnley lads were waving blades about and Blackpool started to get on their toes, with Burnley giving chase. The police appeared on their horses and charged us down the street. Police vans started to pull up and police leapt out of them and they steamed straight into us.

Our driver was waiting, so we jumped in his car but as we were about to set off one of my mates ran over and asked for a lift to the train station. He said he'd slashed someone but he thought it was a Burnley lad. We dropped him off at the station and got the driver to wait on a side street while we looked for any Blackpool fans. As we approached a junction, two lads walked past and one of my mates banged one of them. I don't know what was said but I just punched the other. A copper ran towards us. We got on our toes but he was close behind me. I ran across a petrol station forecourt but slipped on the greasy surface and he was on me.

I was nicked, taken to the police station and charged with actual bodily harm. They kept me in the cells until Tuesday and then took me to court. I had other charges pending at Burnley so I knew I was looking at a remand in custody. The magistrate didn't disappoint. I was taken to Risley Remand Centre and then to Preston jail. Seeing as I had more serious charges at Burnley, they transferred the Blackpool case there so I could be sentenced on all charges on the same day.

Me, Simon and Ade all appeared in court together. Our main charges were for the fight in the Sidewalk. Simon received a two-month sentence for threatening behaviour, Ade was sentenced to three months for police assault and threatening behaviour and I got three months for police assault, twenty-eight days in default of payment and two months for the assault in Blackpool, all to run consecutively. For good measure I also got a £200 fine for threatening behaviour. The court banned the three of us from going into any licensed premises for twelve months, but that meant nothing. If you ask a landlord's permission to drink in his pub and he says yes, there is fuck all the police can do. Nice try though.

The Luton Years – 1988–92

I stayed in Luton for several years but never settled. I'd occasionally go for a drink in the town centre. It was OK but no-one talked to you and when they heard my accent they looked at me as if I was a knob. I didn't take kindly to that. "What the fuck are you looking at, do you want some?" was a typical response and I arrived home so many times with the shirt ripped off my back that I started to hate the place. I had to complete my community service order down there too, and it didn't take me long to breach that. They got me decorating a single mother's bathroom and bedroom. There were three of us, two white lads and an Asian, along with a community service officer. The girl who lived there was sound, made us brews all day and sandwiches for lunch and told us we could watch TV in the kids' room.

The four of us were watching *Grandstand* when the Asian lad started fucking around with the kids' toys and jumping up and down on their bed with his shoes on.

"What the fuck are you doing?" I said. "We're trying to watch TV."

"Just having a laugh, man."

The other lads looked at me as though I shouldn't have said anything. After eating, I went back to decorating the bathroom. I was cutting the wallpaper round the toilet pipes with a scalpel when I heard the Asian lad slagging me off. "He's like facking Tin Tin," he said. I wasn't having that and I got up and walked out of the bathroom. He was standing in the doorway of the bedroom.

"What the fuck did you just say?" I demanded.

"Nothing."

"Yeah you did, you called me fucking Tin Tin. You say a lot but do fuck all."

"You what? I'm in the MIGs." The Men In Gear were Luton's football firm.

That did it. "I'm fucking Suicide, you silly cunt." I punched him in the face and he fell into the kids' empty wardrobe and sat there in a daze. I volleyed him right through the back of it. The community service officer grabbed hold of my hand and I didn't realise that I still had hold of the scalpel. The officer was cut but not badly. The Asian lad got off the floor but he wasn't mouthing any more and the other two lads were just standing there. The Asian was told to go home and I was told to fix the wardrobe. Later, I was charged with threatening behaviour.

I went to two Luton games; West Ham away in the semi-final of the League Cup, and Derby away when they needed to win to avoid relegation. I couldn't even raise a cheer when Luton scored. This wasn't my team, these people weren't my mates. It was lousy compared to Burnley, there was no camaraderie at all. I needed a buzz so I took up boxing. I passed my medical and couldn't wait to get into the ring and feel the adrenalin rush. It was good, but nowhere near as good as when I was at football with the lads.

We soon had a new arrival, a gorgeous little girl. I took different jobs, working at a waste paper merchant's and as a carpet cleaner at Luton airport, but my visits back to Burnley started to get more regular and longer and this affected my marriage badly. The writing was on the wall.

CHAPTER NINE

WELCOME TO BARLINNIE

Scotland v England, 1989
One of my worst memories as a child was watching the Scots invade the pitch at Wembley and pull the goals down. Every time we played Scotland at Wembley they took over the ground; they seemed to take all London over too. When England played in Glasgow, where were the England fans? We were supposed to be top dogs. Well, England had taken a small firm up to Glasgow two years earlier and a few of my mates who went said they had done well. This time it was my turn to cross Hadrian's Wall and go into hostile territory.

I set off with Mick, Simon and Ade from Preston on the overnight train. This would get us into Glasgow at around four o'clock on Saturday morning, which would give us time to get tickets for the game. The journey was full of beer as usual and all the talk was about the Tartan Army. This would be a big test.

With no police at Glasgow Central, we walked into the city centre and decided to find an all-night café. We found one full of taxi drivers. We settled down with our brews and butties and asked the drivers if they knew where we could get some tickets. They weren't very helpful, most wouldn't even answer us. The next question was if they knew if there were any bars open early in the morning, which got a better response. We were told the Budgie Bar, near the fruit market, opened at six. At least we wouldn't have long to wait for a drink. We were just finishing our brews when a Jock came in and came straight over to us.

"You looking for tickets, lads?"

"Yeah."

"How many?"

"Six." Fat Stan and his mate Gwidge, both Palace fans, were coming up on a later train.

The Jock said his mate was round the corner with the tickets, he wouldn't do business in the café. Alarm bells started ringing; there might have been a few Jocks waiting, everyone knows most hate the English, but we decided to follow him anyway. Every corner he took we were expecting to be met by a mob of Jocks intent on doing a bit of English bashing but he was true to his word. On the next corner was his mate, waiting in a phone box, who offered us tickets for the south west stand, the Scotland end. They were priced at £12 each and he wanted £15. We thought it was fair so we took them. Who gave a fuck if they were for the Scotland end?

We got a taxi to the Budgie bar where a lot of English were waiting outside. The doors opened and we all piled in. The bar staff seemed surprised to see us, a load of English drinking at this time, but the banter was good. The Jocks who came in after their night shifts were friendly and talkative, just wanting a relaxing beer after a hard night's graft. More English arrived but there was no sign of trouble.

As the hours rolled by, the English were starting to get pissed. We were talking to some Man City fans from the Young Governors mob. Most of them were drinking outside. We were in mid conversation when one of them came inside,

Daft Donald with his glasses on, and asked his City mates, "Who are these then?"

"They're Burnley."

"Let's do Burnley then," he said.

The four of us jumped up and shouted, "Let's have it then."

Behind us, to our surprise, loads of other lads stood, declaring, "We're with Burnley." Daft Donald quickly changed his tune, smiled and said, "I'm only having you on, let's have a drink," so we all sat back down, situation defused.

The train with Stan on was due at ten-thirty so we got a taxi to the station. It was full of police and Jocks all dressed in their tartan kilts. We waited round for an hour. More English continued to arrive but there was no sign of Stan and his mate. We presumed we'd missed them and went to a pub near the ground. It was packed with Jocks but we managed to find a quiet corner and settle down. The Jocks didn't seem to mind us being there. A few more English, from Carlisle, joined us, all sound lads. The Jocks were getting more and more noisy and a few insults were exchanged, but nothing major.

Mick returned from a piss and warned us, "Be on your guard lads, I've just put one in the piss trough." He'd been in the toilets when this Jock had pissed down his leg, so Mick had knocked him out and left him lying in the trough. Realising what this meant, we turned to face the Jocks. They were all staring at us and started singing their stupid songs, but while they were singing they were moving towards us. The four of us jumped up and told the Carlisle fans, "Don't fucking sit down for these Jock cunts." With all of us on our feet, we said, "Come on then." The Jocks stopped in their tracks. They had twelve English trapped in a corner, there was a door at the side of us but it was locked, the only other door was the one we walked through on the other side of the Jocks. We couldn't work out why they hadn't attacked us, then, through all the tartan we saw police helmets heading our way. They surrounded us.

"Right lads, we have been told that you are carrying weapons, one of you has been seen with an axe so we will take you outside to search you."

Mick said, "If you take us outside we will never get back in the pub, search us in the doorway at the side."

The police agreed, so one by one we were taken into the space between the doors and searched. The pub had gone quiet, all eyes were on us. When the police found nothing they were a bit disappointed. They went to have a word with the landlord then came back over to say we could stay.

The police fucked off and the Jocks started singing again while we tried to work out what was going on. If the Jocks hadn't attacked us because they thought we were tooled up, they had now got the police to search us and establish we were not. Did this mean we were now going to get it? But instead the Jocks tried to make conversation, which was a bit strange bearing in mind they were after doing us twenty minutes previously. Everything settled down and we were left to drink our beer in peace. The Carlisle lads decided to make their way to the ground but we stayed and had another. We still had tickets for Stan and Gwidge and thought we might catch them around Hampden Park, and set off.

Jocks were everywhere, passing around bottles of whisky, sherry and every other drink imaginable. I walked up to a Jock with a bottle of QC Sherry, took the bottle out of his hand, had a good drink from it and gave it him back with a "Cheers, mate." You should have seen the look on his face. I walked away laughing to the sound of, "You English cunt." The others weren't too happy with me.

"What the fuck are you playing at?"

"Just having a laugh."

At the ground, a mob of English appeared and charged the Jocks. The police quickly got hold of the English mob and the

Jocks tried to save face by throwing a few bricks. We walked around the ground trying to find our mates, without any luck, so we made our way to the south-west stand. On the way Mick got pulled by a policeman who asked to look at his ticket. Mick showed him and the wanker took it off him and walked away. Mick shrugged his shoulders. "Fucking Jocks."

We still had two spares, so no harm done. We got to the turnstiles and the police, hearing an English accent, said something to Simon. We seemed to get all the attention. They came up to me and asked, "That your can on the floor?"

"No."

"You've just been seen throwing it on the floor."

"It's not my fucking can."

"Right, you're nicked."

Ade came over and said, "What's happening? He's done fuck all." He grabbed my arm. "Leave him," he insisted, "he hasn't done fuck all."

Two more police arrived and took hold of Ade. "Right, you are both nicked." We were escorted to a doorway leading into the stand, and at the end of a short corridor was a charge desk.

"Put your hands behind your back."

"Fuck off."

They grabbed my arms, trying to get them behind my back to put the cuffs on. They were struggling like fuck and another one came, grabbed hold of my head and proceeded to bang it on the wall. Ade jumped in, it was like a rugby scrum, but they managed to get the cuffs on both of us. They dragged us from the floor, slightly battered and bruised, then they spotted a piece of cannabis on the floor and put it into Ade's pocket.

"What the fuck's that?"

"It's yours now."

They finally got us to the charge desk; it had taken ten minutes to get fifteen feet. They asked the normal shit, name, address. I gave mine no problem, as I had a Luton address.

Ade gave his Burnley address.

"Fucking Burnley, I got a kicking at Burnley with Celtic, you Burnley wanker," said a policeman.

They threw me in a container cell with other English and put Ade in one full of Jocks. All the English claimed they were nicked for nothing, which I can well believe. After around half an hour, the cell door opened and in came Ade.

"What happened in there?" I asked.

"Fuck all, nobody spoke to me."

The police were just taking the piss. They charged Ade with possession of cannabis. I burst out laughing; my brother hadn't smoked anything in his life. Finally, we were all taken to London Road police station and told we would be appearing in court on Tuesday because Monday was a Bank Holiday.

We were all placed in different cells and there was nothing to do except sleep the days away. You only got to see other English in the mornings when you were getting a wash. Tuesday came and we were loaded onto buses. I was put on one for the District Court (their version of Magistrates) but I couldn't see Ade. We arrived at the court and were put into a holding cell. One by one lads were taken up and fined. I was working, so paying wouldn't be a problem. My name was shouted out. I walked out of the cell expecting to walk into a court, get a slap on the wrist, walk out, wait for my brother and hope to be on the train home by the evening. Instead, "Sorry, Mr Porter, you should be at the Sheriff Court [our Crown Court]. Your brother is waiting for you." So I was put in a police car and taken to the Sheriff Court. I was thinking that a fine was looking less likely as were my chances of getting the train home that evening.

There were rows and rows of cells or should I say cages, the most I had ever seen in a court building. I was led down the corridor, cells on either side of me with people staring through the bars. I looked back trying to find my brother.

"Right, in here."

Ade was staring through the bars at me. He was with six others and seemed pleased to see me. I explained that they'd taken me to the wrong courthouse and that all the English were getting fined there. Ade replied, "I don't think we will be getting fined here." Among the prisoners were a couple of Jocks and a few English, including a young Leeds lad who said his mum was a magistrate. He was charged with throwing a CS gas canister through the window of a pub. One of the Jocks was there for knocking an English lad's eye out with a chain after the game and another was getting done for attempted murder. The Jocks went first and got bail. Ade and I were next.

We were taken to another cell outside the court where you could be seen by a lawyer. He told us it wasn't looking good, they were going for a remand into custody but he would try to get us bail. He didn't try hard enough: we got remanded for two weeks in Barlinnie jail. We were fucking sick. We knew we would get a warm reception. We were placed on the jail bus, handcuffed to the seats. Jocks were sat at the back, while me, Ade and some more English were a few seats in front of them. Screws sat at the front.

Halfway through the journey a Jock starts mouthing, "You Chelsea scum, Nazi bastards. I'm going to slash you fuckers." The Jocks around him jumped up and tried to move out of the way. The cunt had a Stanley knife blade in his hand and was leaning over the seats in front of him trying to slash Ade, but he couldn't reach as his other hand was cuffed to the seat. The screws seemed oblivious or they didn't give a fuck. Finally one stood up and said, "What's all this then, have you had your fun?" He took the blade off the lad and walked past us smiling saying, "You know what the Scottish are like, lads. They don't like you coming up here and taking the piss." Then he sat back down with the other screws having a laugh.

We saw Barlinnie approaching fast. It looked dark and dismal. I'd been to jail before but this was different. I knew that half of the jail would be after killing us. The gates opened, the bus went through then the gates closed behind us. We were taken into reception and some of the English said that they were going on protection. The screws were advising them to do so. I turned to Ade and said, "There's no way we are going on forty-threes [protection], we'll take our chances on the wing." Two others decided to do the same, Steve, who was a Rochdale fan, and a Lincoln lad. The screws asked if we were sure. We all agreed that we were and then were told to get a shower.

You put all your own clothes in a box and the reception lads ask what size waist and shoes you are. Your own clothes are taken away and replaced with top quality prison shit, including tobacco pouches for shoes. I put my pants on, they were about ten sizes too big, so I went to get some more.

"Have you got any more pants, mate?"

"What's wrong with them?" he said, looking at my boxer shorts.

"No, not my shorts, my pants, they're too big."

"Oh, you mean your trousers are too big, why didn't you say that." He and his mate started laughing. "Here, these will fit."

I showered and changed and we were given some food and placed in what I can only describe as a dog kennel with a seat in it. If you stood up your head hit the roof. It was a tight squeeze for one, but with two of you, I now know how a sardine feels. You couldn't even eat your food. Then the Jocks would bang on the door yelling, "You're going to get hit when you're on the wing." Well, there was no turning back, we'd made our beds and we'd have to lie on them.

The doors opened. "Right lads, you're going on the wing." We were taken from reception across a bit of a yard and then through some gates onto the wing where we were greeted by six screws. The wing was empty. Everyone was behind their doors except for the wing cleaners and the ones who work the serving areas. "Right, here's the first four English hooligans." We were allocated our cells. I was padded up with Steve from Rochdale and Ade was with the Lincoln lad. We were taken to our landing. "Right lads, one of you go in there and get some sheets," directed one of the screws. In the room were about six lads. Ade walked in and the door started to shut. I saw him get kicked in the bollocks and then the door closed. Ade walked out with the sheets in his hand and a black eye swelling. I went in next and as soon as I walked in I heard, "You cunt." The door closed and they all ran at me. I covered up, protecting my head as punches thudded into my body. The screw opened the door. "Get your sheets, next one in."

We were taken to our cells. Mine and Steve's had one bed. They promised us another. After a while the door opened and a bunch of lads were carrying a bed and a mattress. They must have been holding it two fingers each. With one bed, one mattress and one gang of Jocks inside, the screw closed the door again. The Jocks flew into us, hitting us around the body, but it was nothing major, just a bit of a slap.

The door opened. "Right lads, that's enough." They walked out with smiles on their faces thinking that they'd done their bit for Scotland. Steve and I settled down and got some sleep, wondering what the next day would bring.

"Slop out."

This was the best time if someone wanted a pop at you. I walked out of the cell, piss bucket in hand, swilled it out, got a wash and brushed my teeth. To my surprise there were a lot more English here. I had a chat with Ade about the bed situation; he found it highly amusing. Slop-out over, we were banged back up. The door opened again, it was breakfast. All meals were brought to your cell as Barlinnie is a bang-up nick, twenty-three hours a day. A Jock pushing the trolley handed me two plates. I didn't know what was on them. Steve went for the bowls of cereal. He was passed the bowls and they were quickly followed by a kick in the bollocks. He came staggering back into the cell.

"Don't drop the cereals," I said.

He managed to put them on the bed before collapsing and feeling to see if his bollocks were still there. The door slammed shut again.

"Steve, do you want your cereal?"

"Do I fuck."

"Alright, I'll have it."

Steve finally got the feeling back in his bollocks and said, "Right, you can go for the cereal tomorrow."

Things seemed to calm down after that; we'd had our introduction to Barlinnie. Steve and I had a lot in common, we were both Lancashire lads and I knew a lot of his mates so we always had something to talk about.

The door opened. "Porter, you've got a visit." I thought no-one was going to come from Luton to visit me.

"You sure it's me and not my brother?"

"It's you, the more time you waste the less time on your visit."

I followed the screw. "Right, wait here." He left me on the landing right next to the room where you got the sheets from. I was just standing there when some Jock came from behind me and showed me into the sheet room. It was full of Jocks again.

"What's this, another fucking kicking?"

They burst out laughing. "No, big 'un, what you in for?"

"Fighting with the police."

They thought this was an alright charge. All cons hate the police, after all, it's the police and the courts that put us in these places.

"What's your name?"

"Andrew."

"That's a good Scottish name, Patron Saint of Scotland is Andrew."

The screw reappeared. "Porter, visit." I turned to walk out of the cell.

"Have a good visit lad."

I walked down the steps onto the bottom landing and out to the visiting room. I was on a closed visit, which means you sat in a cubicle with a glass or Perspex panel in front of you so you can see the visitor but you can't have any contact with them. I got to my allocated cubicle and there, staring at me, was my brother's bird, Lorna.

"That's the wrong Porter," she said. "I want to see Adrian."

So I said a quick hello and goodbye and then I was taken back to the wing and put back in my cell. I'm sure the screws do these things on purpose to wind you up. Ade got ten minutes to chat to his bird after she'd come all that way, the wankers.

The days rolled by with the same old shit, day in and day out. One time, the door opened and we were invited to video night down the chapel. Because we occupied the last two cells on the landing, we were at the back of the queue. When we got to the chapel there were three seats left at the back and Ade, Steve and the Lincoln lad took them.

"Right Porter, there's a seat right in the middle."

Some of the lads who gave out the sheets were sitting there. "Alright big 'un?" They all stood up. "Here you are, big 'un, your seat's here."

I was surrounded by Jocks. I sat, my mind racing, thinking, is this it? Am I going to get stabbed or slashed? A Jock's voice snapped me out of my train of thought.

"Big 'un, do you want one of these?"

He passed me a packet of sweets. I took one and passed them on. Then they started asking me if I needed anything like toothpaste, shampoo, newspapers and so on. They said that I was alright for an English lad because I was the only English lad to sit with them. I was thinking it wasn't exactly out of choice. The film was called *Prayer for the Dying*; it was about the IRA. I think the screws were having a bit of a laugh.

The Jocks were sound and true to their word. When I slopped out the following morning, a Jock came up to me and handed me a bundle of newspapers, shampoo and toothpaste. "Here you go big 'un," he said in a friendly manner. I don't know why they called everyone big 'un, I'm only five feet ten. Steve and I would read the papers and pass them next door to Ade.

Finally, we got a court date for bail. We'd been locked up for twenty days. Steve and the Lincoln lad had the same court date. As I left the prison I was hoping that I would never see that place again and if I have to I hope it is only on TV. The four of us were placed in a cell again outside the court. Ade went first and five minutes later came out with a big smile on his face.

"I got bail, you should too. Lorna will wait for you outside. She's got a car waiting."

Armed with this good news, I could almost taste a pint. "Porter, you're next." I couldn't wait to get into court believing I was going home. Then the solicitor came over to me.

"We have a problem."

"What?"

"You're banned from football."

"Yeah, but my ban doesn't apply in Scotland."

He sat back down and the prosecutor started to read out all my charges: attempting to enter a sports ground whilst drunk; breach of the peace; resisting arrest and the obstruction of two police officers in the execution of their duty and struggling violently with them. He continued with my previous convictions, mostly football related, plus I had only been out of jail for nine months. The judge looked at me with contempt. My solicitor argued the case for bail but without success.

"Mr. Porter, you are a convicted football hooligan," said the judge. "You have been banned from football in your own country yet you decide to come up here and wreak havoc on our soil. You will never get bail at this court. Take him away."

I was led back to the cell, totally pissed off. Steve looked at me and said, "I thought it was a piece of piss."

"Not today," I replied wearily.

Steve was next in and came out feeling like I did and the Lincoln lad fared no better.

The solicitor lodged an appeal against the decisions with the High Court in Edinburgh. My wife's family put up a £1,000 surety for me. But back to Barlinnie we went. In reception, "Right lads, you know the score, take a shower and we will get you straight back on the wing." We went in for our sheets, the Jocks were asking how we had got on and explained that in Scottish law they had to put you in court before 101 or 110 days in custody, which cheered us up no end. With this in mind we went back to our old cells and the same old shit routine.

The Jocks were sound but then all of a sudden there was a bang on the door. "Are you the English cunts who threw the flare through the pub window? That pub was full of women and children." Rumours started easily in jail. At teatime I pulled the servery lad to one side and asked what had happened. "Some are saying you threw a flare through a pub window." I got mine and Steve's charge sheets and said, "Let your mates read these." The day after, the problem was solved. We even got an apology.

Another birthday in jail, but a few days later I got my present. A screw walked in and said, "Do you want the good news or the bad news?"

"We'll have the bad news."

He pointed at Steve and said, "Get your gear together, you've got bail."

"What's the good news?" I asked.

"You've got bail too."

We got all our condiments together and gave them to the servery lad. On the landing we met the Lincoln lad, who'd made bail too. The three amigos were out of jail together. We got to the release desk, it was the longest hour you could imagine waiting for the paperwork to be done. I couldn't wait to get fresh air in my lungs. We all signed our papers, but the Lincoln lad was told there were two policemen waiting outside, he had a gate arrest for something else and would be picked up as soon as he walked outside. I was gutted for him but the feeling didn't last long.

The first thing we did was hit the station bar. We had a quick pint and then went to see the time of the next train to London via Preston. We didn't have long to wait. I still had my return ticket, while Steve decided to jump it. We boarded and headed straight for the buffet carriage. There wouldn't be time for sitting down on this journey; we had to stand constantly going back to the bar for more beers.

We got into Preston a bit worse for wear and boarded the train to Burnley. Steve decided to have a beer with me, as it was only £10 for a taxi from Burnley to Rochdale. These little trains were hard to jump, especially with only two of you. Hector came for the tickets, I paid my fare from Preston to Burnley, Steve refused and Hector just fucked off. I knew what was coming. We arrived at Burnley Central station to be met with some of Burnley's boys in blue.

"Right Andrew, what have you been up to?"

"Nothing, I have just been released from Barlinnie."

"Where's your train ticket?"

"Here." I passed him two tickets, Glasgow to Preston, Preston to Burnley, everything above board. Steve, though, didn't have any tickets. The police took his details and he explained that he didn't have enough money for the fare and that he would pay for it at Rochdale station tomorrow. The police accepted this and let us go on our way. We had a few more beers together in one of my locals and then he jumped into a taxi home. We have met up a few times since and had some good drinks. He's a top lad.

The court case in Scotland went on for two years. Every time we went up the judge deferred sentencing for three months for good behaviour. The final outcome was a £750 fine for me and a £1,000 fine for Ade. The judge said we'd been to Scotland so many times we could be classed as Scots. Fuck that!

CHAPTER TEN

TURKISH DELIGHT

Turkey v England - Izmir, 1991

We flew from Heathrow to Istanbul on the Saturday before the game. Mick had arranged to meet Fat Stan and his mates there. They were taking the train down to Izmir, while me, Ade and Simon were catching the next flight down. We had a few hours to kill so we decided to have a drink with Stan and his mates. We had to pay £5 to get our passports stamped. We found the lads in the airport bar, had a few beers and caught the connecting flight. There were hardly any people on the plane. One bloke even had a goat with him that ate the headrests on the seats.

We went through Passport Control again and they tried to make us pay another £5. We refused, but after half an hour they let us through. We waited for our bags to come through but they never appeared. They had gone to Ankara and no-one knew when they would be back. They gave us a phone number for the lost luggage department, which we had to phone every day. Simon and I were now fucked. I had given him my money to hold and he'd put it with his in his bag. It was not a good start. By the time we got out of the airport it was the middle of the night and there were no buses or taxis. We decided to walk.

We got to a junction in the road where we could go left or

right and decided to go left as we could see light in the distance. We walked for miles and when we reached the lights we realised it was an industrial complex. We started back and had been walking for hours when a taxi drove past. We managed to wave it down and were taken to the centre of Izmir. It looked like a bombsite, with demolished buildings everywhere and rubble all over the roads. We found a cheap hotel and believe me, it was cheap. The room had three beds and three coat hooks. That was it. Rats ran over your feet when you went for a piss, but beggars couldn't be choosers.

Ade was the only one with any money and the next day he paid for us all on the piss. The Turks were sound and waved us into their bars. Some had never had English customers and crowded round, touching us and bringing their kids in to touch us and bought us beers. It was mad and a little scary at the same time, because it only took one person carrying a blade to take a dislike to you. Night-time got a bit dodgy as well. We went into one bar full of lads, sat down with our beers and everyone was staring at us. One of the locals plucked up the courage to come over and started talking and waving his arms in the air. I looked round at the others and saw they had knives on the tables in front of them. They were just staring at us and the cunt waving his arms. Then the cunt knocked my beer over. The lady at the bar quickly came over, put it back on the table and, in a scouse accent, asked me for money. I pointed at the lad with the arms who'd knocked it over and told her he was paying for it. She had a word with him and his face changed. He stopped waving his arms about and stared at me. She said that he wouldn't pay for the beer. Ade and Simon were looking at me with a worried look on their faces but I couldn't back down now.

I stood up and pointed at the bloke. "You're paying for that fucking beer," I said. "You knocked it over." I was staring straight at him and he started to smile.

"You crazy English."

He paid for the beer and now all his mates wanted to talk to us. The scouse lady came over to us and told us that she thought we wouldn't have got out of there unless I'd done what I had and the Turks in the bar kept sending drinks over for the rest of the night. They even had Simon dancing on the tables.

Our bags turned up on the Monday. We were stinking so much the beggars stopped asking us for money. We collected the bags from the airport and I was pleasantly surprised to find that the money was still in Simon's bag. We moved straight into a hotel which was like a palace compared to the last place, with TV, an en suite bathroom with shower and even a mini bar, all for £7 per night.

Mick and the rest of the lads arrived on the day of the game and met up at the Euro bar, straight across the road from the train station. Up until this point we hadn't seen or spoken to another English lad. We took everyone's bags to our hotel for safekeeping until after the game and spent all day until kick-off drinking in the Euro bar.

None of us had tickets; we planned to pay at the turnstiles. We got taxis to the ground and were dropped off outside the Turkish end, where we drew a few looks, mostly for Stan in his England top. We walked all the way round the ground with Turks everywhere, but they all moved out of our way as we walked through them and nothing was said. We got to the away end and went up to the turnstiles. There was a line of police in front. They asked to see our tickets and we told them we didn't have any. We were expecting to be told to fuck off but the police took us to another turnstile. The Turks were using the next turnstile along and, as soon as they spotted us, bricks started to fly over. The police just pushed us through the turnstiles and we didn't even have to pay.

I couldn't understand the Turks' mentality. We'd just walked all the way round the ground and they didn't want to know, but as we started to go into the ground, they wanted to brick us. We got onto the terrace and saw we'd been put in no man's land. To our right were the English fans, fenced in, and on our left were the Turks. A line of police sitting on their arses was all that was stopping them coming at us. Missiles immediately started to rain down on us. We spotted Simon and the rest of the lads walking round the ground towards us. Turks were moving out of the way to let them through. The police separating us did the same, but as soon as they reached us, the missile attacks started again. See what I mean?

There were fifty of us in no man's land and we couldn't watch the game because too many missiles were raining down. One lad was hit in the head and it looked like his eye had been taken out. We'd had enough. The police were doing fuck all to stop them so we charged at the Turks and put half the end on their toes. The police stood up with their guns drawn and charged towards us. We stopped in our tracks, while the English behind the fence were going mad. The police returned to their seats and the missiles started to rain down again.

The final whistle blew, thank fuck, and we made our way out of the ground. The police had a massive cordon around the coaches ferrying fans to the airport and a representative from the England Travel Club was directing fans to their allocated coaches. Someone asked him where the coach for the train station was and he replied, "There isn't one." It looked like we would have to walk. There were around fifty of us and we tried to walk through the police cordon but they looked at us as if we were mad and asked if we wanted to die. The main policeman came over and asked us where we were going. We told him the train station and he told us to wait for him where we were. He emptied two coachloads of police and told us to get on. The blinds were pulled shut so that the Turks couldn't see us and we were dropped off right outside the Euro bar.

There were no Turks about so we all went in for a few beers.

One of the lads, Pete, an Arsenal fan, decided to go to the hotel and collect a few bags. A few minutes later he came running back, pouring with sweat, and said, "I've just been run down the fucking street by the Turks, there's hundreds of them." Me, Ade, Simon, Mick, Fat Stan and a few others went out of the door to be greeted by loads of them. They came straight at us and we had to battle like Spartans to defend the doorway. Fat Stan was knocked to the floor and the Turks started to drag him away. We all knew that if they succeeded he wouldn't be coming home with us, so we charged, some lads grabbing Stan's legs and pulling him into the doorway. We were fighting like fuck but no blades were flashed.

By the time we got Stan to safety the missiles had started. The Euro bar was full of windows and the doorway was surrounded by glass panels. Lads were still pushing to get out and we were pushing trying to get back in while every window went through. Finally, the lads pushing to get out realised what was happening and let us through the doorway. A lot of the lads had been cut with flying glass, especially Simon, whose face was covered in blood. We all picked up tables and chairs, expecting the Turks to coming flying through the door, the tables acted as good shields as well as weapons. But they didn't try to come in, they just wanted to see how many bricks they could hit you with. Eventually, the police turned up and charged them off.

I took Simon to the toilet to clean up his face. It looked worse than it was; he just had loads of little cuts on his face. The police surrounded the bar to stop any more attacks and one policeman came in to say they were moving us to another bar until our flights were due. They pointed us to an open door next to the Euro bar. We walked up some stairs and went through another doorway into a big room. The only problem was, no beer was being served. They put Pete into a police van and took him to the hotel to get our bags and once we had our stuff back the bottles of vodka got passed round. We were all buzzing about the night's events. The police took us to the airport when it was time for our flights, and that was that.

England v Poland, Poznan, 1991

This was going to be a good trip. Again we would be travelling by ferry and train, taking in a few stops in Germany. There would be eight of us travelling from Burnley and we loaded up the hired van with beer the night before. One of the lads was going to drive us down to London where he would drop us off and later pick us up when we returned. All we had to do was ring him two days before we got back onto English soil. We weren't following any timetable so nobody knew how long it would take us to get back.

The first pick-up was around 4.30am. The driver stopped at the house, banged on the door loud enough to wake the whole street, then got back in the van to wait for a light to come on. A head popped up at the window with a thumbs-up sign and a couple of minutes later a lad appeared with his bag over his shoulder and beers in his hand, jumped in the back and found somewhere to sit.

Not all the pick-ups went smoothly. On one, the first knock at the door didn't do the trick so the driver started kicking it and lads in the van beeped the horn, shouting, "Where the fuck is he?" The lad in question emerged half-dressed with a woman screaming at him, "Do you know what fucking time it is? You've woken the kids and half the bloody neighbourhood. Enjoy yourself and don't fucking come back!" Once in the van the abuse didn't stop; we all got onto his case and he tried to defend himself by saying, "Come on lads, I had a late one last night and I forgot to set the alarm, give me a break." The beers were then handed out and the laughter began. There were five of us in the back and two in the front plus the driver. Madness was blaring out of the stereo.

We'd just got on the motorway and I realised we were one short.

"We've left Rusty."

"No we haven't. He's not coming. He asked us to drop his ticket off yesterday, he's got a temperature of 104 but said he'll be OK in a day or two and will catch us up."

"What did you say to him?"

"I told him to fuck off. He's already paid for the ticket, and I've got it in my pocket. We'll see if we can flog it and buy more beer with the money. Temperature of 104 and he'll be OK in a day or two, who's he kidding?"

We all burst out laughing. The crack kept on like that all the way to London, making the journey fly. We headed for the North London Tavern, Kilburn. It was an easy pub for the driver to find, plus it was simple for him to get back onto the motorway for his return. This is where the trip really began. Everyone was focused on the journey ahead, discussing good places to stop off at, what problems we may come across, how much money to get changed and what time the ferry left. One of us made a few phone calls to arrange a meeting with some of the London lads.

We sank our beers and made our way to the Duke of York, a big pub right outside Victoria station, where we met Stan, the Palace fan and Alan, a Liverpool fan. More beers were drunk and Alan and Stan checked on train times and the routes into Poland, then it was off to Dover for the ferry. Everybody was starting to buzz as the beer had been flowing for a good twelve hours.

Once the ferry set sail, most went to the bar but I headed for the duty free shop for a couple of bottles of wine and a bottle of Blue Label vodka for the later train journey. I got back from the shop and cracked open one of the bottles of wine. Everyone was in good spirits, laughing about Rusty's temperature. There were a few English lads on the ferry and most seemed to be stopping in Berlin for a couple of days, which sounded good to us. We arrived at Ostend, sold Rusty's ticket for £70 and put the money behind the bar of the nearest pub. We ended up staying there a few hours, which meant the train times went out of the window. We were only leaving when the money had been spent.

We finally reached the train station, everyone pissed by now, and decided to jump on the next train to anywhere in Germany. Once in the country we could catch a train to Berlin. We had two compartments between us so it was business as usual, loads of cans and the bottles of vodka. Some of the lads got their heads down, me included, but it was hard to get kip with everyone fucking about, jumping on each other and steaming each other's compartments. But things like that were what made journeys fly by.

We arrived in Cologne in the early hours of the morning, where we had to change trains, but our connecting train wasn't for another six hours. We got off with our bags and wandered around the concourse. Nothing was open and none of us had any Deutschmarks so we set off to try to find somewhere to change some money. You usually got an odd hotel willing to do it, but as we left the station we realised nothing was open, the streets were deserted. I was impressed, nevertheless, by a massive cathedral which was immediately outside the station. It reminded me of something out of *Batman*.

We walked around Cologne for an hour looking for a hotel or bar. We found a couple of hotels but it was hard work trying to get them to open their doors to ten pissed-up English men. There was no chance of changing any money so we headed back to the station. Unbeknown to us we had walked in a complete circle and as we turned the corner there was a big pub, still open, but full of Turks. The front of the bar was covered in glass panels. You could see it was packed inside and around fifty were standing outside on the corner. We asked each other how much German money we had but we didn't even have enough for a round of drinks. The Turks out front noticed us and there was some pointing over and a little shouting but we stood our ground. We were expecting them to rush us but they didn't move so we made our way back to the station, sat on the seats in the concourse and dove into our bags to find any more beer. I had a few so I was happy and we settled down to wait for the train to come and the bureau de change to open.

Ade and Fuse decided to go for a piss in the toilets about twenty yards away. On the way back from the bogs a few Turks approached them, words were exchanged and one of the Turks went to punch Fuse. He missed but Ade caught the Turk with a head-butt. The two Turks headed off towards the pub where all the others were congregated. Fuse said, "Fuck knows what that was about, they came up pointing and mouthing, I asked if they were batting or bowling, he then goes to hit me but misses and Ade butts him and they fuck off, no problem."

We all looked at each other. Right lads, it was time to get all the bags together and have one of us stay with them. As we were doing this, the first Turks came through the doors. We stood there. Nothing was said. They were getting closer and closer. One Turk came to the front. He was talking to his mates and doing a lot of pointing. Still more Turks came through the door, fifty-strong by now, but we didn't move or speak. The Turk in front of the mob started shouting and pointing at Fuse and started to walk towards us, coolly taking off his jacket and giving it to one of his entourage, who folded it and put it over his arm. All of us were watching this with smiles on our faces. The Turk then took his tie off and wrapped it around his knuckles.

One of the lads said, "Sort it Fuse," and Fuse went towards the Turk.

"Are you batting or bowling?"

The Turk went to kick Fuse but slipped on his arse. We all cracked up laughing, never taking our eyes off the mob. Fuse was dancing around the Turk trying to volley him in the head. The Turk was like a spinning top on the floor trying to keep his head away from Fuse's kicks. The other Turks edged closer; it was time to pick our targets.

We spread across the station; there was a dancing competition going on between us and them. "Come on," the cry went up, and we took three steps and were into them. Each one of us penetrated their mob, took our targets down, then moved onto the next. The Turks were flustered, they could not understand what was happening, there were only a few of us but we were going forward into them. We were hitting everything we saw. They started to back off but we couldn't stop our momentum, we had to still go forward as a group, making sure that no-one got too far ahead of us. The Turks turned and rushed for the doors and we let them go. One of us shouted, "Stick together." We turned round to see Fuse still dancing around his attacker. Someone ran over and volleyed him. The Turk scrambled to his feet and ran down towards the opposite doors.

A big bloke ran towards Stan and Stan shouted, "Do you want some?" The man raised his arms. "No, no I'm American," he said. "I can't believe what I just saw, there were so many of them and only a few of you. I'm from New York and I've never seen anything like that." He then went round every one of us and shook us by the hand. After that he moved down to the other side of the station where a group of people had gathered, probably to see what all the noise was about. Meanwhile we checked that everybody was alright and made a decision to get into the centre of the station concourse so we could easily see both sets of doors. There were also two sets of steps on each side of us leading up to the platform.

We knew they would be back, this time with more. Ten minutes elapsed before the doors started to open and close with groups of half a dozen coming through. This time they were coming from both sides and we would be stuck in the middle. More and more came in. This must have been the full mob from the pub. They came towards us from both sides and we backed up against the bottom of a set of steps. Some of the Turks had armed themselves with glasses which were soon flying through the air and shattering on the floor, showering our legs with shards. Bricks started bouncing off the walls, whizzing past our heads. The whole station seemed full of them, a few pulling blades out, waving them at us and making signs as if they were going to cut our throats. We knew we had to stand firm and together.

We went to front them on both sides, standing in a semicircle in front of the steps. We took a step towards them and they backed off a little. Some of them tried to grab us but individually, we'd run into them and make them back up a moment, but they were pushing us back towards the steps. There must have been well over 100 of them, which was actually better for us as you could see the ones at the front didn't want to be there and the ones at the back were pushing them forward. Once we were on the steps we knew they had to come to us, face to face. We had the high ground and time after time we flew down the steps into them punching and kicking. They tried to grab our legs to pull us down the steps but there were so many of them they couldn't get to us as they were kicking and punching each other more than us. They'd back up when they saw their mates in trouble, then launch a search and rescue mission using sheer numbers. They were pushing us up the steps again.

I burst out laughing when at one stage a gap opened up

between us and a Turk ran out, pulled out an empty can from his coat, threw it on the floor, jumped on it and then threw it at us. All the Turks cheered and patted him on the back; he was jumping around as if he had scored a goal. But they were still pushing us back up the steps and I knew we couldn't let them get onto the platform.

I looked up and noticed the railing running around the entrance to the steps. I turned and ran up on to the platform, picked up a luggage trolley and threw it over the railings. It landed in the middle of the Turks who scattered. Again, another trolley went over the railings. There was no way they were coming up the steps again as I had another trolley balanced ready to let go. Then one of the lads shouted, "Pot, put the trolley down, Old Bill are here." I put the trolley back down on the floor and walked to the top of the steps. Old Bill were on the steps pointing at the trolleys and then pointing at us. We replied saying that the Turks had thrown the trolleys up the steps at us. We carried on arguing for about five minutes.

The outcome was that we had to board the next train out of Cologne. They took us back down on to the station concourse which was littered with broken glass and bricks, pointed at the floor and started shouting at us. We tried to explain that it was the Turks that had thrown the missiles. More police arrived and stood by both sets of the doors stopping us from leaving the station and the Turks from entering. We had been lucky; if the Turks had used their heads and come up both sets of steps leading onto the same platform we would have been fucked. Instead they just came to the same set of steps where we were and concentrated their efforts there.

We all sat on the concourse reflecting on what had just happened, discussing different scenarios. People were starting to filter into the station, going to work or whatever. A clean-up had begun, the cleaners picking up all the broken glass and bricks. They kept giving us dirty looks. "Fuck off you Kraut bastards," one of the lads shouted at them. At that loads of police come through the doors and I thought, this is it, they have gathered some more information, and we are fucked. The police made a beeline for us but said nothing, they just looked us up and down and stood at the bottom of two of the stairways coming from the platforms.

During all this, a big German idiot (that's the best way I can describe him) came up to us trying to start a conversation. He could speak a little English but he looked like he had been on the piss all night. "You English hooligans, fuck off," then he moved on to the next one of us. You always get one. Apparently the police were there for this German, he was one of Cologne's top lads.

A train pulled in and the police start to move, some went up the platform, and some gave us anxious looks. There was a little shouting and the police formed a line between us with the mad German and the two stairways. Then we heard singing and all these lads appeared wearing scarves. The German explained they were Munchengladbach fans, then he started shouting and pointing at them, then at us. It looked like he was saying, "I'm with the English and we are going to fuck you." The police escorted the fans out of the station, then came up to us, dragged the German to one side, gave him a good talking to and fucked him off through the opposite doors. Then they came back over to us and told us our train would arrive in an hour and that we'd better board it.

By the time our train arrived the station was up and running and we had changed some money and bought a few beers. The police watched us until we boarded the train and stayed until it started to move off. Once on board we were back to the usual drinking and sleeping. It had been a long night plus Fuse had a problem, he had lost his passport. There was fuck all we could do about it now but when we got to Berlin we would find the British Embassy to try and get a temporary one and then go to the Polish Embassy to sort out a visa to travel to the match. We got off at the Zoo Garden train station, put our bags in the left luggage lockers and headed for the Euro bar, directly opposite the station. We were greeted with, "Alright lads, you finally made it then." There were a lot of familiar faces and we all settled down with our beers explaining what had happened in Cologne and asked for directions to the British Embassy.

It was late afternoon and we'd had a bit to drink so we thought we'd go to the Embassy first thing in the morning. Our first priority was somewhere to sleep. The other English lads had got digs so we were going to jump in with them and sleep on the floor. Until then it was time for drinking beer and having a laugh. More and more English people were coming into the bar, which seemed to be the main meeting point in Berlin. There were probably around seventy of us and we decided to move to the red light district. We'd been told it was full of bars and that the Germans were supposed to be showing up.

It was getting dark. I'd noticed a good landmark in case I got lost, a large church steeple covered in blue lights that really stood out in the night sky. We were rowdy and a bit loud and the Germans gave us a wide berth. We went into the first bar and settled down having a few beers when one of the lads suggested taking the till. It was a wooden box with a drawer. So a plan was sorted, we would stage a diversion. Everyone got another beer and some of the lads started to get a little louder. The German bartender looked over with concern on his face and the next thing a few punches were thrown and some lads rolled over a table, a few glasses hit the wall, tables and chairs went flying and everyone ran into each other with smiles on their faces. The bartender ran over to try and sort out the situation, shouting in German. Everyone stopped and apologised and told him it was sorted. He seemed happy about this and returned to the bar very pleased with himself. We quickly left and waved at him and he waved back. I would have loved to have seen his face when he opened the little drawer and realised it was empty. We went to another bar where all the drinks were paid for courtesy of this episode and couldn't help laughing at the idea that the bartender thought he had made a load of money and stopped a fight, when, basically, he had just given us free beer.

We moved on to an Irish pub called the Footballers bar and had all just got a drink when the police arrived outside. Obviously the bartender who was out of pocket hadn't found it as funny as we did. The police lined up outside the bar and one of the lads decided to let off a can of CS gas before they gassed us. Some glasses were sent flying through the doors and the police backed off and waited for reinforcements. Everybody was up for the battle that was to come, arming themselves with glasses and table legs. We pulled scarves over our mouths and noses. The police returned, this time gas-masked up, and with shields and helmets and their truncheons drawn. They let a gas canister off in the doorway and everyone surged through, glasses flying. Soon we were face to face with the police, just their shields separating us. We hit them with our own makeshift truncheons but they had their own and theirs were doing more damage than ours. I was pushed through the doors onto the street by the lads behind us who were feeling the effects of the gas. The good thing is that when you are face to face with riot police they can't grab you because both their hands are tied up with holding their batons and shields. They rely on snatch squads to come through the shields and grab you. Once outside I could see they had cordoned off the whole street with line after line of police on both sides.

We were still spilling out of the bar when the police charged us. You couldn't get back in as people were still coming out, so there was only one thing for it. I wasn't waiting to be nicked, so I just waited for the police to get a little closer then I ran straight at their lines and through their shields and over a police car. Someone gave chase down one street then another but eventually I lost my pursuers, plus I had got myself lost. I was wandering around the streets and noticed all the bars had bouncers on the doors by this time. As soon as they heard I was English they wouldn't let me in. I didn't know where the digs were or whether the lads had been nicked and I had no key for the left luggage so I was fucked in that direction. But I had my train ticket, passport and money so I still had a little smile on my face. The time was getting on now so I decided to get some kip in a wank booth. I wandered in unnoticed and got my head down. They are proper warm and usually no-one disturbs you. I woke up early in the morning, dying for a shit. Fortunately, wank booths always have loads of tissues in them so I dropped my pants and my guts, wiped my arse and walked out laughing at the thought of the next person going in.

I quickly made my way back to the train station expecting some of the lads to be there but there was no sign of anyone. I tried to get the left luggage attendant to open a locker but he was having none of it. The only thing for it was to go to a kiosk and get some cans, crash outside the station, knowing that if any of the lads came to the station they would spot me. After there was no sign I got to thinking everyone had been nicked. The Euro bar had opened its doors so I finished my last can and I made my way down, thinking this would again be the meeting place, but it was dead. I ordered a large beer, finished it and ordered another, but still no sign.

I must have fallen asleep with my head on the bar because I was woken up with a tap on the shoulder and half a warm beer in front of me.

"Who are you with?" asked two strangers.

"Just waiting for my mates," I told them. "I lost them last night."

Then I explained what had happened, where I'd slept and

so on. I went to the bogs and threw a load of cold water over my head to wake myself up, then returned to the bar where the lads had bought me a beer. They had been in the bar the night before but stayed in there when the rest of us moved. They were Dermott, a Chelsea fan, and Norman, a Newcastle fan. You could tell they weren't up for a battle but they were good lads. They were boarding a train for Poland that day, so I told them that I would wait to see if any of the lads turned up and if they didn't I would jump on the train with them. Fuck the bag. If they had already gone or if they were following they would bring it with them. None of the lads turned up so I joined Norman and Dermott.

As we crossed from West to East Germany, the contrast was amazing. The West had colour in it but the East was stark and grey. The buildings were rundown, even the people looked different. The train journey was uneventful with me getting quietly pissed and getting to know my new mates. We got off in Poznan and it was like walking onto a film set, with people in berets and overcoats. As soon as we got off the train a man with a hat and overcoat came up to us and said, "English? Me taxi man, take you good hotel." We got into his taxi and, yes, it was a Lada. He introduced himself as Joe and he started driving round Poznan, passing hotel after hotel. I was thinking, here we fucking go, taking the piss already, fuck paying this clown, and then all of a sudden he pulled up into a car park surrounded by flats. Again I started thinking, what's going on here, he's probably part of the Polish mafia or something.

He asked us to follow him and finally we came to a door which he opened and invited us in. There was a woman in a chair and Joe said something to her and she disappeared into another room. He gestured for us to sit down on the sofa then disappeared himself. The three of us looked at each other in disbelief, waiting for what happens next. The woman re-appeared carrying tea and biscuits on a tray, poured out the teas, gave one to each of us and then offered us the biscuits. All this was done in complete silence, all of us just nodding at each other. Then Joe came back with another woman, gorgeous and about twenty years old. Joe gestured for her to speak and she explained in perfect English that she was Linda, his daughter, and was at university in England. So we were in his house, having tea and biscuits with his wife and daughter and we'd only known the man half an hour. I could barely comprehend what was happening, it just wasn't the normal thing for me to be doing when I watched England away. Joe gave us each a card with his number and his daughter gave me another piece of paper with her details.

Joe phoned some hotels and found us a good place in the centre of Poznan with a disco bar underneath. He was going to be our taxi driver for the duration and we would pay him on our last day. Everything was sorted, we finished our tea and biscuits and said our goodbyes to his wife and daughter and he took us in his taxi to the hotel. It looked decent plus Joe's daughter had told us if we wanted any money changed into zlotys we could change it through Joe as he would get us a better exchange rate, also, if you changed it on the black market with the blokes at the station they were adding zeros to make a 100 note into a 1,000 note. A lot of English people had been fooled by this and were about to discover they hadn't actually got that good a deal. I tried to tell people about the zeros but they wouldn't listen, more fool them.

Joe got us booked in and took Norman and Dermott's bags up to our rooms. I had a room with four beds in it. No problem, I could get my mates in if they turned up and other English people might be looking for digs. I had explained to Joe that my friends were following me on from Berlin. I jumped into the shower, got changed and went down to the bar and started on the bottles of Grolsch. It was getting late and Norman and Dermott came down to join me after a couple of bottles. We laughed about our first taxi ride, thinking he could have been kidnapping us or taking us somewhere to rob us, but it had all worked out fine in the end.

A couple of hours had passed when Joe came back into the hotel. He had been back to the train station to find out the times of trains arriving from Berlin and written them down on a piece of paper which he gave to me before he left. I had a few more beers with Norman and Dermott and then headed off to bed. I hadn't had a decent night's sleep in days.

The next morning I awoke to a knock on the door. I opened it and was greeted by Joe who looked at me and smiled and mentioned the train station. I got my shit together and went downstairs where he was waiting. He drove me to the station to wait for the Berlin train. On my way out of the hotel I had picked up a load of cards with its name and address. The Berlin train came in but with no sign of the lads. There were a few English lads on the train and I talked to them about the money situation and gave them the hotel cards, recommending it as a good place to stay. I even got Joe to take a few English back with us.

Once back in the hotel I joined Norman and Dermott at the bar. The place was filling up with England supporters and they were telling us about more trouble in Berlin and that a few English had been nicked. I told the lads I had three spare beds and that they could get their heads down there. I had already been charged for the room so I would just charge them. With that sorted, we sat drinking and talking all night and Joe stayed with us.

The following day Joe again woke me and took me to the station. As the train pulled in I could see Fat Stan's head sticking out of the window and hear his unmistakable voice. As they came off the train I saw Ade was carrying my bag. At last a change of clothes, I was stinking. They weren't surprised to see me and the conversation quickly turned to Berlin. At first everyone thought I had been nicked so they went to the police station to see if I had been but no sign there, then they went back to the pub next to the station and I wasn't there, and finally they went to the station and saw that a train had left and gone on to Poznan and presumed that I had taken it. I realised that Fuse was missing and they explained that he had been unable to get another passport and that he was planning to try to blag it at the border on the train but then had a few more beers and decided against it. He had made his way back to England. I told them about the hotel and the personal taxi service I'd acquired and Joe ran a little shuttle service to the hotel. Everyone got rooms and we all settled in for another night on the Grolsch.

The next day, Dermott and Norman asked Joe to take us down to a place called Peela, around 100 kilometres away, to watch the under-21s. I asked if anyone else wanted to join us but they declined. The lads were a bit rough after Berlin. I loaded up with beer for the journey from a cheap shop that Joe knew. Peela was not a bad ground, we paid for Joe to come along and bought him something to eat; he was well pleased. A few of the locals had turned out as well; they had a decent little mob and threw a few bricks at us but the police soon dealt with them. In the ground Joe was sat with us and other English lads but all of a sudden the police came steaming in, batons drawn, and started hitting Joe around the head and body and dragged him out. The three of us jumped up yelling, "What the fuck's going on?" and dragged him back in to our crowd away from the police. In they came for him again and this time Norman and Dermott explained that he was our taxi driver but they wouldn't listen and made him sit on his own away from the English fans. I was thinking, how fucking mad can you get, this man is no threat to anyone.

There were around 350 England fans at the game and when it finished the Poles came walking across the pitch towards us doing a bit of singing and shouting. I bounced to the front of the terrace with a few more English, ready for it if they decided to come into us, but the police quickly formed a separation line. The Poles leaving behind us threw a few more bricks but nothing major. As the police led us out you could see in the distance the police charging the Poles down the street. If this is anything to go by, I thought, the proper match should be fun. Back in Poznan, Joe pulled up in the taxi, produced a hip flask, poured four cups and gave us one each. I think it was to say he had a good day. I think it was vodka, I know that it went down in one and gave you a warm glow.

We went back into the hotel and all the lads were there, pissed up. The nightclub underneath was open and we headed down there. I can't remember coming out of there or going to bed. The day of the match came, Joe knocked me up and I told him, "No taxi today." He waved at me and went to see Norman and Dermott. I went down to the bar where all the lads were already in full swing, downing beers. After a few hours we all decided to have a walk to the centre. Poznan was a shit place for bars but we found a few and in one we found an English lad who was going to a nearby shop to buy tickets for the game. The English in the Travel Club had paid silly money for tickets, so one of our lads went with this one to the shop and he came back with all of our tickets a third of the price the Travel Club had paid. With that sorted everyone was happy and the beers started to flow. Rumours started to circulate about Polish mobs walking about so we sent a lad out scouting but he came back and announced that fuck all was happening. Even on the way to the ground there was no trouble.

Inside we were well segregated. It looked a decent ground and was pretty full. We were along the side of the pitch from the half way line to the corner flag. Once the game started a scuffle broke out in the end directly opposite us and everyone assumed it had to be English. The scuffle got bigger and a gap appeared but you couldn't see any colours. All of a sudden both sides ran into each other and a full-scale battle took place. The Polish police were quickly in there, long batons drawn, hitting anything that moved and they quickly separated the two sets of fans. Then the singing started, hands pointing at each other and the police in the middle, and both sides singing in Polish. We couldn't believe it; they were more interested in fighting each other than us. As half-time approached another fight broke out behind the right hand goal. The police quickly moved in again. Taking no prisoners and hitting everything in sight they quickly restored order. It was astonishing. I know on a few occasions English fans have done the same, but never when there has been a good contingent of foreigners to fight first. If the Polish got their act together they would have a good mob.

The game finished and everyone was thinking, here we go, they've got to be up for it. The police were trying to keep us in and we got a bit restless so a few seats started to fly onto the pitch. Then everyone pushed towards the exits. Something had to give and the police let us out; they were all around us but there were no Polish fans around.

CHAPTER ELEVEN

CZECH MATES

Czechoslovakia v England, 1992

Saturday morning. I was in my bird's house, pissed off. I had just a tenner in my pocket, Burnley were playing away at Mansfield, and worst of all, Ade, Mick, Simon and Nigel were travelling to Czechoslovakia to watch England – and I wasn't.

There was a knock on the door.

"Are you ready Pot?"

"What for?"

"You're coming to Czechoslovakia, Caddy has dropped out."

That should have been great but I only had that tenner and my passport was in Luton. "Don't worry, we'll sort it." That's what friends are for.

I went back into the house got my coat and told my bird that I was going to the game; she didn't mind. I got into the car and asked what the plan was. "We're going to Mansfield first, then down to Dover for the late night ferry. We have to pass Luton on the way, so we can get your passport. We've got a spare Inter-rail ticket and we'll all sort you with some money."

We got to Mansfield around forty minutes before kick-off and headed straight to the game, lowering the chances of getting nicked. Burnley were everywhere and the Burnley end was packed. The game started with hundreds of Burnley fans

159

still outside the ground. The police didn't want hundreds of lads walking about so they put them in the Mansfield paddock, under their main stand. My mind wasn't on the game. I was thinking about another expedition to Europe. Burnley won 3–2 (I think). Walking out of the ground the lads warned me, "Pot, no fucking about, we've got a ferry to catch." We were walking past the Burnley coaches towards the car park when a lad came up to me and told me that Mansfield had got a mob together and that they were waiting for us round the corner. All the lads looked at me.

"I'll meet you at the car," I said. "I won't be long."

If a mob turns up you should have the decency to front them.

We walked in between the coaches into a small park with a path running through it. The Mansfield mob was gathered at the end of the path below us. We had the advantage of the high ground. Burnley had a good mob now. We jumped over a stone wall surrounding the park singing, "Su, su, Suicide," and running towards their mob. It must have looked like Custer's last stand to them, loads of lads running down a grass bank at them. It did the trick, they bolted, not a punch was thrown. Job done, I went back to the car.

The lads looked a bit impatient. "Right, you've had your fun, now let's fuck off."

We got to my house in Luton at seven o'clock.

"You're not going to be long are you?" the lads asked.

"No," I replied.

I hadn't seen my wife and kids for a month. I walked in and they were all sat there.

"Finally come home have you?" she said.

"Yeah, where's my passport?"

"You fucking what?"

"I'm going to watch England, the lads are waiting for me outside."

"The kids haven't seen you for a month."

"I know, but I'll be home next week."

I spent five minutes with the kids and emptied my bollocks into the wife. "See you next week." Out of the door and back into the car.

"Thought you weren't going to be long?"

"You know how it is, kids all over you and the wife wanted a jump, I haven't seen her for a month."

Back on the road it didn't take long to get to Dover, especially with Mick driving. We were all gagging for a beer. We parked up at about ten o'clock and headed for the nearest boozer. The beers went down well. All the lads had chipped in with some money for me. I had at least £100. "It's your round Pot." They all cracked up.

We had decided to board the ferry one at a time. We had arranged to meet Fat Stan on board but everyone was pulled. I showed my ticket and walked through, past a room with mirrored windows. Two police walked out of a door and said, "Excuse me, can we have a word? Where are you travelling to?"

"Germany."

"Travelling on your own?"

"Yes."

"Well, isn't that funny Mr. Porter. Your brother and your friends, Mr. Massey and Mr. Moore, are travelling on the same ferry and you are all travelling alone. Can you explain this?"

"No. I have just travelled down from Luton, I haven't seen them."

"Right, on your way."

We all met on the ferry pissing ourselves but deep down we were wondering who was going to be waiting for us on the other side of the Channel.

It didn't take us long to find Stan; we heard him before we saw him. He has a cockney accent that is like a foghorn. He had boarded without any checks. We settled down at one of the bars taking it easy on the beer. The main thing now was getting through Passport Control in Ostend. Before we got off we purchased a bottle of vodka. If we got through we would need something for the train journey. The ferry docked and we all sat quietly finishing our beer when three of the ferry crew came over to us and pulled Stan to one side. "Can you come with us sir, it won't take long." Stan went with them, not making a fuss. We wondered what it was all about. Four of us got checked, Stan didn't. We must have a reception committee waiting for us, we thought. But we all walked through individually without facing any checks and headed straight for the train station. Mick decided to wait around for Stan and soon after walked back onto the platform shaking his head.

"Somebody used a dodgy £20 note and they think it's Stan," he said. "They are holding him until they sort it out so he will have to catch us up."

Our route was a twelve-hour train journey to Frankfurt and then on to Prague. We got a compartment and the train moved off without Stan. We'd lost one already. Nigel was buzzing, he had never left England before; he just kept talking about brothels and prostitutes. I drifted off to sleep and was woken up coming into Frankfurt. We put all our bags into a left luggage locker and headed for the red light district. Nigel couldn't wait. We found a bar and got some beers.

"Where's all the brothels?"

"Fucking hell, Nigel, chill out, you've got loads of time."

After a few more beers Nigel was still going on about it, driving us mad.

"Let's just find him a brothel and shut him up," I suggested. We found one. "In you go, Nigel."

"What do I do?"

"Bang on the door and ask how much, that's it."

"Fuck off. You don't just bang on the door. What happens if a bloke opens it?"

"You're in trouble."

"You lot are taking the piss."

"OK, we'll come in and hold your hand."

A spiral staircase went from floor to floor. When he got to the first floor he knocked on the door and asked how much. She told him the price and he turned round with a smile on his face and a thumbs-up sign and disappeared through the door. Ten minutes later he was out.

"That was brilliant, I want another. Let's go up to the next floor."

Upstairs, he did another prostitute and yet another on the next one up. The higher up you went, the worse the girls looked. On the top floor a big black mama appeared dressed in a leather basque and sussies, carrying a big whip. Nigel looked at us, he was no longer smiling. The big mama then suddenly grabbed him and dragged him into her room. He tried to hold the door frame but the door slammed shut. I was in hysterics, so much that I stepped back and fell down the stairs. I was still laughing when I hit the floor at the bottom.

Ade, Mick and Simon came down. They had been laughing at Nigel and now were laughing at me. They picked me up.

"You alright?"

"Yeah. Did you see his face when he was getting dragged in there?"

Nigel reappeared looking a bit worse for wear.

"She raped me, then fucking charged me!"

We all looked at each other trying not to laugh. "Come on we'll find a bar."

"There's just one problem, lads, I've blown all my money in here."

We weren't too impressed but decided to find a cash machine and sort him out until we got home. I was still laughing anyway.

We found a table in a bar where there was a big German on a stool. The door opened and a lad walked in asking if we were English. Then he said, "You haven't seen a mob of Chelsea have you? I went to buy a gas gun and now I have lost them." We hadn't, so he decided to join us for a drink. Then he turned to the big man on the stool.

"Hey, you, German fucker, I want to sit at the bar."

The German pointed to another stool.

"No you German cunt, I want to sit there, fucking move."

The German looked at him, then us and then fucked off. No wonder they lost the war. The lad picked up his beer and came and sat with us. He called himself PJ and had travelled over with a big mob of Chelsea. It worked out that his mob were boarding the same train as us. He was a sound lad but said he had some kind of illness.

We had a good drink and walked back to the station. On the way back PJ decided to get his gas gun out. He fired it at a German walking down the street and it hit him right in the head, knocking him clean out. PJ kept pulled the trigger. "Wankers told me it was a repeater." Some German tramps on the other side of the road were laughing at the one on the floor. This incensed Mick, who he ran over and told them, "Look at you, laughing at one of your fellow countrymen on the floor, you're not worth a wank." Mick and Ade picked up the German while me, PJ, Simon and Nigel carried on walking to the station, our eyes streaming. PJ was still going on about the gun saying that he had been ripped off. We got to the station and he found some of his mates. Mick and Ade returned, saying that the German had given them about £40 for helping him.

We got the overnight train to Prague and got some sleep. Hector the collector woke me up going mad shouting, "Tickets, tickets."

"Who the fuck are you shouting at?"

We soon discovered why Hector was in a bad mood. Loads of lads were jumping the train. As it pulled into Nuremberg there was a reception waiting for us. Even if you didn't have a ticket you were ordered off the train and police surrounded us and the sixty-strong Chelsea mob on the platform. Ade decided he wanted a piss and tried to get to the bogs but police pushed him back. He started arguing and three of them surrounded him. They told us to sit and we all did as we were told.

Then the dogs turned up. One cunt walked up to Ade with a dog, it was going mad, barking and trying to bite him but it was muzzled. Ade was trying to head-butt it. Seeing this, I jumped up, a few more came with me and then we were all on our feet.

"Let's fucking have 'em."

We started walking towards them. The police were blocking the exits but they looked worried as we well outnumbered them. Ade was taken to a room. The noise level was rising, one of the policemen shouted that we could leave the station and they moved away from the exits. We got out of the station but we weren't going anywhere without Ade. A few of us went back and walked up to the police and I asked, "Where's my brother, we aren't going anywhere until he's released." They explained that he was getting released as we spoke. Ade walked out of the room, not too happy, calling them wankers.

We got back outside and decided to walk into town to find a boozer, but everything was closed. Someone saw a light on in one, the door was shut but it was unlocked. We walked in and the barman was waving his arms in the air, "No, no, no bar shut." One of the Chelsea lads went up to him and said, "We are police, we are on a training course," and showed a card. There was a downstairs room full of football and pool tables and a bowling lane. Most of us made our way down there and started playing. Some lads were trying to get their heads down, some were still trying to get beers but there was no chance.

Then the police steamed into the bar with their batons out. They weren't taking any shit. "Move, move." If you moved a bit too slow you got a crack. They got us out and marched us back to outside the train station. The police wouldn't let us back onto the station but no-one wanted to sleep outside. There were a few buses parked up and the emergency doors were soon opened. Lads jumped on to get some sleep. The police realised what was happening and moved us off but now tempers were getting frayed, something the police wisely realised.

Their top man came over and told us they were trying to sort us somewhere to go. Five minutes later a fleet of taxis turned up. The top man spoke with the first driver and told us that the cabs would take us to a bar that was open all night. We jumped into the taxis but the journey took ages, through forests and up mountains. "Where the fuck are we going?" I asked. Then, in the middle of nowhere, a bar appeared, nothing around it but trees. We walked in and there were beers lined up ready for us. We were expected. We picked up a beer, threw our bags in the corner and sat at a table. There were around twenty locals in the bar. I say locals, I hadn't seen any houses on the way, only trees. Taxi after taxi turned up, bags were thrown into the corner and the pile soon reached the roof. Everyone started drinking and having a laugh, though PJ was still going on about his gun.

Mick knew a lot of the main Chelsea lads from previous England games and we talked all night. The barmaid was sound and phoned the train station to find out the times for us. Every time our glasses were empty she would replace them with full ones. We only left the table to have a piss. Mick and Ade did a head count to see how many taxis were needed and then asked the woman to order them. The cars arrived and everyone had room except us; either some lads had been asleep under the bags or Mick and Ade hadn't counted properly. We walked back into the bar and got another beer. The woman explained that it would be another hour before we could get another taxi.

Two Americans who had been drinking all night in the bar offered us a lift to the station. They were both pissed but time was running short. If we waited we would miss the train. We finished our beers and went outside while one of the Americans went round the back to get the car. We were expecting something big but he came round the corner in a little hatchback with a big, fuck-off telephone receiver on the roof. We piled in and after a few detours we finally got to the station. We'd missed the train but it wasn't long to wait for the next one. Most of the compartments were full but we found one with only one occupant. He turned out to be a Nottingham Forest fan. We quickly got out the vodka, cans of orange and plastic cups. The bar was open! We passed him a plastic cup and got talking. He was only young and travelling alone. The vodka was going down well, but when Nigel went for a piss he came back and told us he'd had some shit off a few English. We asked the Forest lad to look after the vodka and went to find them.

We had to go down the corridor in single file as it was so narrow. We got to the next carriage and we could hear them singing, "Leeds, Leeds, Leeds." A chorus of "Who the fuck are Leeds United" went up. The lads standing outside their compartments turned to look at us, with a surprised expression. Mick was leading us. "Come on lads, we're fucking Burnley." He flew straight into them, knocked them on their arses and proceeded to walk right over them. A few Leeds tried to get out of their compartment but Mick was into them. "Do you fucking want it?" They backed off.

Ade and Simon hit another compartment. The Leeds fans were waving their arms in the air saying, "Leave it, lads." Mick launched into one of his speeches. "Who the fuck are Leeds? You mouth off when there is only one but when there are a few of us you don't want to fucking know. You're not worth a fucking wank." Enough said, we went back to our compartment. I think Leeds got off at the next stop. I started to get greedy on the vodka and fell unconscious. I was woken with a slap on the face. We'd arrived.

I managed to stand, get my bag and get off the train. The platform was packed with people making their way to the exits. I started walking with the crowd, caught someone's foot, fell down and took twenty others with me. Ade picked me up and Mick got my bag. I started walking again; there wasn't far to go but I hit the floor again, though not as many people fell on me this time. Some kids tried to help me get up but when I looked up there were four gun barrels pointing at me. Simon and Ade grabbed hold of me and Mick explained, "English, too much vodka, we will find a hotel and go to sleep, we will take care of him." The police went and the lads gave me a severe bollocking, telling me to get my act together.

We still had a hotel to find and weren't having much joy on that front. They'd take one look at me and say they had no rooms available. The lads changed tack, leaving me outside on the steps of one hotel while they tried to book rooms. It was looking good; they had been inside for a while when a security guard came up to me and ordered me to move. I tried to explain that my friends were inside and that we were staying at the hotel. He didn't believe me so he took me inside to check. All the lads looked on in disbelief at me being frog-marched through the front door.

"No rooms available."

The lads went mad. "Fucking hell, Pot, we told you to wait outside." I explained it wasn't my fault. Mick waved down a taxi, had a word with the driver and another taxi pulled up. "Get in lads, they know a hotel that has rooms available. Don't fuck this one up, Pot." The hotel was well out of the centre and a proper dive so we had no problem getting in, or should I say

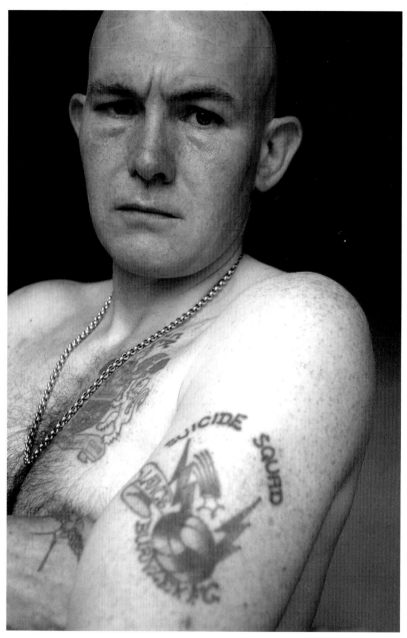

Suicide Squad for life: the author, aged 38.

How it began: in the back of vans on raucous away trips. This one was going to Derby County in the early 1980s.

Burnley's casual firm swarming up a railway embankment at Blackburn on the night of Norman Bell's testimonial match against Bastard Rovers.

GET MOVING: Police round up England fans in Amsterdam's Red Light district last night. Six officers were hurt in clashes.   Pictures: ARNOLD SLATER

'THEY JUST WANT TO FIGHT'

The author (circled) in a line of England fans being rounded up by police during the so-called Battle of Amsterdam before England's World Cup qualifier against Holland in 1993.

That's me (right) in the centre pages of a Sunday newspaper after hours of rioting with German fans in Dusseldorf. The caption read: 'NICKED: A German riot cop holds a Millwall fan and mate'.

(L to r): Billy Redmond, Mark Holden and our top lad, Mick Moore, in Amsterdam in 1993, just after Mark had fallen off a statue (see Chapter 14).

My brother Ade (left), who was often by my side, and Millsy (RIP)

The Suicide Squad made plenty of headlines from the late 1980s onward, once the press had cottoned on to the name and our callings cards

FOOTBALL BANNING ORDER REGISTRATION CARD

Name:

Porter, Andrew Francis

Date of Birth:

27/06/1966

Registration No:

FBOA/3844

22/11/2004

My banning order registration card, an occupational hazard.

Have gun, will travel: fooling around in the Albanian capital, Tirana, before another international game (see Chapter 16).

Another trip, another cheap hotel room, this time in the Greek capital, Athens. Following England took me all over Europe.

Wigan, 1999, and part of the massive Burnley mob on that memorable day.

A gathering of the lads, including some of our young element, the Suicide Youth Squad.

I'm banned from football now but can still hear the crowd at Turf Moor from my doorstep in Burnley Wood. I suppose that's something!

me getting in. I was put in a room with Mick; he took his boots off, his feet stank. I lasted twenty minutes and then went to sleep in the bath, the smell was that bad.

The next day we caught a bus into the centre, changed some money and set out to find the Chelsea mob. It didn't take us long. They told us that 500 skinheads were supposed to be turning up to greet us, so we decided to find them before they found us. After a few beers at fifteen pence a pint, it was hunting time. We headed for the old town where the locals drank and bars were cheaper and away from the tourist places. We encountered a few small mobs of skinheads and a few words were exchanged; lads were breaking bottles on their heads for fun. There were no police and none of the locals gave a fuck; we well outnumbered them. It was better to take the confidence out of them before they got mobbed up.

We got into a bar expecting retaliation for what had just happened, they knew where we were, but hours passed and no-one came. A few of us had a scout around, plus we wanted some CS gas. We couldn't see any mobs of lads anywhere, but we soon found a shop that sold gas. The assistant serving a local went in the back and returned with an open bottle of wine. I asked her for two bottles of wine and when she went into the back Simon put a full crate of twenty-four cans of gas into his coat. The wine even tasted good.

Back in the bar a few windows had been smashed and it was clear some of the lads were getting impatient for a fight. The gas was given out. A chorus of "Rule Britannia" rang out, lads on tables threw a few glasses against the wall and a couple of chairs went over the bar, swiftly followed by a spray of gas from someone eager to test it out. A table flew through a window and landed on the pavement and we soon followed to escape the effects of the gas. It was time to find another bar.

Blue flashing lights were approaching and our numbers halved as lads chose other bars further away. We stayed in a pub until the police activity died down. The bar was full of locals all eating goulash free of charge and it wasn't long before most of us were tucking into the local cuisine. We made our way back to the centre, hoping to bump into the rest of the lads but without success. There was still no sign of any mobs of skinheads so we decided to have a look at the nightclub scene. Ade, Mick, Simon and a few Chelsea lads paid to get in the first club we tried, then one of the Chelsea lads walked back out and said, "It's full of Munich." Someone decided to gas them. When the canister blew, the lads ran into the bouncers, but they weren't moving. Then the gas hit them, and us. A few punches were thrown in the doorway and the lads got out. I was trying to hold my eyes open. We made our way onto the street and the bouncers didn't follow. We quickly caught up with the others but my eyes were still streaming. The Chelsea lads now wanted to go pussy hunting but I don't go to football to look for pussy, so we decided to go back to the hotel. Again, I slept in the bath. No-one would go into Mick's room.

The day of the game came and Simon was on about tying some sheets together and climbing out of the window so we didn't have to pay for the hotel room. The only problem with that was there weren't enough sheets to reach the ground. We got our gear together and went downstairs to reception. The room bill was about £2.40 each, definitely not worth climbing out of the window for. As the next bus wasn't for another hour and a half we decided to try the underground. I led the way as we got on one train, changed at the next station, went three more stops, changed again and got off at the next station. Beside it was the bar where we had all arranged to meet. To this day I don't know how I managed it, but the lads never doubted me again on away trips.

We walked to the main train station, put our bags in left luggage, then moved to the bar. Ade and Mick were talking to some Chelsea lads and Sheffield Ian, a Sheff United fan who used to run with the Blues because he married a mad Chelsea bird. A Chelsea lad called Gatwick walked through the door and went over to Ian and the other Chelsea lads.

"What are you talking to these northern dickheads for," he said, before walking out.

Mick wasn't too impressed. "On your feet lads, we're fucking having it."

Sheffield Ian quickly followed Gatwick out. We walked towards the doors and Ian and Gatwick came back through. I don't know what had been said by Ian, but Gatwick turned round and said, "Sorry lads, I didn't know you were Burnley," shook our hands and fucked off back through the doors. Problem solved.

There was no sign of any skinhead gangs, only Czechoslovakian tramps coming over asking for money. All they got was a spray of CS gas and a kick up the arse. We moved to a hotel bar that had Sky TV. England were playing a one-day final at cricket, I think, and the bar was full of posh people in suits eating food. I don't think we went down well with the guests because they quickly finished their meals and left. Somebody turned the TV over to the cricket and one of the hotel staff turned it back over to the previous channel and walked away. It was turned back to cricket then back over again. This went on for a couple of minutes but the lads got to watch cricket in the end.

I went with Simon to change some money; £10 each would see us through the day, and we decided to do business with one of the street dealers. You got a better exchange rate. I gave Simon my £10. He went over to a dealer and handed the money over and came back over smiling. "We've got a good deal, we'll split it at the bar." We got back to the hotel bar and Simon ordered the beers and handed over the note. The bartender looked at it, shook her head and started laughing.

I took the note off her and looked at it. I knew what it was straight away.

"You've paid twenty pounds for fuck all Simon."

"How do you mean?"

"Well look at it," I suggested.

"What's wrong with it?"

"Where were we six months ago?"

"Poland."

"Well go and spend it there then."

We'd paid £20 for about twenty-five pence in Polish money. Simon was fucking raving, he took the gas out of his pocket and said, "Come on, let's go and find the fucker." He ran up and down the street gassing everyone that looked like the guy that ripped us off. I burst out laughing and this sent Simon on one again.

"Fuck it," he said. "I am going to find him and I am going to take all his money off him."

"Simon, you won't find him, he will be getting pissed with all his mates courtesy of you."

He finally calmed down but, every so often, it would get mentioned again and Simon would look out of the window and ask, "Do you think that looks like him, Pot?" He never did see the funny side.

England got beat by Pakistan. A Czechoslovak came into the bar trying to tap drinks off everyone, going around the tables drinking the leftovers. Some of the lads dived on him and stripped him to his underwear. He got up and started looking for his clothes. A few people bought him some beers and after half an hour they gave him his clothes back, no harm done. At least he got some beers.

Time was getting on and there was fuck all happening so twenty of us made our way to the ground. We walked to the England end and the Czechs didn't want to know. Finally, a mob came walking through. Not skinheads, more like punk rockers with flying jackets on. We were all straight into them. They had the numbers but not the bollocks. They split up. Every one of us was having our own individual battle and the police just watched. People were getting slapped all over. The Czechs were on their toes around to their end. Every time a mob walked through, the same happened. If the Czechs went to the police, the police just hit them with their batons. It was as if they wanted them to get a good kicking. The English numbers swelled to around 100 and the police decided to cordon off the square. It was time to get in the game.

You could pay at the turnstiles, no ticket required. The Czechs were mobbed up behind the opposite goal. They had turned their flying jackets inside out showing their bright orange linings. They looked like the Dutch. The Chelsea lads made their way to the top of the terrace and walked round to the Czech side. The Chelsea lads then appeared at one of the terrace entry points in the middle of the Czech mobs. Orange coats were running away but the police charged Chelsea out of the end.

This was the coldest game I had ever been to. You couldn't hold your beer in your hands, you had to leave it on the floor until you wanted a drink. The ground was three-quarters empty so you couldn't even group together to get warm. Then we heard Fat Stan's voice. He walked out onto the terrace wearing an England top. He must have been freezing. They couldn't prove the dodgy £20 came from him, so they had to let him go after a couple of hours. He got a bit lost on the train journey and had only just arrived. The game finished a draw. Nothing happened afterwards, no mobs waiting, nothing. We made our way to the train station. Stan wasn't happy he'd only been in Prague four hours, but he forgot about that after the first bottle of vodka.

CHAPTER TWELVE

THE BLACK ARMY

Euro 92

My second European Championship. Three of us were making the trip by train – me, Ade and Simon – while the others were flying to Denmark and were to meet us at the ferry port in Malmo, Sweden.

We set off on the Saturday. The first game would be played on the Thursday so we had plenty of time to stop off at a few places and have a beer or two. On the way to Dover the conversations were about whether we would be let in or refused. We all had criminal records for football violence, we didn't have any tickets for the games but we were willing to take the risks. If we did get in, beer was £8 a pint so it would be a very expensive couple of weeks on the piss.

I was amazed there were no checks on the ferry and we were all smiling waiting for the bar to open. We were the only England fans on board, which we thought would work in our favour. If there was a big mob of lads together getting rowdy, you could expect a warm reception off the Belgian police. Before the ferry docked we relieved the duty free shop of three bottles of Blue Label vodka for our train journey ahead. Again, no police were waiting, a flash of the passport and we were on foreign soil.

All you hear about from the media and the police on the run up to a major championship is about stopping people travelling and getting into these countries. Well, three convicted football hooligans arrived without a check or a policeman in sight. We checked the route and the train times, wanting out of Ostend as quickly as possible. We would go first to Hamburg, then to Copenhagen. It would be a long train journey to Hamburg so it was an opportunity to sleep. The idea was to use the train as a bed for the night and avoid the price of a hotel.

We arrived in Hamburg mid afternoon. The train to Copenhagen was twelve hours away so the only thing for it was a quick wash, brush the teeth, put the bags in left luggage and then a day on the piss. We settled down with a beer each in a nice little cellar bar when all of a sudden a bloke runs in covered in blood, screaming. We looked at each other wondering what the fuck was going on. All the other people in the bar seemed to ignore him but he made a beeline for us. Ade jumped up and said, "Fuck off, don't get your blood on me," then pushed the bloke to the floor. Then the barman came over, explained an ambulance had been called and told us to drink our beer. Then he went over to this man, picked him up, took him outside and dumped him on the pavement. He came back in and got a mop and bucket and started cleaning the floor as if nothing had happened.

Simon asked, "Is he alright?"

"Yes," said the barman. "He's just been stabbed, there are a lot of fights between drug dealers and pimps, it happens all the time."

We finished our beers and moved on to another bar. We saw the ambulance crew put him in the back, but before we'd walked another fifty yards down the road we heard, "crack, crack". A bloke was running down the other side of the road firing a fucking gun at someone. Police arrived from everywhere. We had just walked into the middle of a major turf war.

The police ran up to us and started pushing us down the road.

"What the fuck's going on? We're English, we want a beer."

"No, no, it's not a safe road, go down there."

We quickly found another watering hole, a rough-looking place. As we walked through the door everyone's head turned to look at us and it all went quiet. We couldn't just turn round and walk out, it would have made us look like cunts, so we pushed our way to the bar in silence. "Three big beers, mate." As soon as they heard we were English everyone started talking again although we couldn't understand what they were saying. They were staring at us whilst they were talking so we naturally presumed that they were talking about us. We made our way to a table against the wall so if they came at us we could see them. We sat down and nervously sipped our beers. But nerves soon turn to a rush and with that rush your attitude changes. If they wanted us out they would have to get us out, so fuck 'em. The beers went down easily.

Most of the eyes stopped staring at us and the atmosphere changed, but we did notice one lad with two birds staring all the time. We all looked at him, so he walked over with the two birds.

"You're English hooligans."

"Yeah, we're English hooligans."

The lad nodded his head and said, "Alice Clarke," pointing at the two birds. He kept saying it until Ade jumped up, said, "What the fuck are you on about?" and punched him. He staggered away and Simon and me jumped up waiting for the rush of punches, but none came. A German waving his arms in the air said, "No, no, he's offering you his women, no charge, he respects you." With this we all apologised. Ade shook the bloke's hand and told him we didn't want his women.

The man nodded his head, walked to the bar and came back with three beers for us. We didn't have to buy another beer, they just kept on coming.

We decided to go and have a look at the Reeperbahn, you can't go to Hamburg without seeing that. We stood up to leave the bar and every German there seemed to want to shake our hands, saying, "English hooligans good." Finally, we left and headed towards the red light area. It was nothing like Amsterdam. You had to walk through alleyways of steel shuttering. Once out of these we were on a street that I can only describe as a multi-storey car park, with prostitutes everywhere. It was dodgy as fuck with Turks all over the place, eyeing you up. We had a look round but time was getting on and we made our way back to the train station to catch the connecting train to Copenhagen.

Once on the train we found an empty compartment and quickly got our heads down. We had arranged to meet Millsy by the Mermaid statue. The thing is, the statue's in the middle of the harbour.

"Who the fuck said meet him here?"

"Well I didn't know the fucking statue was out there, I've never been here before."

We decided to find a bar and see if he was in there. Three beers cost us £24. "Fucking hell, we aren't staying here long." We got a round each so no-one could complain and decided Millsy would have gone straight to Malmo, so we jumped on the next ferry. We decided not to have any more beers, as you don't want to go staggering though Passport Control.

Ade got through, Simon got through then it was my turn.

"Excuse me sir, can you come with me."

He took me into a small room, took my passport and asked, "Can you empty your bag?" I knew I didn't have anything I shouldn't so I emptied it onto the table. He went through every pocket of my clothes and found fuck all. He told me to put my stuff back into my bag which I did, sharpish. I zipped the bag up and went to take it thinking that was it.

"No, no, give the bag to me."

He put it onto the floor at the side of him and told me to empty my pockets. Again, I knew I didn't have anything so I emptied my pockets on the table.

"Now take your top off."

Now the shit was going to hit the fan; I had Suicide Squad tattooed on my arm plus a can of CS gas that I picked up along the way, which was down my pants.

"Take your shoes and socks off."

I put them on the table and he checked them. "Right, trousers." I dropped my pants and, because I was wearing boxer shorts, the CS gas fell out of the leg of my boxers onto my pants. He clocked it straight away. I put the gas and the pants on the table and he put the gas to one side and checked my pants.

"Right, now the shorts."

"You fucking what?"

"Shorts, give me your shorts." So off they came onto the table.

"Turn around."

I gave him a bollock-naked turn.

"Right, get dressed." With that, he took the gas and went into another room.

Getting dressed, I was thinking, that's it, they're going to send me home and I'm going to miss all the action. After about ten minutes the bloke came back in with a piece of paper.

"You can go to court in the morning or you can accept a fine."

"OK, I will accept the fine, how much is it?"

"Twelve hundred kroner."

"How much? Do you expect me to pay that now?"

"No, we have your passport details, we will send the fine to your address."

Fucking real do, I couldn't keep the smile off my face, it was the quickest signature I had ever given. He gave me my passport back and told me to pick up my bag and follow him. He took me to another door, opened it and said, "Have a nice time in Sweden." I walked through the door and into a waiting room to be met by Simon, Ade, Fat Stan, Gwidge, another Palace fan and Millsy. Fat Stan was the first to speak. "Fuck me, Pot, I thought you were on your way home, son."

A bloke came into the room and started speaking Swedish, then said, "Suicide Squad." We all burst out laughing.

"Come on, let's get out of here, Gwidge has got the car outside."

We walked out towards the car, buzzing. We were in, let the fun begin. Then all of a sudden the police came running out towards us.

"Mr. Massey, come with us please, you are not entering Sweden."

Simon's face went from smiling to totally pissed off. I felt for him but we all knew the chances of being stopped.

"Come on, let's fuck off from here before they come back out and get someone else."

We quickly got into the car and set off to the campsite. It wasn't far away, we had a tent set up for us and there were beers waiting.

The campsite had its own beach, a nudist beach at that. It was full of people from every part of England. Tents were covered with flags with team names on them, the weather was hot and the atmosphere was great. We chilled out, lads were sunbathing quietly getting pissed. We got our gear into the tents and then got straight into the beers. The talk was about Hamburg, Simon getting stopped and whether Mick and Shaun would get through. There were around fifteen Palace lads, they had hired camper vans and driven all the way, they were a good set of lads but not as much into violence as we were.

The second day was all about waiting for Mick and Shaun who were flying into Copenhagen. Stan and Gwidge went to the ferry port to pick them up but only Shaun returned with them. Mick had been refused entry. They took him back to Copenhagen and put him on a plane straight back home. So out of the original six only four of us had made it. The Swedes had set up a big tent in the middle of a square selling beer at £4 a pint; the trouble was the beer was only one-and-a-half per cent proof, like drinking shandy. It made you piss a lot but didn't get you pissed, so we decided to get cans from the supermarket and then make our way to the beer tent. There was a fountain nearby which we used to keep the cans cold.

Everyone was talking to each other. The atmosphere was different than most England games; this seemed like a carnival and all the Swedish girls wanted to be with an English hooligan. One girl even did a striptease in front of about 100 of us. Everyone was egging her on. She got down to her underwear and all the lads ran up and dived on her; she disappeared under a sea of bodies. I don't know if Swedes are stupid or naïve. A ticket tout came over, "Tickets, tickets," and then proceeded to set up a table and put loads of tickets for the Denmark game on view. We looked in disbelief. Needless to say, he didn't last long. A mad rush had him on the floor, table knocked over and no tickets left. He picked himself up scratching his head, looking at his table and wondering where all his tickets had gone. He then ran over to the police waving his arms. The copper looked at him, shrugged his shoulders and fucked off. We all pissed ourselves with laughter.

When night came we made our way into the beer tent. I had found a garage five minutes' walk from the square selling Carlsberg at £1 a can, so we decided to get a crate each and take them back to the beer tent. One of us went in, got to the side of the tent and passed the cases under the side. Once all the beer was in, we followed, then sold the cans at £2 each, cheap at half the price. The others were paying £4 for shite so business was good, it was a free day out. The beer tent was full of lads. You would get the odd little mob of Swedes thinking they were something, walking around and bumping into people but they were soon done over and sent out on stretchers.

The day of the game arrived and again there was a carnival atmosphere; the police were out in force but they weren't heavy handed. We walked up to the ground, there were beer tents all around and big hot air balloons, people were sat on the grass drinking, after all we were playing Denmark who weren't into fighting. Not one of us had a ticket so we waited for the game to start and then the touts were practically giving tickets away. We acquired ours well under market value. A shit game ended 0-0 and there was no sign of trouble. We made our way back to the beer tent, the mood was still good, at least England had got a point. We loaded up with cans and went back to the campsite for a good night's rest.

The next day was a lazy one of sunbathing and getting pissed. Millsy and a few Palace lads had gone over to Copenhagen to score some weed so it was a chilled-out day. More and more England supporters were turning up, a lot of whom I knew from other England games. They didn't bother about the Denmark game, everyone knew it wouldn't go off against the Danes. We just hoped the French would turn up. If not it would be off to Stockholm to do battle with the Swedes on their own turf. The atmosphere was changing, you could feel it in the air. Everyone was on about the Swedish firm, the Black Army, who were supposed to be well up for it. The campsite was now home to a lot of English mobs but there was no sign of trouble. Mobs mingled with others from different teams and the drinking and talking went on all day and night.

Everyone had arranged to meet on Saturday at the beer tent

as usual and we called into the garage to collect our beers. The weather was red hot and there were mobs of English fans all over, the atmosphere was still good but you could feel something else was there, you knew it could kick off at any time. All it would take was one small spark. We met up with more Burnley lads plus a few from Walsall, Arsenal and Leicester. The police were there in numbers but they all seemed to have smiles on their faces as they walked through the crowds chatting to people. I've never known a more friendly police force, they were so laid back. As the afternoon wore on people were getting pissed and choruses of "England, England" roared out. This seemed to get the Swedish police a little nervous, you could sense that something would happen tonight. As we downed our last cans a Norwegian couple approached us, they were probably in their fifties or sixties.

"When does it all kick off?" asked the man.

"When does what kick off?"

"All the fighting, we've come on holiday to see it kick off."

"Later on," I said. With that the couple made their way into the beer tent. Everyone seemed to want to watch England in action.

Me, Ade, Shaun and Millsy went to the garage to load up for the night shift. Walking to the garage I moved to one side to let some people past; as soon as I took a side step I went flying and landed in a heap on the floor. I looked up to see the lads laughing and then saw some cunt and his bike on the floor. I jumped up and ran over to him, called him a fucking dickhead, punched him and then jumped all over his bike.

The Swedish people that I had moved for came over to me. "No, it is your fault," they said. "That side of the pavement is for walking, this side is for bikes."

"What?"

The other lads were still pissing themselves watching the lad carrying his bike up the road, wheels bent. So with me bloody, bruised and pissed off we carried on to the garage. The lads couldn't wait to get back to the beer tent to tell everyone that I got run over by a bike. I took hours of stick.

Day had turned to night and the mood of the lads had changed too. There were little groups of Swedes about, two lads appeared on the roof of the beer tent and everyone was laughing at them. The police started to line up across the square, then Mark, a Walsall fan, came up to me.

"Come on Pot. Let's do these Swedes, who the fuck do they think they are?"

Some other lads had the same idea but Mark and me were straight into them. The police saw what was going on and started to come towards us. The Swedish lads ran towards the police with chairs, tables and bottles following.

Attention now turned to the police. They tried to surround the beer tent. They had riot shields and dogs but we pushed them back towards the street; the air was full of missiles and the sound of sirens could be heard everywhere. The police held their line and fans turned their attention to a few jewellers' shops. The windows went through, pushbikes were being thrown through restaurant windows, film crews were running for their lives. One cameraman couldn't run that fast and was caught and slapped. His camera was smashed and the video was taken from it and smashed too. A motorbike was set on fire. The police were trying to contain us, blocking all the streets leading to the square. Undercover snatch squads appeared from nowhere, then came the horses, coppers on top with their truncheons drawn, hitting almost anything that moved, innocent and guilty alike, male and female, there was no discrimination. Tables, chairs and bikes were thrown at the horses.

A mob of around 100 of us broke down a side street and put every window through. We ended up near the ferry terminal where another line of coppers tried to push us back to the square. We flew straight into them, there was no fucking about. They tried to batter us with truncheons and we only had our hands and feet but we were not retreating. A few of the police had lost their truncheons; these were now being used on them and their workmates. Now it was us pushing them back. A copper went down at the side of me, a volley caught him on the head and his helmet came flying off. I thought, fuck me, he's kicked his head off. The police line started to break. One was on his toes, then two, then three, leaving their mates on the battle lines. We knew we had the edge. "Come on." Now all the police who could run did run. We didn't bother giving chase, it is not advisable to chase a load of coppers.

We made our way up another street, putting windows in all the time. At the top of the street we were close to the square again and met up with another English mob. Police in full riot gear were everywhere and came into us with the snatch squad right behind them. Our numbers were dwindling fast. It was time to evade the police, not encounter them. Me, Ade and Shaun decided to get to the bus station. We turned the corner and saw Millsy walking down the street with two carrier bags full of cans. "I thought you might need a drink after," he said. We made our way towards the bus station while all of the police were up at the square containing the situation up there.

We had just got to the bus station when we noticed some Blackburn fans in front. One of them said, "I know you hate us, but look behind you." We turned to see loads of Lebanese armed with sticks. "Right lads, stick together." We walked to where the buses picked up, we had a bus shelter at either side of us and railings behind us. Over the railings was a graveyard. I got a can out of the bag and sat on the kerb, waiting.

A Lebanese lad walked down tapping a walking stick on the floor and stopped directly in front of us.

"Who's the best hooligans?" he asked.

"Us, fucking English."

I jumped to my feet and the Blackburn lad ran towards him. The cunt then pulled a sword out of the walking stick. We both stopped. The swordsman came towards us, swung and missed me but he got the Blackburn lad right down his face and then stabbed him in the chest. Ade and Shaun flew into the sword merchant and Millsy threw all our beer at him. A few more English came running down the street and then some guardian angels attended to the Blackburn lad. The lad with the sword was getting backed off. We charged and he ran into a little park in front of McDonalds. We didn't follow; we went to see how the Blackburn lad was.

We all knew this wasn't over and more English started to appear, increasing our numbers to twenty. Every one of us knew the score; they would be back and we had nowhere to go. Then out of the park they came, proper tooled up. This was a fight for your life. You couldn't back off in a situation like this. A Lebanese lad ran at me and Shaun. We fronted him, although he had a machete in his hand. Shaun and I were bouncing up and down and he kept lunging at us. Ade ran in from the side and banged the Lebanese guy and he landed on the floor, getting what he deserved. There were bodies and blood all over. A lad ran up to Shaun with a blade in his hand and caught Shaun on the neck but it wasn't too bad. I ran up to the lad and ripped him to the floor by his hair. I started pulling him across the ground, everyone was kicking him. The trouble was I couldn't get my hand out of his hair, I literally had to stand on his head and pull my hands free, needless to say a lot of hair came out as well. We kept chasing them off and they came back with more but our numbers were swelling too. People were stabbed on both sides.

Another group of English appeared, getting run down the street by the Lebanese. We ran towards them shouting, "Stand," and they all turned to face their pursuers. With us coming up behind, the Lebanese realised that they were outnumbered and started to back off, but more English had appeared behind the Lebanese. They were trapped. We all ran into them, there was fighting everywhere. One lad was chasing three English with a blade when Shaun ran up to the side of him and caught him with a pearl of a punch. He was out cold. The three lads then proceeded to jump all over his head. A rumour went round straight away that the lad had his throat slashed with his own blade. I wouldn't know about that, I never saw it happen.

We got the better of the Lebanese before the police turned up and pushed them towards McDonalds. The English now numbered more than eighty and we marched through the park towards McDonalds, where we met a wall of police surrounding the Lebanese, who still seemed to be well tooled up. Bricks and bottles flew over the police lines towards us. We tried to get through them but we couldn't, we were taking a lot of casualties.

Suddenly, the police line opened and all of the Lebanese came pouring through. The police seemed to be on their side; it was their turn to outnumber us. Some English started to run and this set others off. It soon spread and we were all on our toes, chased from street to street, losing numbers all the time. Me, Ade, Shaun and Millsy decided to head straight for the campsite, knowing any English walking round the city centre would be easy prey for the Lebanese. We got there without encountering any trouble. Once at the site we could relax a bit, safety in numbers and all that. A lot of English were walking around with blades as rumours started to fly around that the Lebanese were on their way up after one had died. There wouldn't be a lot of sleep tonight.

Fires were being lit everywhere. People sat there drinking with knives stuck in the grass and there were lookouts at every entry and exit point. The fire brigade then turned up wanting to put out all the fires. This didn't go down well and as soon as the fire engine pulled up to the first fire it was pelted with bricks and bottles and the crew wouldn't get out. The engine quickly turned round as lads chased it, throwing things. It left the site without putting out a single fire. Some lads turned their attention to the site shop; the till was soon smashed on the floor but it only contained change, no notes. The shop was soon well alight and this time the police turned up, coaches full of them on every exit and entry point. I don't know if it was to stop the Lebanese coming in or stop us from getting out but at least we could get some sleep.

I was woken early by a plainclothes policeman poking his head through the tent.

"Come on, out," he ordered.

We got out and saw four more Old Bill, two with camcorders.

"Sit down. Passports."

We gave them our passports then in turn they videoed each one of us. They seem fascinated with Ade, probably because he had a lump missing out of his ear.

One of the police asked "How did that happen?"

"It dropped off when my mother was giving birth to me."

They looked at each other a little bewildered and then fucked off to the next tent. They were everywhere with their camcorders. If you got up to walk to the pisser you were videoed.

After a shit, shower and shave and a bit of food it was off to the beer tent. We walked into the square, which looked a lot different than it had the night before. Most of the windows surrounding it were boarded up and vans of police were down every street. Undercover police mingled with us but were easily recognisable. You won't get a typical Swede Old Bill to look like an English hooligan; they all looked like Dolph Lundgren in *Universal Soldier*. Every so often you would see lads snatched from the crowd and marched off with Old Bill either side of them.

We decided to make our way to the ground in case the police decided to nick one of us, and we still had the small matter of tickets to sort out, but it didn't take long to acquire some from a tout. Then it was down to the beer tent in a field at the side of the ground. We got a few beers and sat outside on the grass trying to catch some sun. A few lads I knew said a mob of English had just attacked a Lebanese mob outside McDonalds, and the Lebanese were supposed to be coming up to the beer tent after the game, so we all agreed to meet back at the beer tent for Round Two.

The game wasn't much to talk about, finishing 0-0 again. The French didn't want to know and our thoughts were on what the night would bring. Back in the square we followed the usual routine, down the garage, pick up the beer and smuggle it into the tent. The tent was full of lads, top lads at that. This was a good mob, the atmosphere was tense and spotters were sent out to see where the opposition was, though there was no early sign. The police put lines across the street leading down to McDonalds and behind the lines were horses and dogs at the ready.

The night was getting on when one of the spotters came back and said, "They're on their way up." Someone grabbed the microphone from the guy on the stage, "Right lads, they're here." Within seconds every table and chair was demolished and, armed with table legs and chair legs, we charged at the police lines. We could see the Lebanese down the road. Missiles flew from either side. We repeatedly charged the lines but they held firm and, in turn, they charged us. We weren't getting through here so smaller mobs tried different streets but still we got pushed back; the police had us well and truly contained. Then they sent in the dogs, the horses and the snatch squads. It was time to get out of the containment zone.

We found a street at the opposite side of the square, split up into ones and twos to make it easier to argue with the police that we were going back to our campsite. Around twenty of us got through using the same method then met up around the corner. It was safer to stick together. Walking back to the campsite nothing happened, we just kept bumping into other English mobs who'd had the same idea as us. I couldn't believe what we found at the campsite, it was half empty and some of the English had left in such a hurry, obviously thinking the Lebanese would be turning up, they had left clothes and tents. This left between 200 and 300 of us. Everyone was tooled up and people were in the trees or in bushes. You would walk past some bushes and a voice would say, "Alright mate, you seen any sign yet?" Lads lined up their cars, pointing them towards the main entrance with the motors running. It was a good feeling, total togetherness, everyone looking out for everyone else. Other people were passing cans around. Then someone said, "They're here." Taxis pulled up and lads charged out of them from every direction, but the taxis were soon full again as they all turned and fled.

"Is that it? Fucking wankers."

Soon after the police turned up in large numbers and sealed off the campsite again. Morning quickly came and all the tents were packed into the camper vans. Millsy decided to travel to Stockholm in the camper vans because they had some weed. Me, Ade, Shaun and a few others would be going by train. At this point I would just like to say to Assistant Chief Constable Malcolm George, then of Greater Manchester Police and the chief national police spokesman on football violence, that the riot in Malmo wasn't pre-planned and there certainly wasn't a whistle blown to start it.

After many checks, we finally boarded the train for Stockholm. Police were on the train constantly walking up and down, looking at you and studying photos, probably from the video footage. We kept our heads down, we wanted to get to Stockholm, this was the big one. We had it on good authority that three firms were joining up to do us: the Black Army, the Blue Saints and an outfit called Bagarm.

We got into Stockholm at nightfall and got out of the station no problem. Now it was time to find a beer. We bumped into a small mob of English who told us that there was a beer tent down the road but it was being run by the Black Army. "Fuck 'em, we'll go and have a beer in there." Off we marched and bumped into a mob of Wolves on the way. They told us it had just gone off at the tent, asked where we were staying and told us there was a bit of a sports stadium down the road, where everyone was camping. With the knowledge of the campsite nearby we decided to carry on to the beer tent.

There were a load of little stalls selling crap around the main tent. One was a hairdresser shaving people's heads then giving them a Black Army tee-shirt. We walked towards the main tent. There was no chance of a beer here, the Swedes were putting it back together, it was trashed. The police started to turn up so we made a hasty exit and headed for the campsite. The Wolves lads were right, there was a bit of a stand full of seats surrounding gravel pitches and there was a large grass bank where all the tents were set up. We made our way to the grass bank and soon bumped into Mark and some of his Walsall mates, who had a good fire going and plenty of beer. The lads told us that the beer tent had been half full of Swedes and half English. The Swedes got a bit brave and started singing a few songs and the English just steamed into them and ran them all over. We drank and slept round the fire all night. Our tents hadn't turned up yet.

We all woke early, first things first, shit, shower and shave. Underneath the seated area were showers, a sauna, washing machines and a café. I put all my clothes in the washing machine, went to get some food and waited for my washing to finish. On the way back to the Walsall lot I spotted a lad with a bottle of Strongbow cider. He explained that there were government-run shops called System Brogan, or something like that, that sold imported beers and I hurried over and told the others. We were in the shop within fifteen minutes. I love Strongbow and I couldn't wait to get a taste of England. We bought a crate each, six bottles to a crate at roughly £4 per bottle, which I didn't think was too bad for imported beer, especially for the stuff that you drank at home.

Back at the campsite a few more Burnley lads had arrived. The camper vans followed shortly after with Millsy and the tents on board. The weather was hot again and football games were being held all over. Lads were sunbathing, drinking and smoking a few spliffs. It made you laugh. The English Travel Club put their members in a tent city in the middle of a gravel pit twenty miles from Stockholm with fuck all around. We were in a campsite in Stockholm centre and it was free. What more could you ask?

Forty of us decided to have a drink in the city centre to see if anything was happening. The only problem was that the beer was still £8 a pint. The night was shit, no Swedish mobs anywhere and we got to thinking, what a load of bollocks, they gave it the big one and couldn't even turn out the night before the game.

The day of the game, we went straight to the shop and bought a crate of Strongbow, which we started drinking on the camp. Someone had a great idea for a north v. south football game. The Red Cross tent set up on the campsite was very busy that morning as twenty-two pissed up lads tried to play football. There were a few late challenges, people running into each other, some collapsing from the heat and me, silly bollocks, doing a sliding tackle on the gravel. My legs were already sunburnt with water blisters coming up and after the slide I didn't get any blisters as I had no skin left. What a great game though, it should have been televised, no-one knew the final score.

Afterwards a lad came up to us and pointed out Millsy, who was unconscious.

"We can't wake him up," he said.

"Cheers mate, we'll sort it."

Millsy was a diabetic and when he drank a lot he used to miss his insulin. There was no chance of waking him so I got him on my shoulder and carried him back to his tent. On the way back I felt warm liquid down my back and onto my legs. He had been sick down my back. I got him to the tent and threw him on the floor. He mumbled, "Black coffee and a Mars bar," he was off to the land of nod again. Fat Stan came up with the idea of a cold shower.

"Who's going to carry him over there?"

"You, he's already spewed, he must have fuck all left in his stomach."

We sat him in the shower but soon realised that there was a big hosepipe connected up. I put it on full blast straight in his face. He started to splutter and his eyes opened.

"Fuck me, Pot, you're drowning me."

I threw the hose down and shoved a Mars bar in his hand.

"Get your own fucking coffee, I'm going for a shower."

Twenty minutes later, after his coffee and insulin, he walked up to us sober as a judge. "Right, are we going to set off to the game at midday?"

Forty of us set off together and made our way to the train station, where police were everywhere and clearly expecting something to go off. We got the underground to the stadium and the train was full of England fans, hardly any Swedish. We came out of the underground and there were lines and lines of police. English and Swedes mingled together. A large mob of English stood on the grass banking with a line of police in front of them. A Swedish mob had gathered outside McDonalds with another line of police in front of them. Nothing was going to go off here, there were far too many cops. Some of us had to get tickets so we left the other lads on the grass banking whilst we went looking for touts. It didn't take long to get the tickets, some paid, some didn't. The only trouble was we were in the Swedish end. We went back to the grass banking to meet the rest of the lads. It was full by then and songs were being sung. More police arrived, looking anxious. Then one of them appeared with a loudhailer telling us to move towards the stadium.

Everyone on the banking started to move off peacefully and go to their turnstiles. Ten of us had tickets for behind the nets, adjacent to the English side terrace. We gained entry and walked onto the terrace expecting a bit of a reception but none came. The Swedes weren't interested. They just wanted a sing-song. We got a spot halfway up the terrace next to the England fans. The teams came out and the game started. Five minutes on the clock and England scored. The English went mad, we went mad, but the Swedes just looked at us. As soon as the game started again in came the police, straight over to us. "English, come with us." They took us up to the fence, opened the gate and put us in with the rest of the English.

One up at half-time, at least we had scored a goal. They equalised in the second half, Gary Lineker was substituted and we went 2–1 down. England had bottled it again. We were out. Now it was time for our game to begin.

We made our way to the exits but they were shut. The doors were steel roller shutters. All the Swedes were banging on them. Some lads tried to kick the doors open but it was no good. A few of us grabbed hold of the shutters at the bottom, trying to lift them but nothing happened, more hands helped and soon the shutters were up and we were out. The police didn't expect this. We walked towards the underground and the police directed us down the ramp towards the station; there was a fence running down the ramp to stop you climbing over. On the other side of the fence were all the Swedes outside McDonalds. They started spitting at us and throwing things. Fuck that. We turned and ran back up the ramp towards the police and about thirty of us got through before they had a clue what was going on. The Swedes were all around us but we went straight into them. They were well up for it and heavily outnumbered us but we knew what we were doing. There were different one-to-one battles going on everywhere, we weren't backing off. The other English went into the station and came out of another exit behind the Swedes. Finally we split them, we had more bollocks. We had them on the run.

A Swedish guy turned round and kicked an English lad in the head, knocking him cold. Then the Swede was on his toes, with me hot on his heels. They thought they were running to safety but they were wrong. They ran straight into the English who had come out of the other exit of the underground. The lad I was chasing ran straight into one of my mates and got a good kicking. With Swedes all over on the floor, there was nothing more to do.

Around 500 of us decided to walk to another underground station. This was a serious mob, there was no talking, just walking. We found another underground and got on the next train into the city centre. We got off and out of the station. No-one knew where all the police had gone. There was a massive roundabout in front of us with Swedes all around. They hadn't noticed 500 lads walking towards them, that was how quiet we were. "Come on!" The Swedes were shocked at what they saw, cars were crashing into each other, English were swarming over the roundabout towards them. I was right at the front when a car drove past with a Swede hanging out of the window spraying a tin of CS gas. He got me full in the face and I was blinded. I tried to open my eyes with my fingers and all I could hear was smashing glass and stamping feet all around me. Then I heard a friendly voice.

"You alright mate?"

"I will be when I can see again."

I was still holding my eyes open with my fingers, trying to

get some vision back. I was pushed up some stairs and heard voices all around me, not one of them English. Finally, I started to get some vision back and saw I was on a bridge going over the road and the bridge was full of Swedes. They were throwing anything they could get their hands on over the bridge and onto the English below. All I could think was keep quiet or they would be throwing me over next. I was still fucked, still holding my eyes open, but I managed to get back down the stairs. The English had moved down the road. Sounds of sirens filled the air and I walked towards them, knowing that's where the English would be.

I saw a big mob down the street, police were everywhere, I thought this must be the English. I quickened my pace to catch them up and had just got to the back of the mob when I realised they were the Swedes. I was behind enemy lines. I took the next turning trying to get around their mob but down every street there were battles going on. It was dark and you couldn't tell who was who. I'd lost everybody, there were Swedish mobs everywhere. Police were charging down the streets and every time I was in the middle of a Swedish mob. I ended up getting to the main train station which was also full of Swedes, no English at all. I moved down to the underground, found a bench, sat down trying to get my head together when two girls came up to me and one said, "You been on TV" and kept pointing at my shirt. "You been on TV." Then a big skinhead came over and sat on my other side, rocking back and forth. I had two birds on one side of me telling me I had been on TV and a lunatic having a fit on the other side, getting louder and louder and rocking faster, working himself into a frenzy. That was it, I was up and I was running.

I just caught the train doors before they closed. I wasn't looking back. I didn't have a clue where I was going just as long as it was away from the lunatic. I jumped off at the next stop and walked out of the station. Then, out of the blue, I was staring at the System Brogan shop. Thank fuck from here I knew my way back to the campsite. I turned onto the main road leading to the campsite only to find a Swedish mob in front of me. In front of the Swedes were lines of police so there was only one thing for it, walk straight into them. All the Swedes were facing the police lines so hopefully they wouldn't suss me. I decided to walk on the pavement close to the shop. Halfway through I started to feel a few looks but I just carried on walking, staring back at them, head held high. You couldn't show you were scared, that gives them confidence. Only when I had passed the front line did I hear a voice say, "Fucking English."

I had made a bit of a distance by now and I turned round with arms outstretched, "Yeah, I'm fucking English," but no-one approached me. I backed off, keeping my eyes on the Swedes. Eventually, there was enough distance between us and I turned and walked towards the police lines. At first they wouldn't let anyone through but a good little mob of English was gathering and, with the Swedes just down the road, I think they decided it would be better for them to let us onto the campsite.

It was surrounded by police. I made my way to where we were camped, a few of the lads had got a fire started and I settled down with a bottle of Strongbow. All the lads managed to get back without getting nicked. Some were bloodied and bruised and they all had good tales to tell. I was totally fucked, so I jumped into the tent and got my head down. Ade woke me up saying he was going down to the train station to find out the times of the trains. My job was to get our shit together. I climbed out of the tent, stood up and took off my shirt (the one that had been on TV the night before) and, as I turned around, saw police and cameras everywhere. I quickly jumped back into the tent, got a different tee-shirt on, shoved the other one to the bottom of my bag, then left the tent and went to the

Walsall lads. I sat with them, trying to mingle, keeping my back to the video cameras.

Then one of the lads said, "Fucking hell lads, there's load of Old Bill on their way over here." I turned round to see two lines of police, around twenty in each line, crossing the gravel football pitches. You get a sick feeling when you just know that they are coming for you. As the police got nearer they started to fan out and form a circle around us. One of the lads asked, "What the fuck do these want."

"It's OK," I replied. "It's me."

Eight police came through the circle straight towards me, said something in Swedish, asked me to stand and then proceeded to put the handcuffs on. They led me through the circle of the police across the football pitch and out of the side exit. I was told to sit against a wall with other English. After ten minutes I saw my brother walking down the street towards us. As he got closer I winked at him as if to say don't say a word and keep on walking. The next time I saw Ade was when all the Palace fans were driving past in their camper vans and cars, wishing me well before driving off into the distance back to English shores. I got to thinking how long it would be before I got to see England again. I figured I would probably be put up in court the following day, fined and deported so it shouldn't be that bad.

The campsite was empty and everyone had been checked and videoed before leaving. Around twenty of us were left against the wall, cuffed up. The police had obviously got who they were after and we were taken in vans to a massive police station, where we were each placed in our own cells. My mind started to wander, wondering what they had got me for.

The door opened and a voice said, "Come with me." I was taken to an interview room and told to sit. Then he fucked off, leaving the door open. I was staring at the wall when I heard this other voice, "Alright Pot, fucking wankers aren't they, we'll be home tomorrow." It was Donald, the daft Man City fan I had encountered many times on my travels. He was then led away.

Two big fuckers appeared at the door, one carrying my bag, the other carrying loads of video tapes. They both sat down facing me with my bag on the table.

"This your bag?" asked one.

"Yeah."

He opened it and pulled out my shirt, a black and white lumberjack type.

"This your shirt?"

"Yeah."

He looked at his partner and said, "We are getting somewhere." His pal then turned on the TV and put in a video. It was showing outside the stadium after the game. "Is that you?" It clearly was me. I was walking through the police cordon and chasing the Swedes. Then it showed one of them getting a kicking. I was the only black and white shirt on the TV, there was no way of getting out of this one, so I tried to think of a good story. The door on the interview room was still open; it seemed every police person in the building wanted to see me. Some wankers called in, "You like to fight, fight me."

"Fuck off, wankers." After all, what else could they do? I was already locked up.

They took me to another room, strip-searched me and placed me in a cell for the night. I awoke to a bang on the door, the hatch came down and a tray was passed through. I was told a solicitor was on his way and so was the British Consul. The hatch closed again. I sat down to eat my breakfast, which consisted of a bowl of cereal, a carton of milk, a cup of coffee and a bread roll with jam and butter. It looked OK, I opened the milk and poured it into my coffee and it came out in a blob, the fucking milk was off. I thought that it might just have cream on the top so I poured it onto my cereal but it came out the same. I couldn't eat that shit. So it was just a jam roll. The hatch opened some time later. "Tray please." I shoved the tray through the hatch. "Shove your food up your arse, the milk's off." He looked at me as if I was stupid and then shut the hatch.

Time has no relevance in places like these. The door opened again. "Solicitor is here to see you." He spoke good English. I told him my story. It went like this: I walked to the underground and the Swedes were pissing and throwing missiles down on us, we got through the cordon, the Swedes attacked us. One lad kicked an English lad in the head and I chased him, he went on the floor, I went to kick him but I was pissed and I missed him, end of story.

The solicitor explained that I had been charged with GBH and could expect anything up to four years in jail. I would be put up in court in the next few days. Meeting over, I was taken back to the cell. The next meeting was with the British Consul's representative. They sent a Scotsman to see me, who wasn't bad for a Jock.

"Have you any complaints?" he asked.

"Yeah, the milk was off, I want proper milk that isn't curdled."

"Do you want anyone notified?"

"Yeah, my wife." And that was it, meeting over.

The next day breakfast came with proper milk. The door opened and I was handed a razor, towel and a shaving stick. "You're in court today, clean yourself up." You had to walk underground to get to the courthouse. The lad who got the kicking was in a bad way and I was remanded in custody to await a trial date and taken back to the cell. The following day I was moved upstairs to the remand wing where the cells were better with satellite TV and a door leading to the cell next door.

"Do you want door open, English in next cell?"

"Yeah."

The internal door was opened and then the main door was shut. I walked into the next cell. The lad next door was a Wolves fan called Carl. As we got talking I remembered he was the lad who had told us about the campsite and we got on like a house on fire. The door between the cells was open from eight in the morning until eight at night and we had a right laugh.

The days went quickly. Carl had been charged for fighting at the Black Army beer tent. My case was all over the Swedish news. Every day the footage would be shown on the TV. Once, when my solicitor came to see me, I instantly thought it was bad news. He told me that a Swedish film crew wanted to do a documentary on English hooligans.

"Are they taking the piss?" I asked. "I haven't even been in court."

He said they would black out my face and distort my voice. I burst out laughing thinking about *Panorama* programmes with their supergrasses and undercover Old Bill doing the same. I got back to the cell and told Carl; he pissed himself.

Carl's court date came; we had done twenty-eight days so far. We said our goodbyes and I wished him well and hoped he would be on his way home soon. I hadn't even got a trial date through. The door between the cells opened and Carl walked in looking well pissed off.

"What did you get?"

"Six months."

Just as I tried to cheer him up and tell him that it would soon go and all that shit, he started laughing and told me, "I'm going home tomorrow, I've done my time, they're deporting me. I've got to wait to hear when they have got me a flight." I was buzzing for him. The next day Carl got his flight home. What a good solid lad. I've had many a drink and plenty of battles with him over the past thirteen years.

200

The next one in the cell was Andrew from Portsmouth, another good lad. We got on well and had something in common: we had both been charged with the same incident. Andrew was filmed walking up and down with a piece of wood in his hand with a few Swedes around him on the floor. After another four weeks we had our court date. Andrew was up in the morning, me in the afternoon. We said our goodbyes and wished each other well. It was time to face the music.

I walked into court, saw Andrew at the back and he gave me a thumbs-up sign. I had an interpreter, explaining what was going on. I stuck to my story all the way through. The lad who got the kicking broke down, crying, saying he was having nightmares about the incident, but then he admitted he jumped up and kicked an English fan in the head. Wanker. I would understand if he had been an innocent bystander, but he was there to fight. You don't cry over spilt milk. You either give it or get it. They looked at different videos, all taken from different angles, but they couldn't see my foot connect with his head. With this the judge decided that I had done enough time and I was free to go, no deportation. Two policemen took me back to the station.

As I walked out of court a film crew was waiting. A camera was shoved in my face and they started asking loads of questions. All I said was that I was going to find a System Brogan shop, buy some Strongbow and get pissed out of my head. The police then put me in a car and took me to pick up my gear. I couldn't keep the smile off my face. Walking out of the station I met Andrew who had got the same result. We were both buzzing. "Come on let's get a beer." We started walking when this reporter came up to us and asked us for an interview. "Yeah, buy us a few beers and we will give you one," we said. After four beers the interview finished and it was time for the Strongbow shop and the train home. I still had my

Inter-rail ticket so there was no problem for me. Andrew, though, didn't have a ticket.

We boarded the train to Malmo and I kept my eye out for Hector. Every time he passed, Andrew jumped under the seats. He managed to jump the train all the way to Ostend, then paid for his ferry journey. Back on English soil we said our goodbyes and I never bumped into him again. When I got home I found out I had lost my job at Luton airport. No surprise there. I had made the national press. It said, "Five English soccer fans were paraded before a Stockholm court accused of kicking, battering and bottling innocent people in an orgy of violence. Millions of TV viewers were sickened by the scenes after England crashed out of the European Championships. Among those accused was father-of-three Andrew Porter, twenty-six, caught on film repeatedly kicking a man in the head. Porter, a cleaner at Luton airport, was arrested at the England supporters' campsite after being identified by his distinctive chequered shirt, moustache and earrings. He told the court, 'I never hit or kicked anyone, I was so drunk I was not capable of doing any battering.' So I wasn't surprised to lose my job. How can a convicted soccer hooligan get through airport security? The writing was also on the wall with my marriage and I soon moved back to Burnley, where I belonged.

CHAPTER THIRTEEN

DOMESTIC DUTIES

Burnley v Cardiff, 1992

No-one expected the Welsh to turn up for a night game. By six o'clock there was fifteen of us drinking in the White Lion. One of the lads came in saying there was a mob of Cardiff up near to Burnley Central train station. As we approached the station, Cardiff appeared on the other side of the dual carriageway. Both mobs spotted each other. Cardiff jumped over the fence and ran on to the road. We started to back off and Cardiff thought we were bottling it. They jumped over the central barrier and we turned round. "Su, su, Suicide." We charged at them, with numbers equal. The Welsh stopped in their tracks, turned and started to climb back over the crash barriers. We were into them. The Welsh weren't standing, they were on their toes. Some of them were caught and were left in the middle of the dual carriageway. One unlucky lad ran into the loading bay of a supermarket and was trapped, there was no way out. He was battered, then gassed. Some of the lads didn't think he'd had enough so they started giving him another kicking. I think the lads would still be kicking the Welshman now if I hadn't told them to stop. We left him in the loading bay; his mates were nowhere to be seen. We walked back to the pub, job done. No more Welsh appeared that night.

Baby Squad in Blackburn, 1992

Burnley were playing away at Rochdale. We travelled in a Transit van. It was pissing it down. We got into a pub in the centre of Rochdale at midday and had just settled down with our beers when a Burnley fan told us that the game had been called off. We ordered another beer and one of the lads got a newspaper to see if there were any other teams playing nearby. We picked Blackburn v. Leicester City, finished our beers, jumped back in the van and headed for Blackburn, where we got into a pub on the outskirts. There were no police or other fans about and the fifteen of us stayed in the pub until after five, when Blackburn's game had finished. One of the lads went into the centre to find out where the Blackburn lads were drinking and found them in the Adelphi, near to the main train station. We headed straight for the pub.

Me and another lad, Ross, were well in front of the rest and walked straight in and had a look round. It was full of lads. I assumed they were Blackburn as there were no police about. We walked back out and, with the other lads still a good couple of hundred yards away, I went up to the pub window and banged on it. All the lads inside turned to look at me. "Outside, you Blackburn cunts," I said, and walked into the centre of the road, where Ross joined me. Blackburn started to bounce out of the pub and I fronted them straight away, but there was something wrong, they called me a Blackburn cunt. These lads were obviously Leicester. I told them, "I'm fucking Suicide, Burnley." We were still fronting them but they wouldn't come into us. Then more lads came bouncing out of the pub and glasses and bottles started to fly through the air towards us. The two of us stayed and just dodged the missiles. I was thinking to myself, where the fuck are the rest of my mates?

There must have been at least fifty Leicester on the street by now and they charged at the two of us. We stood our ground; we were going nowhere. I was fighting like mad with a few of them, they were trying to drag me down but they couldn't. They backed off, then a lad came running through the crowd with pool balls in a sock and hit me right in the face, knocking me on my arse. I instantly rolled up into a ball and waited for the kicking, hoping that none of them had a blade. I felt the kicks hitting my body and then I heard a voice say, "Leave him, he's game as fuck, get the others."

I stayed on the floor for a while. When I got up I felt like I'd had twenty pints. I was dizzy and staggering all over. I saw an ambulance in the distance and lumbered towards it. Mick Moore was in the back with Ross and Shaun T, and I climbed in to join them. The ambulance door shut and we went up to the hospital. Mick was in a bad way; his mouth pissing with blood. The lad with the pool balls had smacked him too, and as he hit the floor he bit his own tongue. It was nearly split in two. I looked like the Elephant Man, with one side of my face hugely swollen. Shaun and Ross had head wounds. They kept Mick in hospital overnight, Shaun and Ross were stitched up and sent home and X-rays fortunately showed nothing of mine was broken.

Full respect to the Leicester lads.

Burnley v West Bromwich, 1992

West Brom were a big club at the top of the league so we had a massive mob out. The Sidewalk pub near to the bus station was packed with a good couple of hundred and we had mobs in the White Lion and Yates's. No West Brom fans were showing their faces in the centre but reports came back that they were drinking up near the ground. We finished our drinks and headed to the Turf pub and the Princess Royal. A lot of West Brom fans were walking towards the ground full of colours, treating it like a home game. I think they thought we didn't have any lads.

As the traffic came to a standstill, minibuses full of

Brummies were attacked from every angle. The doors of the buses were opened and visiting fans were dragged out and kicked to fuck. The police were soon there to save them. A few of us went across the road to the Brickmakers where some West Brom were drinking. It went off like fuck. There were no bottles or glasses, just fists and feet. The West Brom lads picked up pool cues but they were soon snatched from them. We had the pool cues now and we used them well. The police steamed in the front door and we disappeared through the side door back into the Princess Royal. Burnley were all over the street, banging every West Brom fan they could see. There was so much fighting going on the police lost control. On the way to the ground there were little mobs of West Brom who were easy pickings for the Burnley lads.

After the game it was the same scenario, the Brom lads being picked off for fun and the ambulances kept busy. West Brom underestimated Burnley that day to their loss. Burnley's chief of police described it as the worst outbreak of soccer violence for years.

West Brom v Burnley, 1993
Someone had prepared a leaflet to welcome us. It read:

Meeting Places.
Kings Highway   for the Halesowen section
Scotts Arms   for the Great Barr section
The Talbot   for the Wednesbury section
The Sandwell   for the West Bromwich section
The Dudley Arms   for the Dudley section
The Pie Factory   for the Tipton section
Anyone else to meet at the Throstle Club at 1pm. Everyone must be at the Throstle's by 1.30pm ready to kill Burnley.

It might have been a load of shit but we weren't taking any chances. Coaches were organised, two double deckers and a single decker. Two hundred lads were making this trip. The day didn't get off to a good start. Two plainclothes policemen turned up and pulled Simon about his fines and he had to go home for some money. We waited for him to return and he gave the police £400 and got a receipt. Then the journey was underway. We all knew the police would be waiting for us at West Brom. As we approached Birmingham we told the driver to take us to Wednesbury and noticed the police helicopter was watching us. Everyone got off and we went into the nearest boozer. The police had it surrounded within five minutes, came in and told us to drink up as the bar was shutting and they were going to escort us to the ground. As the police were speaking, Wolves fans Carl and Mark came into the pub. Carl knew I was travelling down. He told me he had found us by just following the police helicopter. All the lads were put back onto the coaches but I jumped into Carl's car and we went into Handsworth for a drink and a chat. He then drove me to the ground in time for kick-off. Some of the lads were stood around by the turnstiles and told me that most of the lads had paid to go on to the stand. I quickly joined them.

The game started. Burnley had packed the away stand and it didn't take long for fighting to break out. It looked like the police had gone into the crowd to arrest someone and the Burnley fans surged down onto the police who drew out their truncheons and the Burnley lads steamed into them. Helmets went flying through the air. The police were getting battered to fuck. More of them came steaming on to the terrace to restore order and Burnley fans were dragged from the crowd and led around the pitch. The game passed off without any more incidents and we came out of the ground and made our way to West Brom's end behind the goal. The police tried to block our path and managed to stop a few, but a good sixty or seventy of us got through and walked to the road outside their end. Loads of West Brom fans were around but none of them were lads. The police soon sussed us and pushed us back towards the coaches. Fun was over for the day. We were put on the coaches and escorted out. The West Bromwich police described it as the worst outbreak of violence at the Hawthorns that year. Fourteen Burnley fans and eighteen West Brom were arrested.

Blackburn v Burnley, Youth Cup, 1993

In 1993, I moved back to Burnley. I had been seeing a girl up there for a while, my marriage was over due to my many trips back home and I hated living in Luton. All my mates were in Burnley. The football violence continued.

This was another chance to have a pop at Blackburn and we all thought their lads would turn out. There would be no segregation due to only one stand being open, plus there wouldn't be a large police presence. Around three hundred of us were drinking in Blackburn at half past five in the evening. The place was like a ghost town, no lads and no police. We headed to the pubs near to the ground. Again, there were no Blackburn. Every pub was just full of Burnley lads. We headed to the ground where the police had a large presence and tried to pay into the Nuttall Street stand but they refused us, saying Burnley had brought so many they had been forced to open the Darwen end (the away end). More than 800 Burnley had made the trip and seventy percent were lads. Blackburn hardly brought any. The game was shit. Burnley were being stuffed and around 300 of us left the ground at half time and headed back into the centre looking for their lads. We thought they had to be somewhere but it seems the only place they were was sat on their arses at home. They were supposed to class us as their main rivals, so why didn't the wankers turn out? That's the difference between us and them. We are a better class of hooligan.

Port Vale v Burnley, 1993

I've always had good battles at Port Vale. This would be no different. Thirty of us arrived in two Transit vans around noon, parked up near the ground and headed straight for a pub in the centre. We were in there for about an hour and a half when ten Vale walked in, giving it the big one. We steamed straight into them, bottles and glasses flying. Port Vale tried to get out of the door but we dragged them back in. They were getting wasted. All but one managed to get out of the pub and the lad they left behind took a beating.

We steamed out and Port Vale were in front of us. "Su, su, Suicide." We charged them across the main road and any we caught were left unconscious in the road. At the top of the street was a pub with loads more of them outside. Police vans started turning up but we carried on charging towards them. We were on the opposite side of the road to them and the police were in the middle, waving their truncheons about, trying to make us back off. A bus pulled in front of us, we ran around it and into the Vale lads. They weren't up for it. Police charged back across the road and the dogs soon appeared. They pushed us down the street away from the Port Vale pub. The police surrounded us and then escorted us to the ground.

Me, Dave Pick and Lee T jumped the turnstiles and got in for free. The teams came out and the three of us decided we'd forget the game and go back into the centre. We jumped back out of the turnstiles, made our way back to town and got into a pub with a few Burnley lads already in. They couldn't be arsed going to the game either. They told us that they'd looked in most of the pubs looking for the Vale lads but it seemed they had all gone to the match. We carried on drinking in the centre until fifteen minutes before the final whistle. The three of us made our way back to the ground and decided that we would go into the Port Vale end behind the goals. We made our way round the ground and Vale fans had started to leave. There were hardly any police around. We walked through the exit gates and up into the stand. All the Vale lads were sitting in the middle of the terrace. We sat down at the side of them, half way up. There was a walkway in front of us. We sat there listening and watching the Port Vale lads singing their songs.

Suddenly, Lee jumped out of his seat and said, "Do you know what lads, I feel like doing fifty press-ups," then got down and started pumping the press-ups out. Three Vale lads walked past, one said, "He's off his head." I replied, "Yeah, he is. We're Suicide, do you want it?" The lads raised their hands saying they didn't want any trouble and walked away. I kept my eyes on them, they didn't leave the ground, they walked up to the top of the stand and across the back into their lads. Lee was still counting out the press-ups – thirty-two, thirty-three – and all the Vale lads stood up looking over. Burnley scored in the last minute of the game and the three of us jumped up. Lee was pissed off he hadn't reached fifty!

The Vale fans stood up looking at us jumping up and down, and then it came, the surge of bodies towards us from every side. The three of us made a back-to-back triangle. "Come on." We headed towards the pitch, battling like fuck. Finally we got onto the pitch but the Vale fans were running towards us. I looked at Dave and Lee and said, "We aren't having this are we?" I jumped back into the seats and some punches flew into me from all directions. I was dragged back onto the pitch and some Vale fans followed. I was wrestled to the ground more or less in the back of the Burnley goalkeeper's net with two fat stewards on top of me. The police soon took over and marched me round the pitch to the detention room. Vale fans soon followed me in. I tried to have a conversation with them but they weren't for talking. I sat there waiting to be processed.

Lee then appeared, accompanied by a copper. I was glad to see him. At least I wasn't travelling home alone – but he was taken through another door, kicked up the arse and released without charge. I was devastated. Dave was then brought in and the same happened to him. I couldn't believe it. I asked the police what was going on and they told me that I was going nowhere for the moment. I was placed in a cell with a couple of other Burnley lads, including my mate, Caddy. I started to look on the bright side again. At least I had company on the way home. A couple of hours later Caddy, charged with threatening behaviour, and the other lad were released. I told them to wait for me and an hour later I was charged with pitch encroachment and released. I went to a pub next to the police station where I hoped to find Caddy and the other lad but they hadn't waited. I had a beer and then went into the centre where I caught a bus to Stoke and then jumped on the train to Manchester.

I travelled down by car with Caddy to Fenton Magistrates in Stoke expecting a £100 fine for my offence and told Caddy to expect a big fine plus a ban from football. Caddy got a £50 fine and no ban, then it was my turn. The judge asked me about the Burnley game, then he asked me about the Scotland-England game when I got nicked. I had just got to thinking that the judge was alright when he asked the clerk of the court if he could send me to prison for this offence. I was thinking, you can't be fucking serious; going onto a pitch is a minor offence. Anyway the clerk said it was not a custodial offence, thankfully. I was given a £300 fine and a two-year ban from all football games in England and Wales. Not that I paid that much notice.

Charlton v Burnley – FA Cup, 1994

It was an all-ticket game and Burnley sold out straight away. I was unable to get a ticket for the home end so I called my mother, who lived near Charlton at the time, and she sent me a ticket for the Charlton end. We all met on Saturday morning in the Burnley Wood club. All the lads on the coach were carrying bottles of spirits and bottles of Coke and orange and they were opened as soon as we set off. The journey down was a right laugh; everyone was pissed and play fighting.

The coach pulled into the services just past Birmingham and we all went in to do a bit of pilfering. I don't know what I was thinking but I picked up a huge, six-foot rubber plant and ran out with it. The shop assistant just looked at me in disbelief. I ran onto the car park up to the coach and stuffed the plant underneath it. I looked back towards the doors and there were a couple of shop assistants looking around so I kept my head down. All the lads came back to the coach pissing themselves. "Why the fuck did you nick that, Pot?" One of the lads on the coach was travelling with his girlfriend. I gave her the plant and the driver put it into the luggage compartment.

We arrived in Charlton shortly after midday and the coach pulled up outside a pub called the Horse and Groom. Around fifteen of us jumped off and went into the pub. The rest stayed on the coach until it reached the ground. The pub was massive and full of Charlton fans. We all got a drink. Two of our lads had their kids with them and weren't after any trouble. We were all mixing and talking to the Charlton fans. I noticed two pool tables covered up, with a mob of lads stood around them, some holding pool cues. One of the lads, who was wearing a red and white striped top, started walking round the pub with the pool cue.

I was playing on the bandit talking to some other Charlton lads but kept my eye on him. Stripes went up to a few of our lads and said to one, "Do you want it, you soft northern cunts?" The lad told him that they weren't after any trouble. He then approached a few more Burnley lads. The Charlton lads around the pool tables were getting ready. I'd been in this situation so many times and I knew we weren't going to get out of the pub without a fight. If we started to leave, the last ones in would get kicked to fuck.

I said to the two Charlton lads that I had been talking to, "It's going to kick off in a minute."

"No it's not," they said. "Charlton is a family club."

"Watch this then."

The cunt with the cue opened his mouth. "Do you want it?" I ran up and head-butted him, knocking him to the ground, and fell on top of him. It kicked off to fuck. One of our lads shoved his child under a table. There were bottles and glasses flying all over. I was still on top of Stripes, punching him, while the rest of the lads were fighting with the other Charlton. The older Burnley Wood lads were big and were knocking them over for fun while people ran from the pub.

The police arrived but soon fucked off back outside, that's how bad it was. I had hold of the bloke while one of my mates was whacking his legs with a chair, trying to break them. I let go and turned my attention to someone else. There was a doorway leading to the toilet and it was full of lads trying to get through. They were climbing over each other; you couldn't see the top of the door. The lads with the pool cues stopped fighting and said, "Come on, Burnley, enough's enough, let's have a drink, eh?" I couldn't believe what I was hearing. Just because the shoe was on the other foot, now they wanted to drink with us. One of ours said, "It's a bit late for that, don't you think?" Then he grabbed the pool cue off a lad and started battering him with it. Another lad grabbed hold of another pool cue and began putting all the windows through. There was fighting all over. Riot police came steaming in and started to nick everyone but Mark and I managed to get out of the pub. We ran off down the road with the police chasing us and jumped over people's gardens alongside the train tracks. I looked over my shoulder to see if the police were still chasing us and jumped a bit of a wall, but my feet didn't touch the ground on the other side. It was a six-foot drop. Lying on my back, looking up, I saw Mark coming towards me. I just had time to move sideways and he landed right where I had been.

A Charlton fan with his son came over and asked if we were alright. We told him we were and set off walking along a little path leading under the train tracks. We followed the Charlton lad and his son to the ground. I made my way into the Charlton end and sat in my allocated seat. I was only there five minutes when the police came up to me and told me I was in the wrong end. They grabbed hold of me to escort me out and, as I turned, I saw my mum and her husband, Tom, sitting a few rows behind me. I didn't say anything to them. I was ejected from the ground and walked round to find another pub. A few Burnley lads were already inside. They couldn't be arsed going to the game so I stayed with them until the final whistle and then headed towards the coaches.

I didn't see any trouble after the game but I did see my mother and her husband. They asked me if I'd seen Ade. I said he'd probably been nicked. Actually he was in hospital with a suspected broken leg. So was Ste Smith, getting his head stitched up, while the police were holding on to Ste Moat, Gibbo, Jawbone and Simon. My mum waited until the lads got out of the police station and put them up for the night. Ste and Ade, whose leg wasn't broken, later made their own way to her house.

When I got back to Burnley I got loads of shit off the lads' birds and wives, all asking why I hadn't been nicked. I told them what went on and they all seemed to chill out a bit. To this day I know I made the right decision. We weren't going to get out of that pub in one piece. Out of all of those arrested, only three appeared before the court. Simon and Ade were charged with affray and Ste Moat was charged with threatening behaviour. They all pleaded guilty at Woolwich Crown Court. Ade and Simon were remanded to Belmarsh jail for two weeks for reports to be drawn up and Ste was given bail. Two weeks later Simon was fined £1,000 and ordered to pay £500 compensation, Ade was fined £750 plus £250 compensation and Ste was fined £250 with £250 compensation. All three were banned from football matches for two years.

CHAPTER FOURTEEN

BANNED
FOR LIFE

Holland v England – Rotterdam, 1993

We set off six days before the game. Me, Mick Moore, Simon, Mark and Billy Redmond all thought that this way we had less chance of being pulled and getting refused entry into Holland. We got the ferry at Dover to Ostend, then drove to Rotterdam and it was a piece of piss, our plan seemed to have worked. We dropped the car off at a long stay car park in Rotterdam ferry port and then caught a train to Amsterdam. The first port of call was a coffee shop to pick up some skunk and then on to find somewhere to stay.

The rest of the lads had organised a coach. They were arriving in Amsterdam on the Tuesday, the day before the game. We spent our days and nights getting pissed and stoned and kept out of trouble. Until Sunday, anyway. We had decided to have a vodka party in Dam Square and had two bottles of Blue Label, a few cans of orange and some plastic cups. It was warm and sunny, lovely weather for drinking. We settled down on the steps leading up to a monument in the middle of the square. The first bottle was opened and the party began. We got a lot of funny looks from tourists and the local drug dealers kept approaching us, asking if we wanted any coke, speed, acid or Ecstasy. They were all told to fuck off. The vodka was going down well.

A big, black drug dealer came walking past, listened to us talking and approached us.

"You English? I know England," he said.

Billy disagreed. "You don't know England. I bet you've never left Holland."

The lad put his hands up, he knew he had been sussed, then, all of a sudden Mark who was half unconscious and lying down on the steps, looked up at the lad and said, "Fuck off you black cunt or I'll kill you." We all looked at each other and shook our heads.

The black lad said, "You're going to kill me?"

"Yeah, you and your mother," said Mark, before passing out.

We started laughing but the lad reached into his pocket, pulled out a fucking gun, pointed it at Mark's head, and said, "I will kill you." We stopped laughing. I was just waiting for the bang when Mick said to the lad, "You shoot him and I will shoot you and all of your fucking mates round here. I've got a bigger gun than you." He patted his chest.

The lad nodded at Mick, put his gun back in his pocket and fucked off. Mark was still mumbling to himself, oblivious to what had just taken place.

"That was a bit dodgy," I said.

"Come on, let's finish this vodka and fuck off into some bars," replied Mick.

We were finishing off the last of the vodka when Mark woke up, got to his feet and said, "I'll be back in a minute." We presumed he was going for a piss. On each corner of Dam Square there are statues of lions on big stone blocks and a minute later we noticed a crowd of people gathering round one of them, so we walked over. Mark had climbed up the stone blocks and was trying to get on to the lion. The tourists were taking photos. As soon as we got to him he fell off and landed sprawled out on the floor with blood pissing from his head.

"Do you think he's dead?" I asked Mick.

"Is he fuck," said Mick. "You can hear him snoring."

The police and an ambulance were quickly on the scene and, as Mark was being put on the stretcher, a load of Japanese tourists turned up and started taking more photos. Mick went fucking mad, screamed at them and tried to get their cameras, so the police bundled him into a police van and took him away. Mark went to hospital and Simon went with him. Billy and I looked at each other. "Fuck it, let's get stoned." We headed straight to Hunter's bar, my favourite red light district coffee shop, and got out of our heads. Mark ended up with a few stitches and Mick was released without charge.

We booked out of our accommodation. The lads arriving by coach had booked into a big hotel for the night and we were going to doss with them. We met up in Hunter's, stayed a while as more Burnley joined us and eventually had a mob of at least seventy. Fat Stan and a few Palace had turned up too. We moved further into the red light district, going into every bar we passed. Mobs of English were all over. The police were out in force too, van loads of them parked up on side streets just waiting for it to kick off.

We were drinking in the Old Sailor pub when the police came in and told us to leave, the bar was shut. I went outside and saw a line of riot police across a side street. All the lads were outside the bar looking at the police. Then a big mob of English came walking down the street on the opposite side of the canal, came over the bridge and joined us. One of the lads threw a bottle towards the police and that was the spark. It went off like fuck. Bottles went flying, everyone charged at the police and they were on their toes, running down the street. As we walked along the canal, every window was being put through. The trouble spread fast.

Everywhere you looked, down every street, there were English lads going mad. A thousand lads were on the rampage. We carried on walking along the canal and cars were being overturned. As we approached a canal bridge, near to one of the British Bulldog bars, we met a large mob of Ajax fans and charged into them. Some were game but they got a battering. Me, Mick and Dave were faced with a clown waving a sword in the air shouting, "Excalibur." Every time we tried to get near he tried to cut our heads off. Dave and I were going fucking mad; every bicycle that we tried to pick up and throw at him was tethered up to the railings. A few Chelsea lads came over and said, "You keep fronting him and we'll get behind him." We started bouncing towards him. His eyes were fixed on the three of us and the Chelsea lads got behind him and smacked him one. He was on the floor, plainclothes police ran in, picked up the lad's sword and dragged him away. I wondered how long they had stood watching.

We headed back up towards Dam Square. Police horses were charging down the streets. The cunts on their backs were hitting every head they could reach with their batons. Riot police followed them. Around ten of us managed to get into a bar out of the way but we didn't immediately recognise the rest of the clientele. All of a sudden they started shouting, "Ajax." One of our lads glassed someone and they instantly backed off, but had nowhere to go. We ran into them, battling like fuck. A shout went up that the police were coming and we left the bar and went back onto the street. Shaun ran up to a big bastard and banged him. The bloke didn't move he just pulled a truncheon out and started chasing him down the street.

The police were starting to seal all the streets. A handful of us headed for the Grasshopper bar. There was a massive mob of English on the main road, battling with the police, and I went to join the fight. The riot police charged at us but everyone stood their ground. The police stopped and we charged into them, forcing them back. They sent in the horses and dogs and the English were on their toes. Duncan and I got stuck in a doorway, riot police hitting us with their batons. We steamed into them and managed to get out but Duncan's head was pissing blood. I grabbed hold of him and started running up the road, dragging him with me. The police were close behind us so we ran up and down the side streets, not knowing where we were going, just running. We came out onto a main street. The train station was on the other side of the road and I knew where we were.

The police were no longer chasing us so we stopped for a breather. I took a bottle of poppers out of my pocket and had a sniff. Duncan asked me if his head had stopped bleeding. I had a look and told him it had. "Right, well give us a sniff of those then." He had a sniff of poppers and blood started pumping out of his head again. I had to laugh.

Flashing lights were everywhere. We decided to go back to the hotel, sniffing poppers all the way laughing our bollocks off. I don't know how much blood Duncan lost, but his top was soaked through.

On the day of the game I was woken by Duncan demanding a sniff of poppers. "Here, have the fucking lot," I said. I suppose he deserved them. I was expecting his head to explode again but it didn't. I got up and went for some breakfast, paid for by the lads who had come on the coach. Simon was already there but there was no sign of Billy, Mick or Mark. I went round everyone's room but no-one had seen them after it had kicked off.

Simon and I travelled to Rotterdam on the coach with the rest of the lads, hoping to bump into our lot at the game. The coach journey down was a laugh, the beer was flowing and joint after joint was being passed round. Lads who had never smoked it were having a go. I watched them, mostly greedy with the joints, and then all the colour drained from their faces and they would go quiet, on a whitey.

"Are you alright lad?"

"Am I fuck. What did you put in that?"

Everyone burst out laughing, buzzing off the non-smokers trying the skunk.

Only around five lads had tickets for the game and they were lads I'd never seen before. They were Burnley but they weren't part of our mob. I managed to get hold of some forgeries. They weren't spectacular but they didn't look bad. As soon as we got into Rotterdam the police on motorbikes started to escort us to the ground. The coach was made to stop under a motorway bridge. A huge cage had been erected and was full of English lads. The police made a circle round the coach and, as we got off, they asked to see the match ticket. If you didn't have one you were put into the cage.

It was my turn. I flashed my ticket and got through, same with Simon, and we made our way straight to the turnstiles. There were a lot of English. We thought this would be the right time to use the dodgy tickets. If they were busy on the turnstiles they usually didn't check your ticket that well. No problems. We were on the top tier in the corner, the Dutch were fenced in on either side of us. The atmosphere was good, we just had to watch out for the flares being fired into us.

What can I say about the game? The referee was worthless. England were getting beat. Lads started to rip the segregation fences down. Around four English in the top corner had managed to get over the fence and ran straight into the Dutch, fighting like fuck, outnumbered thirty to one. The lads then started to climb back over the fence into the English end. One was still battling but taking a good beating. One of his mates steamed into the Dutch, backing them off, then picked his mate up off the floor. The injured English lad made his way to the fence, his mate fronted the Dutch, backing them off, and they both got to the fence. He helped his injured mate over the fence first and then climbed out. Every English lad clapped him. English spirit makes us the best.

The game finished and the police kept us in the stadium. Mark appeared. I asked where Mick and Billy were and he told us they had travelled down by train and it had kicked off in Rotterdam centre. They had got to the ground but their tickets were sussed. That was the last he'd seen of them. We knew where the car was parked so we didn't have a problem. Some of the English must have been cold because some of the seats in front of us were burning away nicely. It started to spread and everyone moved well away towards the exits, watching the fire as it grew. The gates opened and we were allowed out of the terrace. Only eight lads travelled back on the coach, three of us hadn't even booked on the trip, but who gave a fuck. The rest of the lads were all deported. Mick and Billy arrived home safely.

England v Scotland, Euro 1996

This was the game everyone wanted. "Let's do the Jocks." Two minibuses full of lads travelled down the day before the game, though none of us had tickets. We had been travelling for about ten minutes and had just reached the dual carriageway on the outskirts of Burnley when a load of riot vans and dogs vans sped past and pulled us over. Some of the lads were carrying drugs so hid them under seats; everyone was pissed off thinking this was the end of our trip. We came to a stop in a layby with the police vans surrounding us and started to get out of the vans. The police ran over, told us to get back in, then took us one by one for a full body search. When the minibuses were empty they sent in the sniffer dogs who found bags of skunk and a block of resin but no weapons. The buses were full of beer but they didn't give a fuck about that. They didn't even question anyone about the drugs though one lad was taken away for possession of one Ecstasy tablet. Finally we were told that we could carry on with our journey.

The beers seemed to taste all the better. Lads started producing blocks of resin that they had hidden down their bollocks. One pulled out a few acid trips and five of us dropped one each. The minibuses pulled onto the M25 and again police vans appeared from nowhere, blue lights flashing. It looked fucking brilliant, it was like being at Blackpool (I was tripping, remember). Again we were taken out and searched. When it came to my turn I couldn't stop laughing.

"Do you find it funny?" asked a cop.

"Yeah, I do."

"Right, fuck off over there with your mates."

Four of us sat on a grass embankment, tripping. Digs came out of the minibus and his head was flying. The police asked him to step over the crash barrier but he couldn't do it. "It's too big," he complained. "I'm only small." The four of us were in stitches watching him. Eventually the police dragged him over the barrier. The buses were given another once over but nothing was found and we were allowed to carry on with our journey once again.

Fat Stan had sorted out a house for us on the outskirts of London. There was plenty of beer in the fridge so we sat drinking for most of the night. As soon as we woke up on the day of the game, we were straight on the beers and smoking joints. Most of us were upstairs and had no idea that downstairs the police arrested Mark H for breach of bail. When one of the lads came upstairs to tell us none of us could believe it. They must have followed us all the way from Burnley. Anyway, we'd been pulled twice and we were still in London for the game.

We headed up to King's Cross. There were mobs of English all over and a few Scots wearing kilts and silly fucking hats.

We got into a boozer to watch the game. More Burnley had boosted our numbers to a mob of about seventy. Game over, we made our way to Leicester Square, along with all the other English mobs. The police were everywhere. We got into a pub called the Porcupine where Birmingham had a big mob and stood outside, drinking, with a line of police in front of us. Behind the police tourists were taking photos and filming with camcorders. Lads started to throw beer at the police, who drew their truncheons and started to push lads about. Bottles and glasses started to fly and soon it was toe to toe with the police. Reinforcements appeared in full riot gear. Bottles and glasses were still flying but they pushed us down a side street and managed to get behind us. We were trapped and they charged from both sides. I ran at the police behind us. There was a car parked up and the police were running past it, so I ran straight over it. I thought I had got past when, all of a sudden, I got hit in the face with a truncheon, knocking me into some cardboard boxes. Trev, a Chelsea fan from Burnley, dragged me to my feet and we were on our toes away from the area going towards Trafalgar Square.

Some of the lads were bleeding from head wounds, especially Gibbo. Lines of riot police surrounded Trafalgar Square. We tried to charge through but were baton charged back. We tried another street and the same happened. There were English fighting with police on every street. Finally the police swamped the area, with officers dispersing everyone. We all got split up and I ended up with Digs, Mick H. and Wayne (Steptoe). Snatch squads were nicking anyone. We managed to get on a tube, which took us away from the area, and got back to King's Cross expecting the rest of the lads to be here, but none had arrived. We made our way back to where we were staying and found most of the lads drinking beer and smoking. My face was swollen and I couldn't open my mouth to talk. I just grunted and all the lads took the piss, but at least I could drink a can and smoke a joint. When I got back to Burnley I got my jaw X-rayed. Surprisingly, it wasn't broken.

Poland v England – Katowice, 1997

We had a good turnout for this one. Twenty-five of us flew out of Manchester into Warsaw while other Burnley lads used different routes. We got into the country without any problems, had a few hours to kill and tried some Polish vodka in the bars. Two hours later we were all off our heads. We managed to catch the train to Katowice; it was a long journey but we had a good laugh. Joints were being passed about and the beer was flowing. Other English lads on the train were all having a laugh with us. The train pulled into Katowice the day before the game. We had all got off when someone noticed smoke coming from underneath the carriage we had just been in, so we quickly fucked off.

Most of the lads made their way to the Hotel Katowice but Ade, Simon, Shaun, Fat Stan and I all decided to look for something cheaper and found one just out of the centre. We dropped off our bags, headed back to the centre to meet up with the rest of the lads and found them outside a bar. We stayed a few hours and then moved around the centre taking in various others. Mobs of English were all over. A few little groups of Polish punk rockers were also around but no-one took any notice of them.

As the night wore on the Polish vodka started to take effect: lads were falling over tables and some had to be carried from bar to bar. All eventually made their way back to the Hotel Katowice but my group decided to sample a few more bars. A few Leicester City fans joined us; they were sound as fuck. We tried to get into a disco bar but the owner stopped us, pointing at a broken window. There were a few Polish lads inside and one of them, a skinny, specky little bastard, stepped in front of us and pulled up his jumper to reveal a gun. Me and one of the Leicester just looked at each other and we thought the same. We punched him together and he hit the floor, his glasses were smashed into his face and his jumper was up round his waist showing his gun. The Polish lads in the bar didn't move but the bar owner walked up to the lad on the floor, bent down, took the gun off him and put it into his apron pocket. "Very bad man," he said, pointing at the unconscious lad. We quickly left, found another bar and didn't have any more problems.

The day of the game and we had no tickets. The Leicester lads had told us about a shop that was selling them and Ade had had the good sense to write its name down. We got a taxi and bought tickets for around £3 each. A lot of English lads were drinking in a packed bar near the bus station and most of the Burnley lads were there too. Some had carried on drinking through the night and were fucked. I settled down with a pint and a joint and was talking to a few lads from Carlisle when a lad came up to me.

"You're Burnley aren't you?"

"Yeah, I am."

"One of your lads has just been knocked out."

I went over and had a look; it was one of the young lads, on the floor snoring. I knew it could only have been a matter of time before he ended up like that. He was pissed and had been annoying everyone. I went over to the lad who had knocked him out, a Villa fan, shook his hand, then went to wake the young lad up. We told him to go back to the hotel to get some sleep and sort his head out. Mark H took him and I went back to having a drink and a smoke with the Carlisle lads.

Some of the English were having a scout about, looking for Polish mobs and one came back to warn us of a mob of Poles walking down the street towards us. We left the bar and walked up towards them. Police were everywhere. We fanned out across the street. The Poles spotted us and stopped in their tracks. We charged into them. They stood and I went blow for blow with them, getting as much as I was giving. The police steamed in, waving their three-foot batons in the air, then everyone separated. More police arrived and started hitting everyone that looked like an English or Polish hooligan and charged us down the street towards the bar we had just left. The Polish police had surrounded it and all the English were now standing outside. We just walked past and I stopped across the street by the bus station. I heard a few glasses smashing and the police went steaming into the lads outside the bar. Glasses, tables and chairs all started flying through the air and the English were soon getting battered by the police batons. They tried to escape by running through the police with their arms covering their heads.

A few English, like me, were getting pissed off with the police. An English lad came running towards us with two police smacking him to fuck. I'd had enough watching all this shit. I ran over to help him and a few more lads came too. We fronted the police and they stopped in their tracks. The English lad carried on running straight past us and into the distance. Now we had the two police to deal with. I ran into them and a baton was wrapped around my body. They were made of bendy rubber. Another hit me around the waist and I was on my toes, running down the street. A police van sped past me and then came to an abrupt stop, the side door opened and the police were on me. I was knocked to the floor and they jumped on top of me. Another van turned up, the doors opened and the police put me inside. The doors opened again and another two English lads were bundled in. The van started and we were driven away then it stopped and I was taken out and led into a stone building.

This was no police station, it was scruffy as fuck and there was no furniture. I was put into a room and then the police fucked off. A couple of Poles came walking in holding truncheons; there were no uniforms. They told me to strip. "You fucking what?" One of them hit me across the legs. I stripped down to my boxer shorts and the other started to go through my clothes. I looked round at the cunt. The other tapped my head with his truncheon telling me to look forward. I was thinking that I was going to be shagged and abused. Instead I was taken to a cell and put inside. It was dirty and stank. There were no windows, just a couple of filthy beds. I was dying for a piss and I banged on the door but there was no response. I sat down on one of the beds. The door opened and another lad was thrown in. I told the Pole that I wanted a piss and he looked at me and started to close the door. I got hold of the door and pulled it back open, the Pole shook his head and pulled out his truncheon threatening to hit me.

"Listen mate," I said. "I want a piss."

He didn't understand, so I got my dick out and walked into the corner. He just looked at me. "I want a toilet or I will just piss here." He nodded his head and took me to the toilet.

Back in the cell the other lad started to speak to me, but could only say one word, "Hooligan."

"Yeah, I'm a fucking hooligan, now shut up." He didn't try to speak to me again.

Hours and hours went by. Finally the door opened and I was told to follow. I was taken into a room, my clothes were on the floor in the corner and there was a metal plate next to them with my camera and money in it. I put my socks and trainers on first then, as I went to pick up the plate, the cunt whacked me with a truncheon and told me to hurry, pointing at my top and jacket on the floor. I quickly got dressed. The cunt was tapping me on the legs with the truncheon telling me to be quick. I picked up the plate and put my camera in my pocket. I looked at the money in the plate, obviously light, and said to the Pole, "What the fuck is this?" Another Pole came into the room, smacked me with his truncheon and pointed at the money. "Put it in pocket," he said. I picked it up, put it into my pocket and was led out of the building and left alone.

I was in the middle of fucking nowhere and all I could hear was cowbells. I looked at the money in my pocket: out of £300 in Sterling plus £100 in Polish money, the robbing twats had left me with about £2.50 in Polish. I could see lights in the distance and walked towards them. I walked for fucking miles in the pitch dark, there were no street lamps, just derelict buildings on each side of the road. The odd open-backed van drove past, full of people in the back. I eventually got back to civilisation with streetlights and proper roads and buildings but still didn't have a clue where I was. I carried on walking, heading towards the brightest lights. I got onto a main street with a few cars driving up and down. I spotted a taxi approaching, jumped into the middle of the road waving my arms in the air and went round to the driver's side.

"Hotel Katowice," I said, showing him the Polish money that I had left. "Is this enough?" He nodded and five minutes later I was outside the hotel. There was a mass of police outside and I walked up to them, explained that I was staying there and they let me through. I went straight into the hotel bar and all the lads were there, pissed up. It was two o'clock in the morning. Everyone was pleased to see me. I was quickly passed a beer and it tasted brilliant. I told them about me being robbed and battered. My back was killing me, so I took off my jacket and top and I asked the lads to have a look. They all said the same, "Bet that fucking hurt." There were mirrors on the walls of the bar and I had a look for myself. My back was badly bruised, the worst one around my kidneys. I was a right mess but there was no use crying over spilt milk, I had some catching up to do. We stayed in the bar all night and the lads bought me beer.

We still had one lad unaccounted for, Mark H. No-one had

seen him. Me, Ade, Simon, Fat Stan and Shaun staggered out of the hotel at nine in the morning, went back to our hotel, collected our gear and headed straight for the train station. We couldn't wait to get back to Warsaw to catch our plane. I slept for most of the journey home. Mark came home a few days later. He needed to get someone to send his credit card details over so he could pay a fine.

Burnley v Preston, 1997

I was in the White Lion with thirty other lads when someone said Preston were drinking in the Bridge, so we downed our beers and walked past Yates's heading for the Bridge. We turned a corner and the Preston lads were walking towards us in equal numbers. No-one backed off. Lads were put on their arses on both sides and the police were quickly on the scene to separate us. They escorted Preston out of the centre and we went back to the White Lion. We moved towards the ground calling in at the Clog and Spindle (previously the Princess Royal) and the Turf, both of which were packed with Burnley. We had a good mob out but so did the police.

Turf Moor was now an all-seater stadium. Four of us were walking past the Bob Lord stand when four Preston lads passed us. One of them said something and I turned round, "What the fuck did you just say?" I started to walk towards them but the next thing I knew my arm was being forced up my back.

"Porter, you're nicked."

"What for? I've done fuck all."

A police van appeared but I was insisting, "Listen, I've done fuck all, what are you nicking me for?"

"Shut up and get in the van."

I started to struggle and more officers gathered round me and my head clashed with one of theirs. I was handcuffed, placed in the van, taken to Burnley police station and charged with threatening behaviour and police assault. I was released on bail with the condition that I didn't enter a football ground in England and Wales.

I was in court in September 1997, fully expecting a jail sentence, but my solicitor worked wonders. I received 100 hours' community service and one year's probation and was ordered to attend a ten-week alcohol awareness course and a ten-week anger management course, along with receiving a one-year ban from football. I don't think the police were happy with my ban or my sentence.

I got a letter from Burnley FC the day after the court case, which read, "Dear Sir, I have received information from the police in Burnley that you were convicted at Stoke-on-Trent magistrates court on January 14, 1994, for an offence of pitch invasion under section four Football Offences Acts 1991 and you were subsequently made subject of an exclusion order from all football grounds until January 13, 1996. This sentence followed your arrest at the away fixture at Port Vale when you encroached onto the playing area. Andrew Porter, I have to inform that you are banned for life from attending football matches at Turf Moor."

Blah, blah, blah. The wankers banned me for something I'd done three years before.

Millwall v Burnley, 1997

Thirteen of us made this trip. I got into the Transit van early on Saturday morning as rough as fuck. There was no beer, I was gutted. I started putting skins together to make a joint, rooted in my pockets for my cannabis but couldn't find it. I must have left it at home. I was totally pissed off. I was passed a few cans, drank them and got my head down.

We were driving down a main road in London when we spotted a pub on a corner called the Three Bells and parked the van outside. It looked rough but there were only about five locals drinking in it. I was gagging for a joint. I looked round at the locals and spotted a lad on his own. I don't know how you know but you just do, I went over to him and asked him if he had any cannabis for sale. He did and I bought an eighth block of resin off him. I skinned up and went outside to smoke it and he came with me. The stuff was top quality and the lad was sound. We stayed in the pub till about two and then walked up to the ground. We never saw one policeman or Millwall lad until we approached the ground and got in without getting any shit from anyone.

After the game we walked straight out onto the street. Millwall were all around but no-one bothered us, probably as we weren't giving it the big one. But then a Burnley police spotter clocked us. The police came running over and rounded the lads up. I fucked off away from them. As I was walking around twenty yards in front of the lads and their escort I passed a pub on the left that was surrounded by scaffolding. A few Millwall lads were outside and one shouted over, "You facking Burnley?"

"Yeah," I said. "I'm Suicide."

The lads in the escort noticed this and so did the police. Horses and the Burnley spotter came charging towards me. The Millwall lads fucked off back into the pub and I was put into the escort. We got back to the van without any problems. The police videoed us one by one as we got into the van, then took one of the lads out and put him into their police van. The copper explained that if we stopped or tried to leave the escort then the lad in the van would be nicked. The escort consisted of two vans in front and two vans behind plus police motorbikes. The bikes blocked every junction, roundabout and set of traffic lights. We had to drive on the wrong side of the road, stopping the oncoming traffic. The escort finally stopped at the entrance to one of the tunnels leading under the

Thames and the police returned their hostage to us.

We headed straight for home but by the time we had got on to the M6 there was no chance of us getting back to Burnley for last orders. I called a mate of mine, Carl, a Wolves fan whose brother ran a pub in Willenhall, near Wolverhampton, and we got there for ten o'clock. A few Wolves lads were waiting for us and we all had a good drink until one in the morning. Carl invited me to stay as his mates were having a lads' day out with some strippers at a club in Tipton. I explained I didn't have enough money but he said he'd sort me out. Enough said. The rest of the lads carried on back to Burnley.

Sunday was fantastic. The Wolves lads were sound and bought me beers all day. When the strippers had finished the lads even collected enough money to get me home. Cheers lads.

Halifax v Burnley – pre-season, 1997

It was a Saturday game and I had been partying all night on the Ecstasy with a friend of mine called Nigger. I knew all the lads had gone over to Halifax for the game and a day on the piss, so Nigger and I, still off our heads, decided to join them. Fuck the game, I was banned from watching football and Nigger had never been to a match in his life.

We made our way to Yates's, where all the Burnley lads were drinking, and had been there for about an hour when one of the lads said Halifax were outside the pub. Burnley went out and chased them off, then the police turned up. We both knew we couldn't have a smoke with all the police around so fucked off into another bar for a good smoke, then moved to various pubs with no hassle at all.

The game had started. We went into one pub where a few Burnley lads who couldn't be bothered going to the game were drinking and we joined them. A few more lads who were not

Burnley came into the pub. Nigger made a joint, the Burnley lads sat in a corner and I sat at the side in an alcove. A few words were exchanged between the two sets of lads but I thought nothing of it. I was leaning forward, talking to Nigger, when all of a sudden a boot came round the corner and volleyed me right in the head. I was knocked back into my seat. Bottles and glasses started to fly into the Burnley lads, pinning them into the corner. I was stuck in the alcove, battling like fuck. One of the lads had a blade. Nigger just fucked off, still making his joint. I picked up a stool and used it to keep the lads away from me when, suddenly, the lads fucked off out of the door. Sirens could be heard coming in the distance. Blood started running into my eye. I touched my face, there was blood everywhere. I had been slashed above the eye. My head went, I ran out of the pub looking for the lads. Covered in blood, I went in nearly all of the pubs, but couldn't find them. A police van pulled up at the side of me and I was told to get in. It was full of policemen, all smiling at me. "That's a nice cut, Andrew," said one. "Who did that?"

They took me back to the pub where an ambulance was already outside. A few of the Burnley lads were in there getting cleaned up and I went in and waited my turn. They told me it needed stitching but I couldn't be arsed going to the hospital. I got out of the ambulance and fucked off to another pub with the others. Nigger was nowhere to be seen. The police followed us for the rest of the day. All the lads came back from the game and we got the train back to Burnley. My wound healed well, it was a clean cut. Must have been a sharp blade.

Wrexham v Burnley, 1997

We set off early Saturday morning by coach. One of the lads was running a pub in Chester city centre and opened early for us. The idea was we would leave the coach in Chester and get the train into Wrexham. We were drinking in Chester before ten o'clock and by eleven most of the lads had decided to stay in town on the piss. Twelve of us got the train into Wrexham, headed straight for the centre and found a pub. There were a few Wrexham lads in, all wearing Stone Island, but they didn't bother us. I got a joint together and went outside with Mick to smoke it. While we were outside a Wrexham lad wearing a Burberry hat walked by.

I shouted over, "Where's your boys?"

"Give us five minutes," he replied.

We finished the joint and went back inside to get another beer. Fifteen minutes went by and we decided the Burberry lad was full of shit, so six of us moved to another pub around the corner. I got served and took my beer outside. As Mick joined me six Wrexham lads walked around the corner. Mick went back into the pub to tell our other four and I ran up the road to meet the Wrexham lads.

"Come on," I said. They did. They flew into me. I was battling with them in the middle of the road when another forty Wrexham steamed round the corner. I couldn't back off; I was too committed. Someone put me on my arse and I curled into a ball. The kicking seemed to go on for ages.

I waited a while and then got up. I could see an ambulance outside the pub. One of our lads was getting in it and I went over to see who it was. Digs was in the back getting his busted nose cleaned up. I headed back into the centre to find the rest of the lads and saw a big mob of Wrexham outside a pub with police stood round them. I walked through the police and into the Wrexham lads. "I'm fucking Burnley Suicide," I shouted. A space appeared around me, all the Wrexham lads were looking at me. Some policemen came over and dragged me away.

The police told me to fuck off towards the ground but when I started to walk the Wrexham mob followed me on the opposite side of the road. The police took a position in the middle of the road between us. Wrexham made a few attempts to break through the police line. When this happened I stopped and fronted them but the police pushed me away, telling me to carry on moving.

I got to the ground and the police tried to get me to pay in but I explained that I couldn't as I was banned. One of the policemen got proper pissed off and told me to wait where I was otherwise I would be nicked, then he fucked off. I was waiting there when another copper told me to move or I would be nicked. I walked towards the pub outside the ground and the policeman who told me to wait came running over to me.

"I told you to fucking wait there," he said.

"Yeah, and he just told me to move."

I pointed at the other policeman. The two had a chat and I was allowed to go into the pub. The rest of the lads were drinking in there along with a few more Burnley. We left just before the final whistle and the police got us straight away and escorted us to the train station.

Wrexham lads were trying to get onto the station and we ran out to meet them. A policeman grabbed hold of me and said "Listen, you'd better fuck off out of Wrexham." He dragged me over to a waiting taxi, opened the door and shoved me in. Another Burnley lad jumped in. The policeman told the driver to take us to Chester and warned that if he saw me in Wrexham again that day I would be nicked. I took heed and we went straight to Chester, getting out at the train station. The Burnley lads that had stayed in Chester were drinking outside a big pub across the road and I went into the beer garden to see them. A lot of them were pissed out of their heads and some started to get a bit loud. The rest of the lads arrived from Wrexham and the police told us we were being put back onto our coach and being escorted out of Chester.

I woke up the next day black and blue and aching from

head to toe. You win some, you lose some. It was still a good day.

Mick Moore's 40ᵗʰ Birthday – 1997

The events on this day changed my life. I did time for something that I didn't do.

It was a Saturday night and fifteen of us were celebrating Mick's fortieth in the White Lion. Half of the lads moved on to the Sidewalk and I was just finishing my drink when a load of birds walked through the door. I knew all of them, as they were from Burnley Wood. An argument started and one of the girls glassed Mick, cutting his head open. He went mad. We managed to get him outside of the pub, where I was talking to him when Doz ran past with two bouncers chasing him. I wasn't having that. I grabbed hold of one of the bouncers, we had a bit of a scuffle, nothing major, and more bouncers came out of the other pubs nearby.

The police turned up and the situation was defused. We made our way to the Sidewalk, where the rest of the lads were outside arguing with the bouncers, who wouldn't let them in. When we got to the door we thought, fuck it, it's our pub, who are you to tell us we can't go into our own pub? We charged into the bouncers and were battling like fuck when the police steamed into the pub. Lads started to get nicked. I was straight out of the door, jumped into a taxi and went to a pub in Burnley Wood.

The day after, I found out that seven of the lads had been arrested. The police were looking for one more – me. It didn't take long for them to find me and we were all charged with violent disorder. I already had a Section 18 wounding with intent, but by the time we got to Crown court seven of us had the violent disorder charges dropped to threatening behaviour. My charges had been dropped to Section 20, wounding with intent plus affray.

They said I had hit a bouncer with a bottle. In fact everyone knows the lad who did it, but the bouncers, police and judge put the crime down to me. I'm no grass, I wouldn't go to the police and say, "Listen, it wasn't me, it was him." It was up to me to prove my innocence, but I couldn't do it, while the lad who did the crime kept quiet.

Those charged with threatening behaviour were fined; the lad who kept quiet was one of them. Doz got four months; he went to jail with me but got out on appeal. Rightly so, he should only have been fined as he was on the same charges as the rest of them. I received an eighteen-month sentence for affray plus eighteen months for wounding (GBH), the sentences to run concurrent.

I didn't give a fuck about the jail sentence, I needed it. This book would still be in my head if I hadn't gone to jail. I needed to be off the streets for a while. I was getting into the drug scene too much, not smack but ecstasy, trips, coke and phet. The lads at football started to pull me, telling me to sort my head out. I was looking a mess, so I would like to thank the lad that kept quiet. Cheers mate, you did me a favour. I have a clear conscience; have you?

CHAPTER FIFTEEN

LIFE'S A RIOT

World Cup 1998, Marseille, England v Tunisia
Seven of us went: me, Simon, Gricey, Tony M, Mick H, Shaun T, and Mick R. Our first port of call in France was Eastenders to stock up with beer, and it took us an hour to get out of the car park. No-one could understand the signposts. Not a good start. We had hundreds of miles to go but finally we hit the road for Paris. The beer started to flow and joints were being rolled in the back of the van. We spotted the Eiffel Tower lit up in the night sky.

While driving down a dual carriageway, we all wanted a piss and asked the driver to stop. He pulled the Transit into an underground car park and we had a piss and jumped back into the van. As we tried to drive out, the roof of the van kept hitting the barrier; the van wouldn't fit. We were all stoned and pissed, except the driver. We had got it in the car park so we had to be able to get it out. We asked the driver if he was sure he came in the same way and then all got out and started looking for other exits, but there weren't any. Some of the lads started going mad, worrying about missing the game, but I just burst out laughing. What a situation this was, stuck in the middle of a car park in Paris getting stoned. Even if someone did come to help us, what were they going to do, chop off the

239

top of the van? There was only one thing we could do; drive out at speed and hope that it didn't do too much damage. Everyone got back into the van; no-one wanted to sit in the front with the driver. We hit the ramp at speed, there was a loud bang and we were free. We got out to inspect the damage but, apart from a few dents, there was nothing major. A loud cheer went up. We were back on the road to Marseille.

We arrived in Marseille mid-afternoon, two days before the game, parked the van and headed towards the harbour. Loads of English were already in the bars and everyone was in good spirits. The bars were expensive so we decided to find an off-licence. It didn't take us long to find one with an open front, no door and only one bloke on the till. A few people were waiting to be served. We walked in, picked up a few bottles and walked straight out again. We headed back to the harbour where everyone was buzzing and there were TV crews everywhere, mingling with the crowds. Tunisians were mixing with the English and there were a lot of police around but they seemed laid back. We just sat on a grass lawn getting pissed and stoned and chatted to other English lads. There was no sign of any trouble.

As the night went on more and more local youths started to appear. A car drove past with a big Moroccan flag out of the window. A few bottles were thrown at the car. Police quickly moved in and the mood started to change. The local youths started singing and chanting, trying to wind up the English. Missiles were thrown at them and police moved in heavy-handedly, pushing us away from the harbour. We decided to make our way back to the van for some sleep and passed a few gangs of locals on the way but nothing was said. In the van a few lads jumped straight into their sleeping bags. We got the beers out and started rolling a few joints.

Suddenly, a few locals appeared and started throwing missiles at us. The lads soon woke up and we charged at them.

Bricks, bottles and massive ball bearings were thrown at us. I was at the front with the locals on their toes and was in hot pursuit when one of the lads shouted, "Pot, get back here, Mick's been hurt, his leg's fucked." I ran back to the van and the lads were carrying Mick H. I looked down at his leg, it was shattered and his bone was sticking out of his shin. A ball bearing had hit him.

We got him into the back of the van. It was clear we had to get him to a hospital and get the van away from the vicinity in case they came back in greater numbers. Everyone was pissed but one of the lads volunteered to drive. We drove round looking for hospital signs without success. We turned onto a narrow street with cars on either side. It was a dead end and there was nowhere to turn round. The driver started to reverse but he hit a car, he pulled forward and hit another one. I jumped out of the van to guide him back. Car alarms were going off and lights in the houses started to go on. People were looking out of their windows. I told the driver to spin the van round. He did and went straight into the side of another car. People started to run towards the van, the side doors were opened and I jumped in and we were away, leaving some pretty pissed off French folk looking at their cars. Mick H wasn't too good in the back, he looked like he was going into shock. I was holding his leg together and there seemed no way we were going to find a hospital. I told the driver to pull up at a phone box. Gricey jumped out and phoned an ambulance and I told the rest of the lads to fuck off away from the van.

Shaun started to get out of the van, proper pissed. As he tried to get out, he put his hand on Mick's leg to push himself up. Mick cried out in agony. "Fucking hell, Shaun, watch his leg." Shaun was on his feet now and staggering towards the doors. This time he stood on Mick's leg. "Fucking hell, Shaun, get out of the fucking van." I pushed him out. The lads fucked off and left us. Gricey came back from the phone and said he'd phoned the ambulance but he didn't know where we were.

A police car pulled up and four coppers jumped out, they slapped the cuffs straight on me and Gricey, took one look at Mick and got straight on their radios. More police and an ambulance arrived. I was bundled into a police van with Gricey and taken to the station where we were placed in a room to get processed. We were told to sit and the cuffs were removed then put back on, just on my right hand. Gricey was sitting next to me and they put the other end on his left hand so that we were cuffed together. They started to interview us, claiming I was driving the van. Fuck that. I told them to get the British Consulate down. They breathalysed me and I passed, God knows how, but they kept us there for hours. I was getting proper pissed off. The coppers started taking the piss, taking photos of us with Gricey's camera. I jumped up, dragging Gricey with me. "What are you doing, you fucking knobheads?" The main man came in and told me to calm down and explained that we would shortly be going into a cell. I sat back down. The handcuffs were taken off.

The cell had a see-through plastic front and consisted of two benches with a foam mattress on each. There were four locals taking up both benches. Three sat on one of them, one lay on the other. I walked into the cell and up to the lad with a bench to himself and told him to move onto the other bench with his mates. He seemed a bit reluctant to move but finally got the message. Gricey opted to sit on the floor. I just got my head down and waited for the British Consulate to arrive. It was a long wait; these people don't rush.

When he arrived I explained that they were trying to say I was driving the van, but the van was fuck all to do with me as I had travelled down on my own by train. I said I had just bumped into these lads; they might have been from the same town but I didn't know them. He asked if I had a ticket for the game and I told him that a friend was bringing it down for me the next day. He seemed happy with my story and told me that I shouldn't be locked up much longer and I was placed back in the cell. It was then Gricey's turn. A couple of hours later we were back on the streets with no charges to answer.

We headed for the harbour where we knew the rest of the lads would be and a coach load of Burnley were arriving. It was a riot zone. There was tear gas everywhere stinging your eyes and English fans were fighting running battles up and down the road with the police. We made our way into the English mob and soon saw the lads but police kept on firing tear gas into the English. Cars were being overturned and the police charged several times, sending in snatch squads. The English started to disperse and we made our way to the train station, where mobs of locals were attacking English lads and missiles were flying across the road. We walked through a group of locals, who just stared at us. We carried on walking with our heads held high, expecting it to kick off at any moment, but they let us through with no words exchanged.

We got near to the station and found all the Burnley lads who had arrived by coach drinking in a bar. They had sorted us out with rooms for the night. One Burnley lad came running in to tell us that there was a large mob of locals coming up the road and we all ran outside with bottles and glasses in our hands and ran into the locals, throwing the lot at them. They backed off, then charged back, throwing their own missiles. It turned into a missile battle. You couldn't get close enough to fight because of everything flying through the air. The police turned up in numbers, charged the locals back towards the harbour, then made a line across the road to prevent it from happening again. The night was getting on and we went to the hotel, leaving most of the Burnley lads still drinking in the bar. We were just getting our heads down when the door flew open.

"It's kicking off to fuck, Pot. There are hundreds of

locals attacking bars with English lads in. You coming down or what?"

I'm not sure what he expected but I said, "No, fuck it, I'm knackered," and with that the lad disappeared back out of the door. Someone opened a window and we could hear the noise of battle outside and the roars as the lads charged. To the sound of smashing glass and sirens, sleep finally took over.

I felt great after a good night's kip. We headed for the station to check the times of trains. A lot more Burnley were due today, the day of the match. We settled in the nearest bar to the station with loads of English lads around. We needed to locate our van. The driver phoned the police and discovered they had it in a compound and that he could pick it up after the game. He wrote down the address on some paper. It was going to cost fuck all as he told them that we had to flee and leave the van as we were in fear of our lives after the locals attacked us. Good result. The lads, including Mick Moore and Mark H, who had my match ticket, arrived by train. The rest joined us and told how one lad's throat had been slashed but they didn't think it was that bad. We were about eighty strong, not a bad turnout. As we stayed in the bar for a few hours, more and more English turned up. Soon there were thousands of us.

On the way to the ground we saw a few running battles and little skirmishes but nothing major. Stories started to circulate that the game was being shown on a big screen on the beach. Most of the lads didn't have tickets so they made their way down there. Me and Mark H went on to the ground. English fans outnumbered the Tunisians by at least ten to one. They had a little section behind the goals but the rest of the ground was English. The atmosphere was friendly, England won the game and we headed back to the train station. As arranged, we arrived back at the bar where we had started the day to meet everyone. The lads who had watched the game on the beach came back telling us it had kicked off big time with the Tunisians. Seats were ripped up and there was a full-scale battle. I was proper pissed off that I had missed it.

Our driver got a taxi to the police compound and after an hour or so we saw our van coming up the street. It was a right fucking mess. The bumper and wing mirrors were hanging off and there were dents all over it. The rest of the Burnley lads were pissing themselves. "Who the fuck is taking that back to the garage? I don't think you'll get the deposit back." We all looked at the driver and burst out laughing; he wasn't impressed. The police started closing the bars, trying to avoid more trouble, and lads started catching their trains back to their camp sites. The van was parked on the train station car park and around ten of us were walking to it when a mob of locals appeared from round the corner. They outnumbered us, but not by many. They started mouthing, expecting us to fuck off, but we ran straight at them. They dropped like flies and took a bit of a beating in revenge for Mick. After that, we said our goodbyes to the rest of the lads, got into the van and fucked off. We still had plenty of beer to drink.

The journey home consisted of drink and sleep. Every time you closed your eyes you could hear sirens in your head. It was weird. We stopped just out of the ferry port of Calais and stretched our legs. I was smoking a joint and we were just about to get back into the van when the police swooped in from all over. I started to think about Marseille; maybe they weren't letting us out of the country. We were all searched then they brought a sniffer dog along. It found nothing and we were allowed to go on our way.

Our police friends pulled us at Dover. "Alright Simon, alright Andrew, did you have a good trip? The van hire company has been informed about the state of the van. Did you know you aren't allowed to take this van out of the country?" I was amazed.

"Why not?"

"Because it's not insured."

Lecture over, we were allowed to carry on. Mick H followed a few days later. They had had to put a pin in his leg and he had to have an ambulance back to Burnley. I don't know how much it cost, but his mum wasn't too pleased. Nowadays, Mick walks with a limp.

Lens, England v Colombia

Fifteen of us travelled by minibus the day before the game. We got the ferry over from Dover and there weren't any checks. The papers and the media had said no alcohol would be on sale on the ferries. What a load of bollocks. The bars were open and you could buy crates of lager, bitter and wine from the duty free shop. We got down to some serious drinking. Before the ferry docked we even loaded up the minibus with beer and had no trouble at Calais.

It wasn't a long drive to Lens, where we had arranged to meet the rest of the lads at the train station. We arrived early morning, parked on the station car park and sat round in the minibus drinking and smoking. It was quiet until the English started to arrive by train and the police turned up in vans. Hundreds of police, kitted out in riot gear. We just kept on drinking in the van and the police ignored us. The Burnley lads arrived, gagging for a beer but we had more than enough for them. Ade, Hodge and his son turned up having driven over in a car and said they had sorted out a hotel for all of us. We carried on drinking throughout the day with no hassle.

Kick-off was drawing nearer and, as most of us didn't have tickets, we decided to head towards the ground to try and acquire some. The touts were asking silly money but we spotted a lad shouting, "Tickets, tickets." He looked like he was holding them in his hand. Dave P and I went over, the lad got banged, the tickets were snatched and we were on our toes through the crowds. We stopped, happy as kids that we had tickets for the match, but we looked at them; they were only fucking train tickets. We were well sick. The only thing for it was to try again. We spotted a tout with a group of lads around him. Tickets and money were being exchanged. We walked over. Dave's hand went over the top and he snatched the ticket quick as a flash. The tout thought one of the lads close to him had taken it and was going mad. We now had one ticket but there were two of us.

The police had a cordon around the ground. Dave went through first but got caught trying to pass the ticket back to me and the police fucked me off. I quickly bumped into Ade, Hodge and Hosker. One of the lads had taken Hodge's son to the game. Hodge drove us to the hotel where they had plenty of beer in the room. I got stuck into the vodka and Ade and Hosker hit the beer. Hodge wasn't drinking, he had to pick his son up at the train station after the game. Me being greedy, the vodka went down far too easily and I only saw the first fifteen minutes of the game. The next day we headed home with hangovers but without incident.

England v Belgium – Stadium of Light in Sunderland, 1999

A lot of lads drove up in cars and minibuses and everyone had managed to get a ticket. We went into a pub in the centre of Sunderland near to the bus station called Chaplin's Bar and settled there for the afternoon. More and more Burnley arrived as the day drew on. The pub had a big screen showing Burnley play Scunthorpe live. Other lads from different teams were in but the crack was good, especially when Burnley lost. We didn't give a fuck. It seemed that every time we played on Sky TV we lost.

It was getting near to kick-off time and we moved towards

the ground, with a mob of at least eighty. I was about twenty yards behind the mob with Mick Moore and his son. The Burnley mob passed a pub with around twenty lads stood outside and one of the Burnley threw a glass in their direction. We carried on walking. More lads started to come out of the pub, but the Burnley mob hadn't realised this as they were facing forward. Still more lads came pouring out. None wore colours and I had no idea who they were, but I noticed what was happening and ran up to the Burnley lads.

"What are you fucking doing?" I said. "They want it."

They all turned and looked at the approaching mob. I shouted, "Su, su, Suicide," and ran straight into them, expecting all the lads to be behind me. I was fighting ferociously with a few of them and looked over my shoulder to see the Burnley lads getting run down the road. I was dragged to the floor, rolled up into a ball and got kicked to fuck. I looked up to find Mick Moore's son trying to help me up off the floor. The lads who had chased Burnley off were walking past me, going back to the pub. A few of them ran into me again and gave me another kicking. Mick went fucking mad. "Do you not think he's had enough, he's on his own." The lads must have thought the same because the kicking stopped.

I got to my feet and walked to the ground with Mick and his son. Ade, Fat Stan, Duncan and a few others saw me and came over. They told me that around ten Burnley stood at the bottom of the street and had a little bit of a battle but the rest just fucked off. When we all met up in Chaplin's Bar at the end of the match, I gave the Burnley lads a piece of my mind. "If you want to be a firm, fucking act like one." I had a beer and fucked off back to Burnley for a hospital appointment. I had a few broken ribs but that was the gamble. I would just like to know what the fuck happened to Burnley on that day. Too much quantity not enough quality, that's what I think.

Wigan v Burnley, November, 1999

We travelled by service train, and 100 lads were drinking in the Moon Under Water pub in Wigan by 11.30am. The police soon sussed us and surrounded the pub. We were escorted to the ground around 2pm. Burnley tried to break out of the escort but the police came in heavy with their dogs.

Burnley had brought thousands and the away end was packed. Wigan's lads sat to our right. Burnley fans tried to get into their seats via the pitch but the stewards and police pushed them back. More and more were coming into the stand that was already packed, yet the stand to our left running along side the pitch was empty, so Burnley fans invaded the pitch and went into the empty stand. Then they started walking towards the Wigan end behind the goal. Police and stewards quickly ran into the stand, forming a line to prevent them getting to the Wigan fans.

After the game, police lined up to prevent us getting to the Wigan end. Everyone charged them, their line was broken and we were through – but there were no Wigan lads about. Burnley charged past the cinema onto the main street and took a left turn, hundreds of us. Then Wigan appeared.

There was no backing off. The two mobs just steamed into each other. You didn't know who was who. I ended up on top of a lad who said, "Fucking hell Pot, it's me, what are you doing?" We both got to our feet. Bricks started flying through the air. Burnley started to back off, then more Burnley came charging to the front. Now Wigan backed off. It was going off all over.

One of my mates Jimmy went running past me. He had a police dog on his back with the handler in pursuit. The dog was running free, that's how bad it was. It was toe to toe all over. Eventually the police arrived in numbers, pushing us down the street. We were rounded up and escorted to the station. A young Wigan lad wearing his clubs top walked past the escort. Some Burnley cunt punched him to the ground. I went over and picked the young lad up asking him if he was okay. The police ran over.

"Fucking move."

"I was just seeing if he was okay."

"I don't care, fucking move"

I apologised to the Wigan lad and moved on. Full respect to Wigan, it was one of the best battles I'd witnessed, toe to toe all the way.

Oxford v Burnley, 2000

Eighty of us made the trip by train from Manchester. Earlier in the season Oxford had brought a little mob to Burnley. I was told that Burnley gave them a slap but a few of us thought they were cheeky bastards and decided to go down and see them on their own patch. We pulled into Oxford around midday and found the police waiting. We headed for the nearest pub with uniforms following. Everyone settled down with their beers and a game of three-card brag started up. We were there for around an hour and a half, during which time more police turned up. One of them told us that they had put two buses on to take us up to the ground, which a lot of the lads were pissed off about.

The two buses pulled up outside. I was still playing cards, I had a good hand and there was a fair bit of money on the table. We were sat by the window and a lad came up to me and said, "Pot can you just lean forward for a minute." I bent forward and a chair just missed my head and went sailing out of the window. More started flying all over the pub and the bandit soon went over. I took all the money off the table – I was sure I had the winning hand anyway. The lads started to leave and the police didn't know what was happening. We tried to get through their cordon but had no chance and they finally got us on the buses. Five minutes into our journey someone kicked one of the windows through. The bus pulled over, the police surrounded us and told us to get off. We were then told to wait and by now the dogs were out in force. Horses arrived and we were escorted to the ground.

The police were making us walk slowly and this pissed everyone off even more. Lads started to walk fast and the police started pushing back. Fighting broke out, the police steamed into us using their truncheons and order was soon restored. We passed a pub and we could see lads looking through the window. We tried to break the escort but the horses and dogs charged us back. Lads were getting nicked and others were getting battered to fuck by the police. Again order was restored and we were taken to the ground without any more problems.

And that was pretty much it for the day. We couldn't find a single Oxford lad after the game, and the cops had us boxed off all the way home. A definite result for the police.

Cardiff v Burnley, 2000

Forty of us met up at Manchester Piccadilly train station early on Saturday morning for the trip to Cardiff. At Newport station a few police were waiting on the platform and we clocked a Cardiff spotter. He took his hat off to us to show he knew he had been seen but no-one gave a fuck. None of us had come down for a picnic.

The train pulled into Cardiff, we walked out of the station and there were police everywhere. We all expected to get stopped but, amazingly, they let us through and we walked into the centre. Cardiff suddenly appeared, running at us from round a corner. We charged towards them chanting, "Su, su, Suicide". Police vans appeared and came to a stop in the middle of the road, the doors opened and the police steamed out blocking the road off and stopping the two mobs from meeting. The police quickly surrounded us and more arrived and started to push the Cardiff lads away. We got to the ground without any problems.

The away end was an open terrace with no roof and the Cardiff lads were stood to our right. Nothing happened during the game apart from us getting pissed wet through in the rain. The game finished and we walked out of the ground. Again, the police were everywhere and we were escorted back to the station. The police outnumbered us by at least four to one. I'd never seen an escort like it for such a small mob. One of the lads asked a copper if it was always like this and he explained it was a dress rehearsal for Cardiff's game against Bristol. We got back to the train without seeing a single Cardiff face, but on the way back one of the lads got a call off a Cardiff lad saying, "Fair play to you Burnley. At least you came down for a go. You weren't to know the police would be out in force."

CHAPTER SIXTEEN

GUNNING FOR TROUBLE

Euro 2000

We flew into Amsterdam the day before the England v. Portugal game in Eindhoven and the five of us – me, Simon, Ade, Fuzzy and Andy T – got through without a hitch. We had arranged to meet Darren, a Burnley lad who lived in Elmond, a small town on the outskirts of Eindhoven. My first port of call was a coffee shop to purchase a good amount of skunk. We met Darren in the Grasshopper bar and spent the day drinking in Amsterdam. I was getting stoned but the other lads didn't really touch the stuff. We caught the late train into Eindhoven and I got Fuzzy smoking the skunk on the way down. When we boarded a train from Eindhoven to Elmond, Fuzzy was again smoking the skunk and got paranoid, saying a Dutch lad kept looking at him. Eventually, Fuzzy got up and banged him. We all pulled him off, saying he was just paranoid. The train pulled into a station in the middle of nowhere and Fuzzy went on one, shouted, "Fuck this," and jumped off just as the doors were closing. That was the last I saw of him until I got home.

On the day of the game we made our way back into Eindhoven, where we had arranged to meet Mark H and

Mick Moore plus PSV Eindhoven fans Patrick and Angelica. Patrick was one of PSV's main lads. It was sunny and hot and there were thousands of English fans walking the streets and standing in front of the bars, drinking. There were flags hung up all over displaying every team imaginable. The police were laid back, not one of them in riot gear. Everyone seemed to be in a party mood. We walked towards the ground with Portugal and England fans mingling together without a sign of trouble. The atmosphere was good and the mood didn't change even when we lost the game. The English were there to party, not to fight.

The day after, Simon, Ade and Andy T flew home and we arranged to meet them again in Brussels by the train station. Mick stopped a couple more days, then flew back leaving me and Mark. We thought it better to stay in the country now that we had gained entry and spent the days getting pissed, drinking with PSV lads, having barbecues and just generally chilling out. We headed into Belgium the day before the Germany game to meet the rest of the lads. We didn't fancy getting the train, especially with the security operation that was on, and Patrick and Angelica volunteered to drive us into Brussels. We saw no border control and no police until we arrived in Brussels.

Patrick and Angelica dropped us off right outside the train station and we headed for the nearest bar. There were a lot of English lads about and hardly any were wearing colours. This was a different class of lads to the ones that had attended the Portugal game and the atmosphere was completely different. You could feel it was going to go off, there were too many lads around for it not to. Gilly from Wolves came over and told us Burnley and Blackburn had just kicked off in the square and that Carl and Paul were drinking in O'Riley's bar. We hadn't seen them for a while so went to meet them and to see what was happening with Blackburn. O'Riley's was surrounded by

English lads. We soon spotted some Burnley, Barra, Lee and Glen F, who said that Blackburn had given it the big one but had come unstuck. I went into the bar to have a drink with Carl and Paul.

I had just got the first one down when it kicked off outside and someone CS gassed the bar, forcing us all to leave. Bottles were flying across the street towards the police, then some lads started fighting with bouncers at the side door of O'Riley's. Both the bouncers and the English had gas so it turned into something of a gas fight. Eventually the bouncers got the door closed, so the lads turned their attention to the windows. A few went through and bottles were thrown at the police who decided they had put up with enough and charged, pushing us down the street. Bricks flew through shop windows and cars got smashed. The police fired tear gas and pushed us towards a dead end. Fuck that, I wasn't getting nicked this early, especially as I'd done fuck all. Me, Mark, Carl and Paul managed to get past the police lines as they rounded up all the English for an early flight home, and settled down in a bar not far from the train station. We had a few beers with Carl and Paul then went back to the first bar outside the train station, where some of the lads were already drinking. We told them it had already kicked off and that the police were getting heavy handed. Eventually the rest of the lads turned up and we decided to move. We had a mob of about twenty.

I was walking ahead of the others with Dave Pick. We still had our beers and Dave asked me to hold his while he went for a piss and not to kick off until he got back. I was in the middle of the street holding two beers when this cunt came up to me and put his hand flat on my forehead and slapped it with the other.

"You alright, mate?" he said, and then did it again.

"Listen mate, fuck off," I told him but he did it again, but harder, and said, "Now that was a slap."

I threw both beers over him and punched him right in the head. Before he hit the floor he was volleyed in the head by Joe, who had seen what was going on. All of a sudden someone else punched me from the side. Tubby and I caught him and he was soon slumped in a doorway. The lad who started it began to get up. "You're going fucking nowhere," I yelled and tried to curl his head round a bollard, which was not a good idea wearing trainers, as I fucked up my foot. Other lads stopped and turned. "Come on! Su, su, Suicide." We charged down the road. Everyone was on their toes. The police didn't give a fuck as it was English against English.

Dave Pick came back from his piss and went mad.

"I fucking told you not to kick off until I had come back."

"What the fuck do you expect me to do? The cunt slapped me on the head three times. I'm pissed off too: I wasted the beers."

Dave still wasn't happy he had missed it. We tried to have a drink in the square but the police had blocked it off.

It was getting dark, and gangs of local Turks began to appear. Before long they had a proper mob together. They came charging down the street but we were straight into them. There was fighting all over the road, lads flying in from all directions and bodies all over the ground. The Burnley lads stuck together, watching each other's backs, as the police struggled to separate us and plainclothes snatch squads came in. Eventually the Turks started to leave and we gave chase. An English lad shouted at us to come back, "Don't split up, stick together, they'll be back." He was right, we didn't have long to wait. The Turks came running down the street throwing missiles. We charged into them again, fighting like fuck. There were little battles going on all over the place. Every club's mob was staying together as one looking after their own. If one of your lads got into trouble it was your duty to get him out of it.

We were all stood together when someone shouted, "Gun!"

A lot of lads quickly backed off, me included. A police snatch squad was soon on top of a Turk and one of them got up holding what looked like a gun. It could have been a starting pistol but who was to know? Eventually, the police separated the English and Turkish mobs. The English were together at the top of a side street and the lines of riot police charged at us. Everyone was on their toes as the police carried on charging. Lads were running down different streets, everyone splitting up. Some went into bars trying to get out of the way only to find that when the police spotted them the bar was surrounded and the English taken out.

We managed to get away from the area and found a bar full of Middlesbrough, who heavily outnumbered us. I got a beer and started talking to them. They were sound as a pound. Everyone was getting on fine when one of our lot jumped up and shouted, "Let's do the Boro." I asked him to sit down and I explained to the Boro lads that this was his first England game and he was pissed out of his head. The explanation was good enough when all of a sudden the lad jumped up and repeated the same thing. This time I gave him a slap and a severe bollocking; you don't need a pissed up cunt who wasn't into fighting bringing it on top. The Boro lads shook my hand, saying if I hadn't done it they would have. Then Dave Pick had a bit of an argument with another Burnley lad and the police were called and bundled him into a van.

We carried on drinking into the early hours. The Boro lads offered to take me back to their hotel, where they had loads of beer, but I'd had enough, plus my foot was killing me. As soon as I got back to my hotel room I filled a bin with cold water and stuck it in.

I woke up on the day of the game with my foot still in the bin of water. It was agony but at least I could get my training shoe on. I limped to the station with the others to catch a train to Charleroi. Every conversation was about the Germans. How many would there be? Would they be up for it? The usual. As we arrived, the police were out in force surrounding the station and everyone had to show their passports to get through their cordon. The ones who didn't have their documents were put to one side and told to wait.

We headed to the nearest bar and found the rest of the Burnley lads had beaten us to it. Some had tickets for the game but I didn't. I had a ticket for the Romania match and one of the lads showed me his ticket and, unbelievably, it was exactly the same colour as mine. Things looked promising. If I used the ticket at the right time I would get into the game. Big mobs of English were walking round, some looking for Germans, others looking for other English mobs. Ours numbered around sixty. A group of lads sat at tables by the side of us and I recognised two of them from the night before. They were a bit bruised and looked worried, but none of us said anything to them.

After a couple of hours we made our way towards the square. The streets were lined with riot vans. We avoided them and went into a bar just off the square. A few Germans stood outside wearing football shirts and scarves round their necks and wrists. They weren't lads, but a German was a German. It didn't take long for someone to punch one and tell them to fuck off, which they did. Then reports came down from the square; the English and German fans had kicked off. Some of the lads went to join the fun but soon came back saying the square had been sealed off. We decided to wait inside the bar until nearer kick-off time.

Everyone was having a laugh when two English knobheads started banging on cars, slagging off the drivers. A lot of the cars had women and children in them but these two picked beers up off our tables and threw them. Ade went up to the first dickhead and said, "What the fuck do you think you are doing, we've just fucking bought those." I sat watching as dickhead number two head-butted Ade from the side. I immediately jumped up and punched the lad to the floor. I was on top of him punching his lights out when someone decided to smack me on the back with a chair. I looked round to see Kev F, a Burnley lad, stood there.

"Fucking hell, Kev, you're supposed to hit him, not me."

"Sorry Pot," was all he could offer before he sat back down as though nothing had happened. Meanwhile, dickhead number two was up on his feet, running up the road closely followed by dickhead number one, who had taken a slap from Ade.

Getting nearer to kick-off, the police let fans into the square. Groups of police fully kitted up were dotted around and police horses were on most entry and exit points to the square. Through all the singing and shouting we could hear Fat Stan's voice and soon found him with Mick Moore. The lads who had tickets went up to the ground, the lads who didn't, like me, stayed in the square. I felt it wasn't the right time to try my ticket. When we had a good mob of around a couple of hundred, we walked up to the ground en masse. I was at the front as we approached a security gate manned by police checking tickets. We started to run towards the gate. I had my Romanian ticket in my hand and was the first there. I flashed my ticket and they didn't even look, they were more interested in the 200 lads running up the road behind me. I was through. I looked behind me and the English were trying to rip the gate down and the police left their positions at the turnstiles to try to stop them getting through. I went straight to a turnstile, flashed my ticket and got through, no problem.

The atmosphere was good, the 1–0 result even better. We don't often beat the Germans. Walking back to the square afterwards, I spied a film crew doing an interview. I jumped in front of the camera and made a mad noise, shook my fists in the air and then I was away, laughing. I got back to the square and found Ade. He told me that the English were battling with each other during the game. We waited round for a few more lads but none came. The square was full of police and we decided fuck all was going to happen so we caught the train back to Brussels. The only problem was that this train didn't go to the main station. We were told to get off at a station in a mainly immigrant area.

Our senses were on edge, it was dark and there were loads of side streets leading off the main road. Lads were walking round saying, "No splitting up, everyone together," and, "Don't fucking run." We all expected an ambush on the way back to the centre but it didn't happen.

The road led us to O'Rileys bar. The Turks were again waiting on some steps leading up to a building, but there were riot police in front. We walked past on the opposite side of the road and it didn't take long for bricks to start bouncing off lads' heads. The Turks charged and some got through the police lines and came straight into us but they were soon on the floor getting kicked to bits. The police were trying to keep the two mobs apart when another Turkish mob charged out of a side street. We met them head-on and were straight into them, kicking and punching anyone in front of us. They backed off and we held our line. Pockets of lads then started to have their own individual battles, running into them, fighting, then backing off. It seemed to take ages for the police to separate us. They used the same tactic as before, trying to contain the Turks and disperse us. We were charged down side streets again, lads splitting up. But this night, if you got split up, you could end up with a mob of Turks in front of you, as thirty of us found out.

We went down one street then turned into another, straight into a mob of Turks walking along, doing every English lad they met. We ran straight at them, hitting them with chairs that had been stacked outside the bars. The fighting was fierce, with casualties on both sides, but they took more. Plainclothes

Belgian police turned up and it looked like they were on the Turks' side, so a few of them ended up on the casualty list too. Finally the riot police charged us down the streets again. Ade and I ended up on our own and made our way to the main train station to get a taxi back to the hotel, where we found most of the lads. They were all laughing, as I had just been shown on TV screaming at the camera. We had a few beers and all got our heads down.

The following day, Ade and Mark made their way to Darren's house in Elmond. They were stopping for the Romania game. I decided nothing was going to happen there, plus Glastonbury started that week so I had a fence to climb. The lads who made their way over by car gladly gave me a lift home.

Birmingham City v Burnley, 2000

Forty of the lads travelled by train. I was supposed to be with them but one of my mates, Mick Nick, was running a coach from his pub. Most of the lads who travelled on this coach were Burnley fans dressed in the club's colours. They wouldn't be looking for trouble and they liked a drink before the game. Mick asked me if I knew any pubs just outside Birmingham where they could stop without getting any hassle. I made a call and got a pub sorted out in Darlaston. When we arrived I met Carl, Paul and a few more Wolves lads and had a good natter and drink with them. The rest of the lads had a drink without getting any hassle. We got back onto the coach and carried on to Birmingham's ground. Burnley had brought a good following. The atmosphere was good too. The lads who had come in on the train said the police were on them as soon as they came out of New Street station.

The final whistle blew and we walked out on to the coach park. Some Birmingham lads started climbing over the fence into the coach park but they didn't get far. The Burnley lads just steamed the fence making the Birmingham lads fall off. I had decided I was going back on the train. As we walked through the coach park riot police were standing in front of the gates, preventing us from getting onto the street and the helicopter was hovering above with its search light on. Birmingham lads started to walk past the gates, taunting us. Burnley surged towards the gates. The police steamed into us using their batons. It was going off like fuck. I was hit on the head by a baton. It started pissing blood and then I discovered I had a big cut across my knuckle, probably from a police helmet, also bleeding heavily. Burnley surged forward again and this time managed to get through the gates. I pulled my hood up so the police couldn't see the blood pumping out of my head.

It was dark and the street was full of bodies. No-one knew who was who. I kept my head down, walked with the crowd and came to a roundabout near McDonalds. I walked across with the rest of the lads and had a look around at the lads walking with me. There were a few black faces and I didn't know any fucker. I was walking with the wrong fucking mob. I turned round and walked back towards McDonalds; a line of police was coming towards me. I tried to walk past them but they pushed me back into the Birmingham mob. I try to walk past again and again they pushed me back. I told them I was Burnley but the police didn't believe me. The Brummies who heard me did though. No one hit me, they just started threatening me, telling me that they were going to cut me up. When I heard this I decided to take my chances with the police and tried to go through them again. They tried to push me away again but I wasn't going anywhere.

"Listen," I said, "I'm fucking Burnley."

"Right, you're nicked."

Thank fuck for that. I was placed in the police van, other police jumped in and the van started to follow the Birmingham mob.

One of the police pulled my hood down and noticed all the blood on my head and hand. He told me that my head looked a mess and told his sergeant who in turn came to have a look. He asked me what happened and I told him that I was walking back to my mates after the game when I was attacked. I was separated from my lot and I wasn't sure where the car was parked so I headed for the train station. I took a wrong turn and ended up in the middle of a mob of Birmingham.

All I wanted to do was get back to the train station but the sergeant told me that they were taking me to a hospital. I told them I didn't want hospital treatment because I would probably miss the last train so, instead, they took me to the police station and made me sign a few papers saying that I had refused hospital treatment. Then they let me go without charge. Kings Norton train station was nearby so I got the train back into New Street and then jumped on another to Manchester. Nothing happened on the way home except the arrival of a massive headache.

Albania v England, World Cup qualifier, 2001

The plan was to fly into Athens, stay in Greece for two days and then catch a coach to Tirana. We arrived in the Greek capital and quickly found a youth hostel. The place stank but we couldn't complain for the price. We washed and changed and headed into the city for a few beers. The bars were full of tourists paying silly money like £5 a pint and none of us fancied that so we headed away from the tourist bars and into areas where the locals drank. We found a bar, well more a café with a few tables scattered around, a small food counter and a large fridge with bottles of Heineken, and ordered a round of beers for around eighty pence each. This became our local for our short stay in Athens. The Greeks who used the bar loved their football and asked us about all the teams in England and bought us beer. Not one of them had any animosity towards us.

The coach journey was a twenty-four-hour drive so we got a crate of beer each – but when we came to board, they wouldn't let us on with the beer. We had to put it in the luggage compartment. We were well pissed off; twenty-four hours without a drink. Imagine how boring the journey was. I skinned up a joint and lit it only to be told I couldn't smoke cigars on the coach. We travelled through the night, trying to sleep through the journey but it was hard on a moving coach, especially on the potholed roads.

At the Albanian border everyone had to get off and walk through Passport Control, where they charged us £5 to enter the country. The last leg to Tirana wasn't too bad as the coach stopped every three hours at roadside eating places selling beer. We always had time to sink three or four and smoke a few joints. On the outskirts of Tirana the coach pulled up and the driver got out, then came back with a crate. "Now you can drink beer," he said. All the other people on the coach started cheering and clapping. We didn't know what to make of it. We opened a can each and then passed the crate round the coach. Everyone who took a can came up to us and shook our hands, wishing us well.

We got off at around four o'clock the afternoon before the game. Walking was out with our bags and a crate each so we got two taxis into the city centre, and were dropped off at a massive square. It was surrounded by banks, hotels and an opera house. In the middle was a fairground. The weather was gorgeous and there were a lot of English walking round, standing outside hotels drinking beer and having a laugh. We didn't bother trying to get into the hotels round the square as they'd be top money but moved away and found a nice cheap hotel where we got our heads down for a couple of hours.

After our much needed sleep we headed out, found a bar

that was friendly and cheap and settled for the evening. Every hour on the hour a lone policeman walked in carrying a big machine gun. I asked the barman if the next time the policeman came in I could have a photo taken of me holding his gun. The barman shook his head. I wasn't sure if he had understood me but bang on the hour the policeman came in and the barman had a word. He shouted me over and started rubbing his fingers together saying he wanted some money. I handed over £5 to the policeman. He took his gun off and gave it to me. I spun round pointing the gun at the lads and they all dived under the table and the policeman ran out of the bar. The barman told me to be careful. The lads got up off the floor and I had my photo taken and gave the gun back to the no doubt highly relieved policeman.

After a few more beers most of us went back to the hotel but Mick Moore and Fat Stan decided the night was still young. We were woken in the early hours by the police banging on the door. Mick and Stan were that pissed they didn't know which door was the hotel's and the police had given them a lift from the bar.

The day of the game saw us head to the square with our bags and cans. It was hot and sunny and a mob of local winos were drinking on the steps leading up to the opera house. We took a seat beside them and got stuck into our cans, while one of the lads went off to find somewhere to stash our bags. A hotel let us put them in a room behind reception for a small fee. Back on the steps with the pissheads, the beer was going down well. Some of the winos were trying to make conversation with us but we didn't understand them so we gave them a can to get rid of them. I noticed a big bloke standing behind us dressed all in black, he had short cropped hair and mirrored sunglasses and looked like an American secret service agent from a Hollywood film. A wino came over who could speak good English and passed Fat Stan a brown paper bag with a bottle in it. Stan took a mouthful and spat it back out. "Fuck me it tastes like petrol," he said. All the winos started laughing, while the one who spoke English became Stan's drinking partner for an hour or so.

The man in black was still behind us, saying fuck all, just watching. Stan and the winos were getting on great and one wino pulled a wad of tickets from his pocket and gave us one each for the game.

"How much money do you want?"

"No, no, you English are my friends, tickets free."

We gave him a can for each ticket. Fat Stan and the wino were by now well drunk and Stan started taking the piss a bit, so the wino got the hump and asked for money for the tickets.

"Fuck off," said Stan. "You've had a can of beer for them."

The wino started ranting and raving and then the man in black spoke.

"Watch it lads, they will try and take the piss," he said in perfect English. Who the fuck was he?

The wino approached me and said, "You can have your ticket for free, I like you, but your friends will have to pay." I told him to fuck off then it got less than friendly. "Me part of the Albanian Mafia," he said. "I know the police, I have a gun." He patted his chest.

"So fucking what?"

I stood up while the rest of the lads laughed. "What's so fucking funny?" I asked. The lads just shrugged their shoulders and nodded their heads.

The wino spoke again. "Me and you go for some food, bottle of wine then fuck." I couldn't believe it, this cunt was after fucking me; the cheeky bastard then went to kiss me. I grabbed hold of his face, pushed him away and he stumbled to the floor. I felt like kicking him in the head but the man in black was staring and there were a few policemen dotted around, so I just walked across the road into a bar full of

English. The rest of the lads took the piss out of me for the rest of the trip but at least we all had tickets. We never did find out who the man in black was.

We had a few beers and headed towards the ground, walking side by side with the Albanians. We got to the away end and they didn't even check the tickets. The ground was a shithole and Norman Wisdom, the most popular man in the country, was walking round the pitch. We were on a terrace surrounded by riot police but the Albanians made no attempt to break through.

At the finish, everyone was let out together. I lost the other lads and the English and Albanians walked back to the square together. I bumped into Mark H from Burnley in front of the opera house. He had travelled alone. Then we heard a few shouts and a few stones started to bounce on the pavement. All of a sudden, English went running past us towards their hotels.

"Don't fucking run, stand," I said.

Some stopped, most didn't. I saw Fat Stan, Mick and the rest of the lads walking through the crowd. Someone punched Stan in the head, Mick flew into the culprit and knocked him right on his arse. Mark, me and a few other English ran in to help but they didn't need it, the Albanians fucked off as soon as they saw the English running towards them.

We headed to the hotel where we had left our bags, had a few beers then got taxis to the coach station. I slept most of the way to the Greek border. At Passport Control all the Albanians started pushing each other trying to get to the front of the queue. We stood at the back laughing at them. A Greek customs officer came out, went mad at the Albanians and then spotted us.

"You English?"

"Yes."

"Come with me."

He pushed everyone out of the way, including the women and children, took us to the front of the queue, through Passport Control and then into a room where he checked our passports. He told us his daughter was studying in Manchester and that he liked the English but didn't like Albanians. We went straight through and the Albanians took hours.

Greece v England, World Cup qualifier, 2001

I managed to get three tickets for the game, one for me, one for Jimmy Craggs and one for Fuzzy. We were going to make a holiday out of it and booked a week in Kos and a flight from Kos to Athens for the game. Everything was sweet at Manchester airport. There were no checks. We had a few beers in the airport bar until it was time to board. We were in the queue having a laugh and a joke, but when Jimmy talks he shouts and sounds really aggressive and when it was our turn to show our tickets we were told, "Sorry lads, we think you've had too much to drink, can you step to one side please." I'd only had four fucking pints. I couldn't believe it. We watched in silence as all the other passengers boarded. Fuzzy had a word with the ticket girl who told him that the air steward was asking the captain to see if we could board. He told us we could, but we weren't allowed to drink on the flight. We boarded the plane looking like three naughty schoolboys who had just had a severe bollocking.

The dinners started to get passed around and the steward came us to us.

"Would you like any more dinner lads?"

"Would it be possible to have a bottle of wine with our food?"

"No."

"Well shove your food up your arse."

He pulled a funny face then fucked off. We asked three

birds who were sat in front of us to buy us a few beers but they refused, the tight bitches. As we had no beer we got our heads down.

Our apartment was in a complex with its own pool and a poolside bar. Jimmy and Fuzzy spent the day sunbathing round the pool. I hate sunbathing and sat under an umbrella drinking beer and smoking joints.

The day of the game arrived and we got into Athens centre for noon. Fuzzy and Jimmy wanted something to eat so we went into a tourist bar and ordered three and a half beers each plus two salads. The bill came to £40. I said, "Fuck this, come on I will take you to a cheap bar," and took them to the bar that we had made our local on our way to Albania. As soon as we walked in the owner recognised me. We ordered our bottles of Heineken and he said, "No money, I buy you these." After a few hours we decided to find out where the English were drinking and took the underground towards the ground. Quite a few English were on the train and they all seemed to be getting off at a certain stop, so we followed. As we came out of the station there was a small square in front of us surrounded by grass and loads of English sitting on the grass, drinking. Some were kicking footballs in the air. We walked through the square, checking out all the Union Jacks to see if we could spot any Burnley. I noticed a Wolves flag and went over to see if I knew any of them. I immediately spotted Gilly, their best-known face, and we had a few beers with him. A few Burnley appeared and we sat round the square for a few more hours.

There were no mobs here, only lads with their birds, all wearing England shirts. Someone said that the England lads were drinking near the ground so we caught the train up there and got off at the stop before the ground. There were five bars all together with seats and tables outside. All the seats were taken by English lads, a good couple of hundred of them. It was a different class of English to the ones we had just left. We bought a beer each, walked outside – and everything just kicked off. I don't know why. Some Greeks in a bar threw chairs at the English, who returned fire with bottles and glasses. A lad at the side of me was hit by a chair. He started whining. "What the fuck are you moaning at?" I asked, picked up the chair and steamed into the Greeks, who backed off into a bar with bottles and glasses smashing everywhere. I followed them into the bar, smacking them with the chair, then Duncan and Fuzzy came running in shouting, "Pot, police." I threw the chair and walked out.

More Greeks were about now, having individual battles with the English, most of which ended up with the Greeks running off. Then the English mob made their way to the train station and the majority got on a train, leaving about fifty of us. The Greeks had taken the opportunity to mob up and came steaming down the road, throwing rocks at us. We waited for the missiles to stop and then charged at them. They were on their toes. We didn't follow, we stayed as a group. The Greeks were soon back with greater numbers, throwing rocks again. The same thing happened, we charged and they ran. Again we didn't chase as a mob, but Duncan did on his own. He carried on chasing up the street, got hold of a Greek lad and was battling like fuck with him. Some Greeks came back to help their mate so Fuzzy and I ran up to Duncan and backed them off. The lad who Duncan had been fighting joined his mates again and the three of us walked back into the English mob.

Another train arrived as we made our way to the platform. The first carriage was full of English and the second full of Greeks. Some came bouncing off the train but we punched them straight back on again. English lads ran down the stairs of the platform with a mob of Greeks chasing them. Fuzzy ran up the stairs and straight into them with Duncan and I not far behind. We were brawling like fuck on the stairs but the Greeks had the high ground. More English came to join us and we pushed the Greeks back, fighting for every step, and got them off the steps onto level ground. The Greeks started to run and then the police came steaming over the bridge and charging us on to the platform. Everyone jumped on the train. The doors closed and the police hit any lad unable to get onto the train.

Fuzzy's head was pissing with blood but the cut wasn't too bad. I was still shaking from the adrenalin but a joint worked to calm me down. The train pulled into the station and we made our way to the ground with police everywhere. Fuzzy kept his head down. There were loads of English lads coming up to us, shaking our hands and saying, "Fucking hell, Burnley, you're game as fuck." I can't explain the feeling of getting recognition from fellow hooligans, it felt brilliant. We got onto the ground without a problem and after the game we were put on the train back to Athens centre. There were no Greeks about and we got a taxi to the airport and flew back to Kos.

The following day, while we were sitting around the pool, I just got the feeling that I had to call home. I made the call and my girlfriend answered the phone.

The first thing I said was "What's happened?"

"Nothing," she replied.

"Yeah, it has, tell me."

"Well, I didn't want to tell you until you came home, but the dog has died."

I was devastated. I had had the dog for seventeen years. I went back and told the lads, then went to the bar, bought a crate of lager and disappeared to my room to get pissed and stoned and shed a few tears for the dog.

CHAPTER SEVENTEEN

THE END OF THE ROAD

Burnley Riots, 2001

It was Sunday, shortly after midday, and twenty of us were in Burnley Wood club. We were rough as fuck after a football trip the day before. We had been drinking in Lancaster until two in the morning and hadn't got home until five. None of us knew about the previous night's events in Burnley, until a few lads came in from Duke Bar and explained how local Asians had attacked the Duke of York pub the night before and were mobbing up again to do the Baltic Fleet and Old Duke pubs, both side by side in the Duke Bar area of town.

We all had mates up there and we weren't going to let them down. We got taxis up to the Baltic Fleet and saw riot vans parked up outside. Lads were outside the pub drinking, singing, "Rule Britannia" and chanting, "England." We got a beer each and went outside to talk to them. More police started to turn up. There was no chance the Asians would attack the pubs, there were far too many police around, and the lads decided to walk into the town centre. Our walk took us past Stoneyholme, a predominantly Asian area. The mob split into two groups, each trying to get down different side streets into Stoneyholme but the police were out in force and had blocked every street, so we carried on into the centre. We went into a pub just on the outskirts of the town centre, near an Indian restaurant, another pub, fast food outlets and taxi offices. The police appeared to be still concentrated up near the Duke Bar. We stood outside drinking and it wasn't long before the windows of the restaurant, taxi offices and fast food shops went through. Police sirens could be heard in the distance.

Fifty of us now made our way to Turf Moor football ground, got a drink in the Turf pub and stood outside. Songs were sung again. Riot vans pulled up and soon a line of police fully kitted out in their body armour, crash helmets and riot shields blocked the way into the town centre. Songs were still being sung and a couple of glasses were thrown at the police but fell short of their line. The police then separated, forming two groups. One approached us from the left and the other was straight in front of us. They looked like marching stormtroopers. Lads started to pack into the doorway. The police then charged, trying to push everyone into the pub with their riot shields. And they had a second tactic. Police with shields were stood behind the officers pushing us into the pub. The first line of shields was right in our faces when, suddenly, the officers from behind raised their shields above the ones in front of us, then proceeded to hit us with the bottom edges of the riot shields. I am sure that they sharpen them. Lads' heads and faces were cut and soon there was blood everywhere.

When the lads in the doorway of the pub saw what was going on, everyone went mad and charged out of the pub into the riot shields, punching and kicking them. Facing increasing numbers from the pub, the police started to back off. Glasses and bottles started flying into the police. They came marching into us again using the same tactic but this time we knew what was going to happen so we attacked the shields. We were taking a lot of casualties while fighting toe to toe. Everyone seemed to have lost their heads. No-one gave a fuck about the police filming us with their camcorders or the police helicopter hovering about our heads. They started to back off. Lads armed themselves with table and chair legs. Some lads managed to get through the shields and traded punches with the police. Lads came out of the Brickmakers pub up the road to join the battle. The police were now shitting themselves (I've got their statements). They were backing off and near enough on the verge of turning and running. You could hear the main officer screaming at the top of his voice, "Hold the fucking line."

They formed a line across the street, again preventing us moving into the town centre. But lads were now joining us from other nearby pubs. Someone pulled a bottle bin out from one of the side streets. Lads started to disappear down the street, then all of a sudden they charged out together. Hundreds of bottles flew through the air towards the police line and everyone charged. They backed off and we were into their shields, kicking and punching them. Again we took casualties and, when the missiles ran out, we backed off.

The mob moved towards Burnley Wood, smashing all the taxi offices and takeaway shops along the route. The police now had their horses on the streets. They came charging towards us followed by a line of officers. We were on our toes, running up Oxford Road, but the police had sealed it off at the bottom. Horses charged up the road towards us. Fuck this, we weren't running anymore. We all charged towards the horses. They realised we weren't stopping, and turned back towards their own lines, which opened to let the horses through As soon as the horses were past, the police were on their toes too. Oxford Road was ours.

The mob overturned cars and set them on fire, blocking the road, then made its way up Oxford Road into the heart of Burnley Wood. The police didn't dare enter Burnley Wood at this stage and the lads were left to do what they wanted. Off licences were looted and shops and cars were set on fire. Oxford Road soon resembled a warzone. Everyone seemed to disperse, looting other shops in the area. I went back to Burnley Wood club, just caught last orders and got three beers. It had been thirsty work.

The next day, the police blanketed the area. The clean-up began and film crews were interviewing residents. I waited for the knock on the door and, inevitably, a couple of months later, it came. Along with more than sixty other white lads, I was charged with violent disorder. We all appeared at Preston Crown Court for sentencing and I was given three years. Thirty-eight of us were jailed on the same day and around thirty more followed at a later date. Most of us went to Preston jail, though the younger lads went elsewhere. Most of us were kept together for the first week and had a wing of our own. No-one seemed bothered about being in jail. Soon they started to split us up, sending us to different jails. I ended up in Haverigg, Cumbria, with Ade, Boris, Eddie Mac and Paul H. Me, Boris, Ade and Paul all got jobs in the building yard and our civvy officer, Richard, was sound and took us around the jail, doing odd jobs. He even stuck up for us when the race relations officer tried to get us sacked.

We had been concreting the floor outside the building huts and thought, with the World Cup coming up, we would use red brick to put a St George's cross in the concrete. Clarky and Danny, two scouse coloured lads who were sound as fuck and doing a painting and decorating course, agreed it looked smart but reckoned it would look better if they painted it. They painted the concrete with white gloss, and they were right, it looked proper smart. The whole jail could see it, but that didn't go down too well with some people. They said we were trying to stir up racial hatred and the race relations officer pulled us into the office asking us if we were racist. We just explained that it was for the World Cup and that Richard had said it would be alright. Clarky and Danny asked us what was going on. We told them and they went to see the race relations officer, explaining that they had painted it and they were coloured, so how could it be racist?

Then Clarky asked him, "What do you know about race relations? What is the difference between me and him?" (Danny was a lot darker skinned than Clarky.)

"I don't know," replied the officer.

"He's done ten minutes longer under the grill, you know fuck all."

Everyone burst out laughing when he told us the story, but we still had to dig it back up.

Back home the people at the club collected money for the Burnley Wood lads so we never wanted for anything. If you needed some new clothes or anything a postal order was soon on its way. I met some good lads in Haverigg, top lads, especially Bob, a Newcastle fan doing life. He'd done fifteen years and was getting ready for his Cat D before release. He introduced me to Dom, a Bolton fan, and Jimmy, a Sunderland lad, both lifers coming to the end of their sentences. I took my hat off to those lads. Jail hadn't broken them. You see some people doing a few years and you can't get a smile out of them but these three lads never stopped laughing and taking the piss out of each other. If you needed anything they would get it for you.

As the months went by, Ade, Paul and Eddie went home and Boris was moved to Kirkham open prison. Another one of the Burnley Wood lads, Greg Foreman, arrived in Haverigg following a conviction for the riots and it didn't take long for him to get on the same residential unit as me. I got a new job for my last nine months, working as a gym orderly. All the rest of the orderlies were sound, so were the gym screws. I used to get Greg into the gym regularly, playing tennis, football, volleyball and step aerobics. Our time flew. You might think I am insane but, honestly, I had a good time. There were hooch parties every now and then and we had a smoke. I almost felt sorry that I was leaving. But when I got out of the gates and I saw Jimmy Cragg waiting for me with a massive joint and a twenty-four pack of Strongbow, I knew which side of the fence I would rather be on.

While I was in jail, things changed. The lads who visited told me about a new mob coming through Burnley youth and the police were said to be well on top, especially as there had been two murders in one season. Tragically, a Forest fan was killed and then an elderly woman died after being hit by an ashtray which had been aimed at the police. These things should never happen at football but, obviously, they do. I don't think any football lads go out purposely to kill another fan. I know I certainly never have and I have been involved in a lot of battles.

Germany v England – Munich 2001

Three of us would be making this journey via Amsterdam: me, Mick Moore and Doz. We flew from Manchester on the Tuesday morning before the game, caught the train into Amsterdam central station and checked the times of the trains to Munich. With a few hours to kill, I needed some skunk for the journey. We went to Hunters Bar, my favourite; I always seemed to get good deals in there. I bought a big bag of skunk, and after a few drinks we bought some cans and boarded the train and found a compartment to ourselves.

As our train pulled out of Amsterdam, I got out my stash and made a joint. Then we got stuck into the cans. Mick never smoked cannabis so it was down to me and Doz to get stoned out of our heads. The skunk and the cans went together well; maybe a bit too well. I soon crashed out.

Mick woke me. "Pot, have you got your passport, he wants to see it"

I looked up and saw a guard inspecting Mick and Doz's

passports. I was still half asleep. I reached into my back pocket, pulled something out and gave it to the guard.

"No, your fucking passport," said Mick, a little desperately.

I looked at the guard; he held my bag of skunk in his hand. He kept looking at the skunk, then at me. I took it off him, put it back in my pocket, got my passport out of my other pocket and gave it to him. He looked at me again, shook his head, then walked out of the compartment with all three passports. After a short mobile phone conversation, he came back in and gave us the passports back.

"Have a good trip," he said, and left.

We all cracked up laughing

"Fucking hell Pot, what you doing giving him your skunk?"

"I thought he might have wanted a smoke."

We got into Munich around 5pm and found a youth hostel near the train station. With our beds sorted, we headed back to the station, where we had arranged to meet some of the lads arriving on later trains. A few English were in a bar facing the station and gradually more and more turned up, including Ade, Fat Stan, Rusty, Simon and Dave Pick. There were no German mobs anywhere, which I thought was unusual. You would expect them to be out in force on their own turf. We drank until the early hours, then got our heads down.

We headed back towards the train station on match day. We got into a place called Schillers Bar, where English were drinking inside and out. The weather was great, Burnley's mob was growing by the hour and I managed to get hold of match tickets for me and Doz off a German for £50 each. They were for the German end but I didn't see a problem about that.

The atmosphere was noisy but good-natured until two German lads walked past in their team colours. Beer was thrown on them and a few lads chased them up the street towards the police. Suddenly it kicked off; it was like someone had tripped a madness switch. All the English charged up the street towards the police, hurling bottles and glasses. Some went the opposite way, smashing cars and putting shop windows through. The police charged through us and if you got in their way you got battered with their big batons, no messing. Plain clothes officers wrestled lads to the ground and nicking them. Sirens could be heard coming from every direction.

It seemed to stop almost as quickly as it had begun, and I headed to the ground with a few others on the underground. As we came out of the station it kicked off again. The Germans were dressed the same as us, many in Stone Island, and you didn't know who was English and who wasn't. Me, Dave, Doz, Simon and Rossy from Tranmere all stuck together as battles broke out all over and bodies hit the deck. Soon the Germans were on their toes.

Our mob of about forty walked outside the German end in a park, with a grassy hill at the side of us. A mob of Germans stood on the hill, talking into mobile phones and looking at us. They had a few police stood with them. We spread out at the bottom of the hill and slowly started to walk towards them. The police moved away. Rossy and I had picked our target. He was big, and he looked like he was giving the orders. As the fighting began, Rossy and I ran towards our target. I was just about to punch him when someone smacked me from the side, and I was rolling down the hill. I came to a stop and got back up, thinking, the fucking cunt, where is he?

I saw Rossy and Dave bang at it with the Germans, and I steamed in to join them. Dave knocked one of them to the ground and I kicked him in the head. It was a big mistake; I had trainers on instantly felt a pain shoot up my leg. I couldn't put my foot back on the floor, and had to hobble to the bottom of the hill and sit down, as fighting went on all around.

As I sat and watched, the Germans started to scatter. The English had taken the hill. Finally, Doz came over.

"You alright Pot?"

"No, I think I've broken my foot."

I stood up but I couldn't put my foot flat on the ground. I had to limp, walking on my toes. It was agony, and by the time we got to the ground I was bathed in sweat.

We were on the terrace behind one goal, opposite all the English fans, and decided to walk round towards them. But as we moved through the crowds I couldn't keep up, and I quickly lost sight of Doz. I thought fuck it, I'm staying here, as I could hardly walk. There were Germans all around me. They started going mad, jumping up and down: 1 - 0 to the Germans. Same old story. I sat down on the terrace to make a joint.

Then England scored - and I went mad. I forgot about my foot for a second, but my cheers soon turned to groans of pain. I sat back down and made another joint. Germans were looking at me, but fuck 'em.

As the game approached half-time, England scored again. This time I remembered my foot and just punched the air, shouting, "Come on England." The Germans just looked at me again, while I rolled a joint for half-time.

Two minutes into the second half and England scored again. Owen got his hat-trick. That deserved a joint. The Germans weren't looking at me anymore. Five-one, fuck the foot, it was worth the pain. I don't think I will ever witness a result like that again. In fact it was worth making another joint for.

By the end of the game I was stoned out of my head and my foot didn't seem to hurt as much. I managed to make my way back to the underground station and bumped into Dave, Simon and Scott. Dave had fucked his hand up. We got back into the centre of Munich and it was pissing it down. There were no Germans about so we went into the bar near the train station. There was no trouble; I think everyone was in shock about the result. We had a few beers then got a taxi to Scott's hotel. Once there me and Dave got a wastepaper bin each, filled them with cold water and put our injured body parts in them.

In the morning, me, Simon and Dave got a taxi to the train station. I was hoping to find Mick and Doz. I walked to the left luggage lockers and Mick, Doz and Ade were asleep on the floor. Some jumped on the next train to Frankfurt and the rest of us went to Amsterdam. I got home and went straight for an X-ray; my foot wasn't broken, just badly bruised. Dave got the bad news, his hand was broken.

Euro 2004

I received this letter from the police a couple of weeks prior to the European Championships:

> Dear Sir,
> Due to your association with football-related disorder on both the domestic and international fronts, you have come to the attention of the police. There will be a high police presence in Portugal for the forthcoming European Championships. Anyone involved in football-related violence or disorder, before or during the championships will be subjected to a rigorous investigation which will involve the extensive use of police evidence gatherers and CCTV cameras.
>
> Any offence disclosed will be prosecuted and banning orders will be sought at court as part of the Football (Disorder) Act, 2000, which prevents attendance at any domestic and international fixtures for a minimum of three years. If you are thinking about attending the Championships please consider the above.

I read the letter over and over again and finally came to the conclusion that it was telling me I could travel, but to make sure I was right I showed the lads. They all came to the same conclusion, so I booked my flight and accommodation with Ade, Simon and the ex-Burnley player Andy Payton.

Our plane left Manchester early on Saturday morning, the day before England's first game against France. I was still apprehensive but I had the letter with me. Simon, Ade and Andy went through Passport Control ahead of me, no problem. I did too, then two plainclothes policemen approached me.

"Can we have a word?"

"Yeah."

"Are you known to the police?"

"Yeah."

"What for?"

"Drunk and disorderly."

They checked on their computer and said, "Right Andrew, you can go." I was thinking, yes, I'm through, and headed to the bar to meet the other three. Just as it came to my turn to get served, I felt a tap on my shoulder. "Andrew, can we have another word?" My head was in bits. They sat me in a room saying that they had more checks to do on me but there were only fifteen minutes to go before we were boarding. The door opened. "Right Andrew you can go now." This had got to be it, I had to be through. I went to the bar, got a beer and sat with the lads. I was buzzing and couldn't keep the smile off my face. We boarded the plane and I fell asleep straight away.

When I woke up, Andy offered me a bottle of Champagne, telling me it was going to be a good trip. It tasted great. As I walked through Passport Control at Faro airport there were two English policemen in a booth at the side and loads of police lined up on the other side of the barrier. I didn't even get to show my passport.

The pair came up and said, "Andrew, you're a known football hooligan, the Portuguese don't want you in their country."

"Listen," I said. "I've had two checks at Manchester and they let me through. I've got a letter here that says I can travel."

I showed them the letter, they read it. One of them thought he was a right smart cunt. "It says you can't travel," he said.

"How the fuck do you work that out, you prick?"

I walked up to him and he said, "Don't get in my face."

"You fucking knobhead. Don't get in your face? I'll fucking punch it off."

The Portuguese police grabbed me, led me onto the tarmac where people were boarding their planes and put me in a newly built bungalow. In front of it was a cage so you could stand outside in the sunshine, waving at the busloads of tourists going past. There were two bedrooms with single beds and bunk beds, a TV room and a bathroom. Once they got me in the place, I was searched, my belt and trainers were removed and I was told they were putting me on the next plane back to Manchester. I asked about my luggage and they told me it would be put on the plane with me (lying bastards). They then locked the door to prevent me from going outside.

I started kicking the door. It opened and the police came running back in. My head was starting to go. They asked me to calm down, telling me they locked the door because they thought I wanted to sleep but, if I didn't, I could sit outside in the cage, which I did. There were three police in with me at all times. One had a big truncheon, one a gun and the other didn't have anything but made conversation with me.

A couple of hours went by. Every English plane that landed I expected to be on, returning to England, but they just kept taking off without me. I had a bit of cannabis so I went to the toilet and made a few single-skin joints that looked like roll-ups. I went back outside and started to have a good smoke and the police didn't have a clue, or if they did they didn't pull me. The chatty one started talking to me.

"You're always smiling, you happy?"

"Yeah, I'm happy," I replied. "I'm stuck in here then I am going home."

He just walked away and I burst out laughing. I was stoned.

Ten hours later, three plainclothes Portuguese police travelled back to England with me. I was handcuffed and sat at the front of the plane. I got the window seat. The police were sound and took off the handcuffs and, when the beer trolley came round, asked if I wanted anything. I said a couple of beers but the hostess informed us the plane had been drunk dry on the way out. I was sick and had to settle for a cup of tea. I asked how come they deported me and they claimed the English spotters had told them to do it – they all blame each other. Then there was an announcement over the Tannoy that the plane's destination was Gatwick.

"I thought I was supposed to be flying back to Manchester?"

"No, no, police waiting for you at Gatwick."

This pissed me off. How was I supposed to get back to Burnley? The plane landed and everyone got off but I was told to wait. Five English police came on for me, signed a piece of paper for the Portuguese and then I was taken from the plane, straight through Passport Control and Customs. They told me I had to appear before Crawley magistrates the next morning.

I asked about my luggage and was told none had come with me. The police sergeant asked if I had anywhere to stay for the night. I told him I didn't. Credit to him, he drove me round different hotels to see if they had any spare rooms, but everywhere was full, or at least they said they were. I didn't look good jumping out of a police van running in and asking for a room. I told the sergeant to take me back to the airport and I would get my head down there. The last thing he said to me was, "Make sure you turn up for court in the morning." Court was the last thing on my mind; getting back to Burnley to watch the game with my mates was the only thing I was interested in. I had a final joint and got my head down.

Two police woke me at five o'clock on Sunday morning. Loads of people were sleeping around me.

"What are you doing here?"

"I'm waiting to go to Crawley Magistrates' Court; I've been deported from Portugal."

"Oh, we're sorry to have woken you."

Actually, they did me a favour. I went straight to the train station, bought a ticket for Burnley and got the next train into London. By the time I was due in court I was on the piss on a train halfway back home.

I got back well in time for the game and no-one seemed surprised to see me. I got a three-year ban in my absence at court. I asked my solicitor to appeal, asking for the reason why I was banned. This is what they sent to me as justification:

Name:	Andrew Porter – Risk Cat B
Alias/Nickname:	Not known (well, you do now)
Tel Numbers:	Home – Known
	Mobile – Not known
	Work – Not known
Occupation:	Unemployed (Oct 2001)
Vehicle:	Unknown
Status – Risk:	NCIS Flagged/follows England home and abroad/Life ban from BFC. Travels to Burnley away matches.
Other Club Contacts:	Tranmere Rovers
Conviction Summary:	
1981–1990	11 Convictions for various offences
02/09/97	Convicted drugs offences
08/09/97	Convicted of assault constable (Burnley v Preston 21.01.97)
04/03/98	Convicted drugs offences
23/10/98	Convicted of affray and GBH – 18 months prison
08/03/02	Convicted of violent disorder – 3 years prison (Burnley riots)

Warning Markers: Violent/Drugs
*Intelligence international: (England games) based on historical NCIS records
and spotter reports.*

Czechoslovakia v	
England 24/03/92:	*Stop checked Dover, en route to this fixture*
Euro 1992 (Sweden):	*Stop checked Malmo*
Euro 1992 (Sweden):	*Arrested in Stockholm on 17/06/92 for assault Received prison sentence*
England v Norway 14/10/92:	*Arrested for affray i/e six other Burnley targets at McGoverns Irish bar in Kilburn High Road, London – pre-match*
Euro 96 (England):	*Stop checked in two minibuses organised by Massey 14.06.96 en route to England v Scotland fixture (i/c Moore, Parkinson, Bradshaw, Holden and Porter)*
World Cup 93 (France):	*Stop checked en route to tournament (i/e Simon Massey) also seen in Marseille (14.06.93)*
Germany v England 01/09/01:	*Sighted with other Burnley targets*
England v Sweden	*Sighted in Manchester with other Burnley targets*
10/11/01:	
Manchester 10/09/03:	*Spotted in Manchester city centre with several other Burnley risk supporters prior to England v Lichtenstein game*
Plans to travel to Portugal 05/04/04:	*Intelligence log*

Intelligence Local (Burnley):

Burnley v West Ham Utd	
02/03/04:	*Spotted with thirty risk supporters pre-match*
Bradford v Burnley 27/03/04:	*In company with approximately two hundred other risk supporters on the day*
Sheffield Weds v Burnley 17/03/01:	*In company with approximately fifty other risk supporters during the match*
Barnsley v Burnley 26/12/00:	*In company with fifty other risk supporters on the day*

Notts Forest v Burnley 28/10/00:	*In company with fifty other risk supporters, disorder on train pre-match*
Huddersfield v Burnley 23/09/00:	*In company with sixty other risk supporters on the day*
Scunthorpe v Burnley	*In company with approximately one hundred and*
06/05/00:	*fifty other risk supporters on the day when serious disorder took place*
Wigan v Burnley 27/11/99:	*In company with approximately two hundred other risk supporters on the day when serious disorder took place*

General Comments

From the above it can be seen that Porter has been associated with the Burnley Suicide Squad for many years and been present when serious disorder has taken place. A lull in attendances at away matches, between 2001 and 2003, coincides with periods of imprisonment.

Extensive intelligence regarding Porter's attendance at England fixtures abroad. He is a known associate of a number of other risk supporters including Massey who has travelled extensively throughout Europe.

You see lads, we've all got these files. Big Brother IS watching.

CHAPTER EIGHTEEN

SUICIDE MEMORIES

Here are some memories from a few Suicide friends, staunch lads who have been there through thick and thin, sometimes at games when I wasn't present.

SIMON MASSEY

Wrexham Away

It was pissing it down when I woke up and I wondered if the game would be on. There were only about forty of us going on this trip but they'd stand against 100 opposing fans. We set off around ten o'clock and an hour later the radio informed us that the game had been called off. We didn't know what to do so just carried on to Wrexham, arriving at noon. We walked into the centre and visited a couple of pubs, looking for trouble. In the Eighties most firms liked a row.

We walked out of the second pub, went down the main road and saw the Frontline, Wrexham's so-called firm. They were surprisingly up for it and tooled up with bottles and glasses. It went off with even numbers for a good five minutes. We put them on their toes but they came back numbering around seventy. Then the heavens opened and it pissed it down. I'd never seen rain like it. The battle continued for a good ten minutes until the Old Bill arrived. We still had the edge but it felt like all of Wrexham was against us. Two of our lads had been bottled but that was the game. The police escorted us out of Wrexham. We were wet through but we were smiling.

Lincoln Away

We arrived at around eleven o'clock and had a few drinks in the town centre. It was surprisingly quiet; Lincoln were normally up for it. There was no action until we got up to the ground and we spotted their firm with all the usual faces. We attacked them first, there were fists and boots flying all over. The police arrived and soon restored order with their favourite toys, their dogs. We were then escorted to the ground and into the away end. Ten minutes into the game twenty of us sneaked round to their boys in the stand. All hell broke loose; there were thirty arrests, twenty-five Lincoln lads and five Suicide Squad. We were chuffed, Lincoln weren't. We all ended up at the magistrates' where jail terms were expected, but with my eight-month pregnant girlfriend sat in court, the magistrates told me I was a lucky man and I was given community service.

Stockport Away – Night match 16/09/88

Over the years we had grown to hate each other. There had been stabbings and slashings on both sides. The thing about Stockport was they had fifty keen lads, always up for it, but on this night our attention was drawn to the police. As we entered the ground they gave us a hostile reception. We were around 400 strong and they knew we were coming. Stockport fans knew we were the firm that night and so did the police. They were on our case as soon as we entered the ground. The young coppers showed us no respect so we had to teach them a lesson. As the teams kicked off, so did we. Two smoke bombs were hurled into the fifty or so coppers. They drew their batons and panicked. It was too late, the full force of the

Suicide Squad was there and they wanted blood. There was fighting all over, the coppers couldn't see us for the smoke. Twenty-nine boys in blue ended up in hospital. The moral of this story is that if you messed with the Suicide Squad in the Eighties and Nineties, when we were in full force, you came unstuck.

Scarborough/York Away, 1994

This quiet seaside resort was in the Football League for the first time. Little did they know what was to come. On their first day Wolves had a running battle with the police and smashed up the ground. Now it was our turn to have some fun by the sea. We arrived in vans early and had a few drinks round town. The last pub we visited the police surrounded, so we smashed our way out with chairs and tables singing our anthem, "Su, su, Suicide." That seemed to send the fear of God through the police, and they backed off down the road.

Somehow, we got to the ground and steamed the gates and turnstiles. Once inside there was no local opposition, just the Old Bill, who by this time had got shields, their batons out and their helmets on. This was where the real fun began. Throughout the match we smashed up the ground and attacked the police. There were casualties on both sides but we got back to our vans together and were escorted out of town.

Sixteen of us decided to detour to York for more action. We had a drink in the first pub and asked a few locals which were the best bars. They suggested a few but warned us not to go into the Squaddie bar. Naturally, after that comment the only place we wanted to go was the Squaddie bar. It was massive and had a virtually all-male clientele, so we all got drinks and started singing, "Su, su, Suicide." Soon, bottles, glasses and tables were flying around – and the great British Army ran away. We ended up battling with the bouncers in the beer garden. They somehow locked us out of the pub so we picked up the big old benches outside and used them as battering rams, but couldn't break open the doors. We heard the sirens coming so we walked away.

Two weeks later, six houses were dawn-raided and four of us subsequently appeared at York Crown Court. Three got community service and one lucky lad got a walkout – me. What a result.

AN ANONYMOUS CONTRIBUTOR – AMBUSH ON PRESTON

We knew Preston would be coming through Burnley after the game at Bradford City. Fourteen of us made our way to a pub near to the Manchester Road station, where their train was due to stop. We knew what time it would arrive so we had a few drinks and then went to the platform to wait. As it stopped with at least 100 Preston on board, seven of us walked up to the front carriage and seven to the back. We banged on the windows, ordering them off, and went to the doors, but they wouldn't open them, so we did it for them. As soon as the doors opened we were into them, battling like fuck. Two Transport Police managed to get between us and created a gap between the two mobs but neither side would stop fighting. Everyone charged into each other and the Old Bill were swept to one side. Preston eventually pushed us up the ramp out of the train station with their sheer numbers. One of the lads shouted that the police were on their way and we fucked off before they arrived.

PHIL HOLMES

Burnley v Wigan 2000
It was Ian Wright's first game for the Clarets. I couldn't get a ticket so we all stayed in two boozers, The Turf and the Clog

and Spindle. There was a real team of us and none of us liked the Wigan wankers.

I have been diagnosed as mentally unstable so a skin-full of ale makes my head go. I don't like being handcuffed and always resist and start kicking off with the Old Bill. Anyway, we had a good drink while the match was on. There was plenty of singing and we were all having a laugh. The lad I was with, Shaun, said he had a deal to sort out in a pub in the town centre, but when we walked outside it was mayhem. There was a big mob of coppers in the middle of the road and a crew of about 200 Burnley lads were throwing bottles, glasses and bricks at them. It looked nasty.

I walked towards the police and got whacked a few times with their batons. One of the coppers said, "Fuck off Holmes." Shaun grabbed me and we moved around the coppers. The next thing I knew a police dog had attacked me. The police had lost control because the Suicide boys were running amok further up the road, attacking the Wigan mob, and the horses were contained up there.

The dog bit me on the stomach and all over my legs and I lost it. I was wearing leather gloves so I grabbed the dog by the neck and fell to the floor with it. I had all my weight on it and started smashing its head against the floor and punching it. My head had gone. The police were smashing me with their batons so I gripped the dog and put it over my head and I threw it yelping at the police. People dragged me away as they attacked the police.

It was ten days before they pulled me in and charged me with violent disorder. I was in a picture in the local paper, showing the violence, but they had blacked out my face. The case went to Crown Court five or six times, a total fuck-up. My brief told me to expect eighteen months but I ended up with a three-month sentence and a six-year ban.

Football violence is like a drug. I've had loads of convictions for it. I can't live in Burnley because of the trouble with the

Asians. I was charged with three racially motivated offences and I am banned from all the town centre pubs. The police are always on my case but I have never regretted anything. If I hadn't done these things I would be fucking boring, living in a nice house with a flash motor – fuck it. In the Eighties we used to turn over the away fans' cars after a match for fun. Those were the good old days.

SUICIDE SECTION FIVES

We, the SSF (Suicide Section Fives), were around and active from 1986 to 1989. We were a very tight unit, numbering only five or six, but everyone watched each other's back. At sixteen you had no fear. The first time the older lads noticed us was when we played Hartlepool. After the game about thirty of the older lads were going down Todmorden Road. We were right at the front and two vans went past with around twenty-five lads in, tooled up with a couple of chunks of wood. I looked behind us and discovering we were miles in front of the rest of the squad. But we thought, fuck it, let's have it, and ripped up some fencing and got into them.

The Hartlepool lads seemed shocked that five young lads were going toe to toe with twenty of them. After their main man was knocked on his arse it was game, set and match to us. I put a couple of windows through on their van as they made a swift exit. As we turned we saw that the older lads had stopped further up the road and had just watched us. They were impressed that we'd done their main boys and from then on we were allowed to travel with them. Most of our best results, though, were when we travelled on our own.

One firm we really rated was Darlington. I don't think the older lads thought much of them but they always showed at Burnley. We were in town, near the Empire, when a van full of Darlington went past us. The next thing I knew, one of our lads was chasing the van. It stopped and I was straight into the back, battling with twenty tooled-up lads who all bailed out of the van and fought with us in the middle of the road. I got my jacket slashed and a screwdriver in the head. They eventually fucked off and we decided we needed to see them again. We didn't have long to wait.

We regrouped around Yates's with a couple of other lads when someone said, "That van's fucking here." It was parked just up the road outside a toyshop. Game on. It drove off but had to stop at the roundabout. Some bailed and were on their toes but some stayed and had a go. The van driver got a bike chain wrapped around his head and was out cold. You could see the fear on the faces of the last ten or so lads left in the van. We knocked a couple of them clean out and started smashing up their van.

The best time we had was when we went on holiday to Lloret de Mar in 1998. For the first seven days it was pretty quiet. We hooked up with some Bolton lads who we'd met in the hotel, they were top class. Two or three of them had been to Burnley when we turned them over. Anyway, on the eighth night it really kicked off. Someone came into the boozer and said there were about forty lads from Barcelona looking to have it with some English. Unluckily for them we were beered up and had the rest of the boozer behind us. Four of us were straight into them before they knew what was happening. We coshed every Spaniard in sight. Four of us and a couple from Bolton did forty Barcelona. After that everyone kept telling us, "You lot from Burnley are fucking crazy."

"Yeah, we are, we're SSF."

I suppose the time when the Fives were going was a golden era. There was no CCTV and no banning orders. It's a shame the football was shite but two out of three wasn't bad. Although, of us all, only Peg Leg carried on doing the football, we still like to know how the Squad is doing. I'd like to mention the Scott

Parkers, a fucking top set of lads who sometimes backed us up. I was really saddened to hear that Cleggy had died. He was a top lad and a right laugh. Also, rest in peace Wayne Howarth and Andy McCrystal. Although they weren't part of the SSF they were part of the scene back in the Eighties.

MICK H, SSF

Hartlepool v Burnley – 1987/1988 season

We were five lads and three girls and went up in two cars, arriving around eleven o'clock and parking near the ground. We sprayed the ground with the Burnley Suicide Section Fives SSF logo, the mark of the Suicide youth section. We took a walk down to the docks and a bus went past with a lad and his bird on the back seat. The lad started flashing us the V sign and telling us to fuck off. When the bus pulled in at a depot, we ran over and pulled open the emergency exit and one of the lads jumped in and punched him. The driver jumped out and grabbed one of the lads, Sutts, in a bearhug but me and Bizzy went over and banged him a couple of times and he soon let go.

The next thing we knew, about fifteen bus drivers were running out of the depot towards us. We were on our toes in case they had called the Old Bill. We walked up the road and went into a boozer full of Burnley fans, stayed about half an hour and then went into the shopping centre. We had a small bet with each other as to who would draw the first blood, so anyone who looked like a boyo got smacked or kicked. We walked along just whacking anyone who we thought would fight back but no-one did and we ended up in another pub.

After a while, Bizzy, who was pissed out of his head, went outside. Moments later another Burnley lad came in and told us it was going off outside. Only eight of us managed to get out before the doors were locked and we found ourselves faced with a mob of around fifty. We had to fight for our lives. One lad nearly got cut but the blade snapped on his back. Jay was fighting with a couple of lads when the Old Bill turned up. One tried to grab him from behind but he cracked the copper with his elbow and was nicked. Me and Sutts were kicking and punching heads all over the place. Sutts was then nicked and Hartlepool fucked off across the road to a boozer, then hid behind some bushes and threw bricks and coins at us.

We set off walking towards the ground and a dog van pulled up at a roundabout, nicked Bizzy and threw him into the back of the van. The dog was in one cage and he was in another. We were down to two lads and three birds but carried on towards the ground and saw all the lads we had just been fighting. They looked at us but wouldn't come across.

After the game we waited for the rest of the Fives to be released. It was about eight o'clock before we set off home. We were all chuffed to bits and buzzing. It was a top result.

AN ANONYMOUS CONTRIBUTOR

Plymouth Away

Quite a few of us had decided to make a weekend of it. Plymouth was always a testing fixture. We met up at Saturday lunch and made our way towards Holme Park. We drank in the Penny Come Quick pub, a favourite of their mob, the Central Element. There were a few lads in, but as there were around thirty of us, nothing happened. Unknown to me, one of the lads had told them we were staying the night and we would meet them up the Barbican area.

As usual for Burnley fans, the game was a boring non-event. Twenty-five of us left the ground, walked across the car park and stood behind some bushes out of the sight of the Old Bill. We could see about the same number of their lads walking towards us. We steamed into them and a few of their lads slipped on the muddy grass and got a good kicking. Plymouth carried on trying to have a do all the way back to the Penny Come Quick, but by then the Old Bill had us.

We started the night at the Barbican and most of us were pissed by eight o'clock. I walked outside the pub and I saw two Burnley lads, K and Buz, with forty Plymouth round them. I went back inside and told the rest of the lads. I didn't expect it, but they all came out. It went mad. Bins, bottles, feet and fists were all being thrown. We ran them up and down the street, backwards and forwards. It was solid toe to toe for about ten minutes. We needed a breather so we went into the Dolphin pub where we met five marines who had been watching the battle. They asked if they could join in against the Plymouth lads.

We went outside again and it was fucking madness for about five minutes. Three Old Bill turned up, one a woman, and by now it seemed all of the Central Element had arrived. I swear the woman copper said, "Come on Burnley, get into them." A couple of us ran down a side street with the Old Bill woman chasing us with her truncheon out. I rolled over a car bonnet and got my best shirt ripped off. The soles of my shoes were also hanging off from the fight.

Eventually it died down. I went back to the bed and breakfast and got changed. We met back up at a pub on Union Street and around twenty Plymouth lads came in and sat down opposite us. They had a drink and acknowledged us but both sets of lads were too fucked to carry on. We went our separate ways. I've since met up with Plymouth in Bulgaria, we had a few drinks together and friendships were made, although one of the lads who was hurt still held a grudge.

ANOTHER ANONYMOUS CONTRIBUTOR

Wrexham v Burnley – 1987/1988 season
I was sixteen years old and it was my first game away with the Suicide Section Fives. We had a good, tight-knit little mob and

we watched each other's backs all the time. We went down in cars for the Tuesday night match and parked up on some hospital grounds. As we came out of the car park, thirty lads were walking towards us. Some had umbrellas. We looked at each other and said, "Let's do 'em." A lad called Jay ran at them and we all followed. As we got closer they panicked and most of them turned and fucked off. We got hold of a few of them and they got a good slap and a few kicks. We chased them down the road carrying milk bottles.

As we reached the bottom of the road we realised we were outside the home end of the ground. I asked Jay what we were going to do but he was already crossing the road towards their lads. As we got into the middle of the road a couple of Frontline approached us. One said, "Let's do 'em," but his mate replied, "They're only kids and they've just done us once." Then they walked away towards the turnstiles.

After the game, we mobbed up outside the ground and a lad came up and said, "If you want it, we'll meet you at Sainsbury's," but everyone got split up by the Old Bill. We headed back to the car and there were police all down the road stopping and searching fans. I think someone was slashed that night. For my first game it was a good result and I was hooked.

PEG LEG

Bulgaria v England – June 1999

I went out to Bulgaria for my stag do. There was eighty-four of us. Only four of us travelled together and had been on the beer for two days solid before travelling. We flew out on the Sunday morning from Leeds/Bradford airport. We arrived at Bourgass without transport but managed to blag our way onto a coach full of Brummies. One lad ripped the baggage rack down and threw it through a window. I knew it was going to be a good trip from then on.

That night the four of us went out for a quiet drink and ended up back in the hotel bar. Two of us stayed up until about four o'clock with around forty Preston lads. We were talking to their lads when some gobby cunt came over and started mouthing off. Dave said to his mates, "Tell him to sit down or I'll knock him out," which he did.

Dave, Scoot and me all went out on the Monday and were arrested for three offences. The police were heavy-handed and gave us a few slaps. We were released fourteen hours later after paying a small fine. On the way to Sofia, I bumped into some Wolves fans I had met before. They had attacked a pub full of Burnley on Monday and were asking if I was there. I told them that I wasn't. I was talking to them for a while but then had to leave to catch the coach.

On the Thursday we were staying in one part of Sunny Beach and all the other Burnley were on the other side of town. They turned up at the bar where we were eating and said they were going to do Wolves because of them attacking the Burnley pub. We arranged to meet up on Friday.

It was about teatime and after a few dozen bottles of wine and pills we saw a few Wolves lads outside a bar, letting off firecrackers. Later, we found them outside a shop. I ran up and smacked one of them but no-one else did anything. Wolves had been bragging all week about doing Burnley but, outside this shop, with even numbers, they didn't want to know, in fact they were shaking quite a bit. Later that night we all fell out of taxis at a pub called the Red Lion and, as we walked up the path, they ambushed us from out of the trees. It was a bit mad, people were "double-barrelled" as we call it, with a can of gas in each hand, and they were just spraying anyone. The next thing I knew I woke up in my hotel room.

Saturday was very quiet, as we were leaving that night, but we had heard that Wolves were at their hotel with bottles singing "We hate Burnley" while surrounded by the police.

That night, with our bags in the hotel lobby, ready to go, and the four of us in the restaurant having a meal, two taxis of Wolves lads pulled up and asked Burnley outside. Some Burnley, West Brom, Preston and Bolton took up the challenge. Wolves smashed all the lights and slung a few gas grenades into the crew. We heard the commotion and ran outside. It was like NATO had gone through.

AF

The Long March, 1983
It became a tradition over the years that each time we played Blackburn Rovers, everyone would meet at Burnley Central train station to catch the local service train from Colne to Blackpool. Easter Monday 1983 was no different and as I stood on the platform with the lads from my local pub, the Rose and Crown, different mobs from all over East Lancashire and parts of Yorkshire were arriving to go on the crusade. That was one of the strange things about supporting Burnley, lads travelled from a wide area to support the club.

Excitement grew as the train pulled into the station. In those days there was no Old Bill with cameras in your face filming every movement. We were the ones who decided how we would travel and what pubs we were going in. The train pulled out of the station with a good 400 lads on board. Within ten minutes we were arriving at Accrington, where no doubt there would be a good turnout from the "Accy Clarets". Accrington is halfway between Burnley and Blackburn and had a divided loyalty when it came to football, split three ways between Burnley, Blackburn and the famous Accrington Stanley.

A cry went up that there were some Bastards (our pet name for Blackburn fans) in the town centre. A mass surge of hungry warriors steamed down the station steps and onto the main road into the centre. "Bastards, where are you, Bastards, where are you?" was the war cry as startled shoppers stared at the early morning invasion. It turned out to be a wild goose chase and there was no sign of our enemy. One bright spark came up with the suggestion that we walk into Blackburn to avoid the Old Bill. Before anyone could argue we about-turned and started walking down Blackburn Road.

After about half an hour we had gone through Oswaldtwistle and were approaching the outskirts of Blackburn. I looked back at the lads and was impressed with the sight. The column stretched back for a good couple of hundred yards. Another half hour and we were approaching the town centre. A couple of patrol cars latched onto us. We set off at a jog to ensure we reached the centre before police reinforcements arrived. One police car knocked a motorcyclist off his bike in a bid to keep up with us. Within a few minutes we had reached our goal but as we triumphantly marched round there was no opposition in site. Many shops were closed as it was Easter and so were the pubs.

We headed towards the train station and two of Blackburn's main pubs, but as we walked across the Boulevard, loads of Old Bill arrived from nowhere and began herding us down Market Street in the direction of Ewood Park. Their heavy-handed treatment was not appreciated and as we approached the railway bridge, it went off. The Old Bill drew their truncheons and used dogs in an effort to restore order. Quite a few arrests were made but it still didn't dampen the enthusiasm of the mob as we marched on to Ewood Park.

It was around one-thirty when we reached the ground, ridiculously early, but there was nothing we could do about it, there was no chance of breaking out of the escort. We were in the ground for two and the Darwen end soon filled up. In those days there were never any all-ticket matches so no-one ever struggled to get into the ground. Our end was packed with nutters. I looked across to the Blackburn end and laughed to myself. It was a typical Blackburn turnout, nothing. How could a town that is one and half times the size of Burnley offer so little resistance? Over the years I have read many books about life on the terraces and I cannot remember any team being run by a mob of Blackburn.

The first half passed without any major incidents, although a few arrests were made for the usual things like disorderly behaviour. Things began to liven up at half time when an old boot that belonged to a guy called "Billy the Werewolf" started being thrown around, resulting in a mass scrum. Billy had got his nickname when he used to climb up into the rafters in the Longside at Turf Moor. He used to swing over no-man's land and hang above the away fans howling like a werewolf. Suddenly, a few police decided to put a stop to this unruly behaviour and made their way into the scrum. What a grave mistake. Within seconds they were set upon and only just managed to get out of the Darwen end in one piece.

The fuse had been lit and now it was about to go off. The snack bar in the corner of the end was invaded and relieved of its takings as well as its stock. Another attempt was made to restore order by the police with their truncheons drawn but this was rapidly repelled as by now there were hundreds of lads of all different ages up for it and determined to show Bastards how mental they were. In the meantime the players were back out and on the pitch. The second half had started but no-one was interested in the football, as off-the-field activities were proving far more entertaining. Some of the younger lads climbed up into the rafters of the roof and began to kick through the old asbestos panelling, which fell on the unfortunate fans below. This then provided missiles which were launched onto the pitch, hitting players from both teams as well as several police. The referee had no alternative other than to take the players off.

Frank Casper, the Burnley manager, tried to calm things down by appealing to the fans but he was met with a barrage of asbestos too. "We hate Bastards, we hate Bastards," was the cry from the away terrace, which was rapidly becoming an open end. Out of the corner of my eye I saw a large force of police assembling with truncheons drawn and dogs on their leads ready to pounce. They made a mass charge across the terrace, hitting anyone in their way; and let the dogs have a free bite of anything that ended up close to their mouths. A counter charge by the Burnley mob was forced back and, despite fierce resistance, the police finally managed to regain control of the terrace. Many arrests were made and many fans had injuries sustained from the crack of a truncheon or a piece of flying asbestos.

The game restarted twenty minutes after the players had left the field. True to form we lost 2-1, but as we left the ground no-one was talking about what had happened on the pitch. There were police everywhere but no sign of the Bastards. They had seen what mood the Burnley lads were in and had made the wise choice to do a quick exit at the final whistle. We were escorted to a local train station, Mill Hill, therefore avoiding the town centre. A special train had been laid on for us for the twenty minute journey back to our town.

When we finally pulled out of the station, the wrecking mentality of the terraces was still apparent among a large majority of those on the train. Seats were going through windows along with everything else that wasn't nailed down. There were only a few police aboard and they were powerless to prevent the destruction. The communication cord was continuously pulled, which to be honest was a pain in the arse as we wanted to get back to go on the beer and celebrate our "victory". By the time we reached Rosegrove station, three miles out of Burnley, the train had to be abandoned as I think the brakes had seized. Everyone made their own way into town and all had a tale to tell.

The next day all the tabloid newspapers as well as the local television stations reported on what had happened at the match. "Animals!" was the headline in the *Burnley Express* and Frank Casper said he was ashamed of the behaviour of the fans. The Darwen End had to be closed for the rest of the season due to its unsafe condition.

Many years have passed since that match, but on the rare occasion we play Bastards, the songs remind them of what happened at Ewood in 1983. They cascade round the ground in celebration of that great day.

AF: The Coldest Away Journey Ever

It was the mid-Eighties and Burnley were due to play Reading away at Elm Park. As this was not one of the most attractive fixtures, due to the length of the journey, I knew our turnout would be low. Reading weren't known to have a particularly good mob either. We hired a Transit van and everybody met at the bus station at seven in the morning for the long journey south. Despite my misgivings, we still managed to assemble thirty good lads.

I managed to scrounge a front passenger seat, therefore avoiding the uncomfortable ride experienced by those in the back. A card game helped them pass the miles away. We reached Reading at one o'clock and parked out of the way. We found a pub not far from the ground that was fairly empty and stayed there before making our way to the ground. We didn't rate Reading as they never showed at Turf Moor and each time we had been there before their lads seemed to be a mixture of every Cockney club going.

We took our place on the open end behind the goal and it was good to see that there was a decent turnout of around 500 in total. Whatever people say about Burnley, we always had good away support and when we were playing down south there was always a good contingent of Cockney Clarets to make the numbers up.

Reading's mob was to our left and things began to get heated, with various threats about what was going to happen outside the ground after the match. I was surprised by how many there were of the opposition but, like I said before, how many were actually Reading? The Clarets lost as usual but that was par for the course. We grouped together at the bottom of the terrace, and, as we exited the ground, we turned right in the direction of Reading's end. As we started walking up the hill their mob appeared from around the corner and we found we were well outnumbered. The usual cry, "Su, su, Suicide," went up to signal things were about to happen when Reading steamed into us, throwing bricks as they ran down the hill. We stood our ground as long as we could, but as both the hill and the numbers were against us, we ended up retreating to the main road. The police soon waded in and separated both mobs. This was no disgrace to us; Reading never travelled to Burnley and they had never had a go at us on our patch.

During the melee we discovered two of our lads, Finny and Ivan, had been nicked. This was a blow as now we would have to travel to the local cop shop and wait for them to be released. We got directions and made our way back to the van. Ten minutes later we arrived at the nick and the desk sergeant informed us that the lads would be released at half past six. This meant there would still be time to get a beer once we were back in Burnley.

Some of the lads went into a pub round the corner for a swift one before we set off but there was no sign of the lads at six-thirty. Another hour went by and we kept getting told that their release was imminent but I think they held them longer on purpose just to piss us off. Eventually, three hours later than promised, they were let out. We rounded everyone up and decided to get some petrol before we set off back.

We found a garage and I jumped out of the front seat to put the juice in. The four of us in the front were all made up that we would be having a comfortable ride home. As I started to put the petrol in I noticed a gang of coloured lads in the corner of the garage who looked a bit dodgy. The next thing I knew, our lads were out of the van and directing abuse at the coloured lads who quickly disappeared.

I paid for the petrol and settled into my front seat for the long journey back but, just as we were about to set off, a car pulled up in front of us and reversed up to the bumper of the van. I looked in the passenger mirror and saw a coloured bloke approaching the door. Before I knew it he had smashed the window with a car jack and he began lashing out at us in the front seat. Another guy had appeared and began smashing the front windscreen with a baseball bat. Unbeknown to us there were two cars directly behind us and the blokes from those were attacking the lads in the back with various weapons. Robbo, the driver of the van, desperately tried to get it into reverse. He managed it eventually, but the van mounted the bonnet of the car behind us. He slammed it into first gear and managed to pull away from the garage forecourt. We had truly had our arses spanked.

We stopped about a mile away from the garage to survey the damage. The van had no windows left and plenty of holes down the side. One of the lads had what looked like a broken cheekbone, courtesy of a baseball bat. Others had various bumps and cuts but they had managed to stop the attackers getting into the back of the van. We put the smashed windscreen in the back and the lads lit a fire on it to keep warm, then we set off back up the motorway.

In the front it was absolutely freezing. Robbo was having trouble driving as the cold was getting in his eyes. We had to stop at every service station to get warm. He even tried driving with a cardboard box on his head with two holes cut out for his eyes. It took ages to get home and we finally landed back in Burnley at eight on Sunday morning. We dropped the lads off, took the van back to the rental firm in Blackburn and dumped it outside. Just as I was looking forward to some shut-eye my car ran out of petrol on the motorway.

AF: The Bus Hijack

A Sunday afternoon in the early Eighties and we were playing Millwall at home. It was also Gaz B's twenty-first birthday and we had hired a double-decker bus to pick us up after the match and take us to a neighbouring town for a drink.

Nothing much happened during the day as, not only was it pissing down, but Millwall had only brought a couple of hundred on coaches and they were escorted straight to the ground. Everyone met in the Park View pub outside the ground at six-thirty and, judging by the quality of the lads on display, an interesting night lay ahead. The bus turned up and the Scottish driver looked apprehensive as he watched our motley crew board his vehicle.

"Where to?"

"Blackburn."

As everyone knows, Blackburn are despised by Burnley, so the idea of going there for a drink without there being any trouble was something out of Fantasy Island. We pulled up on the Boulevard outside the train station at seven o'clock. A couple of pubs in the area seemed lively so we all marched into the Brewer's Arms in the hope of finding some opposition. One of the lads announced our arrival by throwing a stool through a window but none of Blackburn's mob were in and the landlord refused to serve us, so we decided to try our luck up the road.

As we headed back up the Boulevard towards the Star and

Garter a few police arrived and tried to round us up. One of the coppers' helmets was knocked off and snatched by Steve H, which resulted in it kicking off. The police were hopelessly outnumbered and were no match for the baying mob. Sirens were heard in the distance and, before you knew it, snarling dogs were biting everything in sight. Within five minutes the police had managed to force everyone back onto the bus except five of the party who were helping them with their enquiries.

They escorted us to the outskirts of the town and then, miraculously, disappeared, obviously presuming we would head back to Burnley. We had other ideas. We told the driver to head to Whalley, a small village five miles outside of Blackburn which has quite a few pubs for its size as well as being a stronghold for our hated rivals. Within twenty minutes we were marching down the main street to the Whalley Arms. The look on people's faces was a treat as seventy football hooligans invaded their posh pubs, ruining their Saturday night out. Alas, there were no Bastard fans in sight, but the entertainment soon got underway.

A lad with us from Accrington and on leave from the Army ran into a pub across from the Whalley and threw a smoke bomb into the main lounge. It was one of those used in mock battles. Green smoke soon filled the pub, causing a mass evacuation with women screaming and dragging their husbands behind them. "Burnley boys, we are here" filled the night air along with the smoke. Soon the first police arrived in a Land Rover and radioed for back-up. This was when it really went off. As soon as they tried to nick anyone, everyone else waded in to rescue them, even if it meant dragging them out of the car, handcuffed. Windows were going in and there was a mass brawl on the high street. The police, using dogs, eventually forced us back towards the bus. A dog jumped onto the bus but was soon kicked off. Finally, everyone who hadn't been nicked was back on board.

We set off with two riot vans in front of us and two at the rear, and at each set of traffic lights we were waved through by other police. But the wrecking spree wasn't over. Every window on the bus was kicked out in a show of defiance. As we approached the police station the bus slowed down to turn a corner and at this moment some of the lads on board made a desperate attempt to escape by forcing open the front doors. About ten got out and fled towards the canal. The rest of us arrived at the cop shop to be greeted by two lines of coppers. We had to walk through the lines and listen to their remarks about us being a shower of shit from Turf Moor. As there were so many of us they had to put eight in each cell, which was great, as we could all relive the tales of what had gone on that night. We were dragged out one by one and had our fingerprints and photographs taken and our hands checked for signs of blood. The police were trying to track down who had caused the damage to the bus and they assumed that anyone with bloody knuckles had put a window through. As the night wore on, the songs from each cell began to die down as the beer began to take effect and everyone crashed out.

Early the following morning we were let out one by one with a caution, but those who the police thought had put the windows through were charged. Eventually, a deal was struck that if the damage to the bus was paid for, the charges would be dropped. Over the next few weeks a lot of us were £25 lighter as we contributed to the fund. On the Monday after the birthday celebration I read in the local paper how the driver had reported his bus had been hijacked and forced to go to Whalley. He even said that he had worked in the roughest areas of Glasgow but had never seen anything as bad as what he had gone through that night. Hijacked? You're having a laugh!

CHAPTER NINETEEN

SUICIDE YOUTH SQUAD

Like many mobs, Burnley's Suicide Squad has seen a big increase in youth membership over the past five years. This section tries to explain why the Burnley Suicide Youth Squad, or SYS, was held in high esteem by many other youth mobs. Because many of the lads involved are still very active it has been difficult to go into too much detail about events, but it is a fair and accurate account of the bigger picture, and has been written not by me but by one of their main players, who can tell the full, inside story.

The Suicide Youth Squad started at the beginning of a new wave of football hooligans after the Millennium. Anyone who knows the scene knows that mass offs involving hundreds of lads on each side don't happen anymore and weapons are hardly ever carried because of the constant section 60s. Before the police's Operation Fixture in Burnley, SYS pulled forty lads regularly for a home match and twenty for away matches, but had the ability to pull over seventy for big matches when the younger youth lads, who we liked to call yo-yo's, were out. They have used expandable batons, CS gas, pool balls, glasses, bottles, stun guns, chairs, tables, and basically anything they could get their hands on at the time. It was also known to us that a couple would carry knives on occasions; these were very rarely used, but every mob has them.

Contrary to their image of being scruffy bastards, the youth look the business as well as doing the business. This came as part and parcel of the casual culture, and youth lads were easily identified, their clothes acting almost as a uniform. Unfortunately, like elsewhere in the country, townies have jumped on the Burberry bandwagon and we have been labelled with them.

Prior to 1999, different youth lads from different areas and towns around Burnley came to Turf Moor, but none travelled together and, more importantly, none of these lads organised anything. They were, however, on the edge of the action, champing at the bit to get involved. In 1999, home and away against Millwall, youth lads were involved in fighting. Inside the New Den, they took part in ripping up some of the stand and in fighting outside on the walk towards the train station. At home they were part of the massive Burnley mobs that roamed the centre on St George's Day trying to get at the Millwall escort that had tried putting on a show inside the ground; we didn't get at the escort but had it with the police, with whom we were to get very familiar over the next couple of years.

In the next season, Bastards were relegated from the Premiership, and Suicide Squad had huge mobs out for both games. This was no surprise because the last time we played them was April 4, 1983, when Burnley ripped Ewood Park to pieces, before most of the youth lads were even born, but they had heard so many stories of that famous day. At home, lads old and young looked for any Bastard mobs that were about but we were disappointed with the seventy that arrived with the Old Bill. Afterwards, we tried to find any that had slipped the escort, but couldn't, so battling with the Old Bill commenced. Due to the intense and fierce hatred Burnley have towards Bastards, and the frustration at the defeat they inflicted on us, Burnley town centre was trashed. However this was not done by Burnley's lads, but by a load of Burnley's drunken barmies.

In April 2001 Burnley went to Blackburn for the first time in seventeen years with more than 800 lads. The SYS hadn't yet been formed but loads of youth lads travelled. We didn't see any Bastards but the police operation was one of the biggest ever launched. In Accrington, after the game, the Old Bill were attacked when they walked into the pub we were using and one was seriously injured by a glass. In the same month we played Birmingham at home and the SS, with youth lads in tow, tried to attack the escort after the match. The Old Bill got in the way outside the White Lion and came under attack from a shower of glasses. They chased our mob back to the doors of the pub, let the dogs off, and then traded batons for glasses in the doorway for up to ten minutes. This led to arrests and charges of affray, which were many young lads' first football-related dealings with the Old Bill and the courts. That season saw many youth lads catch the football violence "bug" and games like Birmingham just strengthened their desire to form a youth firm.

In 2001, two groups of Burnley youth started to travel together. They had an average age of just seventeen and had several months' experience of using the Internet to keep up to date with hooligan activity up and down the country. The Web was an invaluable tool while setting up the SYS, as it provided easy communications between youth firms and helped recruitment. These lads met up with some Leicester Young Baby Squad at Coventry. The YBS had been going a bit longer than our youth and taught us some lessons. Before long another group of youth lads from Burnley joined the lads who'd previously travelled to Coventry. These new lads also had contacts with Leicester's YBS through the Net. The new mob of lads from Burnley was a couple of years older and had more numbers. This was the first time in recent years that any sort of Youth Mob had crossed the barriers created by the areas people come from, and they agreed that if they wanted to be Suicide then we had to make the older lads sit up and take notice. At the time they didn't realise how much the youth respected them and were in awe of them. The only way to gain their respect was to come together as one and prove they didn't need them to organise or to fight their battles, hence the SYS was born.

A founder member explained: our first objective was to get our own pub, one that none of the older lads ever frequented. We found the Bar Mambo, formerly the Bridge, and soon struck up an arrangement that the landlord would open up early on any match day we wanted. Our first arranged meet in this pub, and probably our most significant because of the feud that it started, was against Nottingham Forest. At the time Forest regarded themselves very highly, as youth firms go, and we realised that these were the youth we were going to have to perform against, because from day one we wanted to be the best mob around and we would stop at nothing to get that title.

Forty of us met in Bar Mambo at eleven o'clock and waited for the Forest Nasty Squad to arrive. All week and even up until around one o'clock on the day of the game they told us that they were coming on their own coach. However, when we rang Forest, an hour before the game, they said that there were eleven of them on a supporters' coach. Most of our lads thought they were bullshitting. However, later we found out that they were a game set of lads. We knew they sometimes travelled tooled up, so SYS also tooled up for the first time with all the usual shit and stun guns. Because the FNS only came with eleven, they asked if we could pick our eleven to meet them. We laughed at them, called them a joke, and told them how to get out of the away end without Old Bill, but they just fucked off on their coach.

The next big home match was against Preston on a Sunday. Their Youth had assured us they were coming so we met up at

Sidewalk early doors. The game was an early kick-off and not many older lads thought Preston would come. We went for beer in Yates's and, although it was a derby game, hardly any older lads were out so early. One of the youth lads went to the Bar Mambo to suss if any more youth were about, came back and said Preston were drinking in the Swan with no Old Bill. As we walked out, the PPS came charging out the doors of the Swan. We shouted the older lads out of the pub and started walking towards them. We were ten SS and twenty SYS, while the PPS had more than forty older lads. Preston charged towards us, got within twenty yards, dodged a couple of glasses, and bottled it. Watching them run fifty yards then seeing their arses go was priceless. We went into them but the police arrived. One brave, sorry, stupid Preston lad ran all the way round the block, reckoning he could attack us from the back while his mates would sweep the floor with us. He didn't take into account his mates' arses going and got a kicking for his troubles.

That was the first time we received any kind of recognition from the Suicide Squad. News spread fast, and an hour later about 300 lads were out asking what had happened. We had gained a bit of attention. After the match the PPS tried announcing themselves under the Culvert, outside the Clogg and Spindle. It was pitch black and nobody knew who anyone else was, so it was a free-for-all, with Burnley youth fighting with older Burnley, neither recognising the other, a real problem in the first couple of years. In the end the police got in the middle and pushed Preston towards TK Maxx but we had split them up and all they wanted to do was get out of town. Some tried fucking off in taxis, so we opened the doors and handed the slaps out accordingly. We roamed the streets in small mobs looking for lads who had got lost and gave the ones we caught a kicking. We got used to hunting down small mobs like this because we wanted Burnley to be a place where lads felt threatened, but we left the scarfers alone, we knew the rules.

At this time the SYS still travelled separately from the older lads but the Preston incident got people talking about us. The following week on the Turf a couple of older lads asked us to meet them for an away match at Stockport, and we knew that this was our chance to make an impact. Thirty SYS met at the bus station at nine o'clock and caught the X43 into Manchester for a meet in the Moon Under Water pub. Some of our lads were a mess when we arrived due to bottles of beer, wine and pills that had been taken at the bus station. This seemed to worry the older lot because we were being on the loud side, but we knew the score, we were just young and excited.

About 100 mixed older and youth waited in Manchester for Stockport to turn up as promised, but they didn't show, so we travelled to Stockport in two mobs. Stockport had recently been relegated so, as it was the last time we'd play them for a while, this was supposed to be their going down party. Lads had been slashed in previous years and they promised more of the same in Manchester. When we arrived in Stockport, the police put us in a pub outside the train station. Stockport made a move on the pub and we tried to get out, but the police forced us back in. We pelted the police with some pool balls and were escorted to the ground.

After the game a couple of youth noticed a group of more than a dozen Stockport bullying scarfers as they were leaving the ground. Sensing this could be their opportunity, they got on the blower and told the other youth where they were. While waiting for the rest of the lads, the two youth fronted the Stockport not really knowing what to expect. A couple of blows were exchanged and the usual flow of adrenalin hit but the OB arrived in due time with the rest of the youth lads. The police pushed us down a terraced street and, in their wisdom, pushed Stockport down the street parallel. Consequently, thirty seconds later we were face to face with the same lads. There was a short stand off, but we didn't need a second invitation and steamed straight into them screaming "Su, Su, Suicide" and trading punches whilst one copper tried to stop it. The youth use the same battle-cry as the older Suicide lads because we have seen it used so effectively in the past. It puts the fear of death into you when you hear 100 lads chanting it whilst charging towards you. It can definitely put a mob on the back foot and when this happens the battle is half won.

We chased Stockport down the street and gave it to the ones we caught. We were a bit disappointed with their "party" but at the same time were buzzing because the SYS had gone there to prove a point, and we had done it in full view of our older lads. The police escorted us back to Manchester city centre where we waited in the Waldorf, because Stockport had been shown up and wanted to have another pop. After an hour, up to twenty lads walked past the windows, looking in. We ran out and the first few got bricks thrown at them before they ran off down Piccadilly Gardens. It turned out that they had planned to mob up at the same pub, but didn't realise we were already there.

The police arrived and tried to contain us in the pub by letting the dogs off and baton charging. We tried to get out through the cellar and the flat above the pub but the police wouldn't let us, even when we set fires for the smoke alarms. Eventually we were escorted down Piccadilly to Victoria, where we saw the Stockport lads shoot off in front of us. At the train station the police formed a tunnel that we were forced down by dogs from behind whilst being hit on the back and legs with batons. All in all that day belonged to the SYS because the older lads who doubted us in the past now had to sit up and take notice.

Now they had started to accept us, we travelled with them for the rest of the season. About twenty-five youth went with them to Sheffield United later that season, accompanying well over 100 older lads who were on a stag do. It was a beautiful shorts and t-shirt day with the sun shining. The usual stop at Bradford made us think the day might be over before it had started when the OB collared us on the train, mainly because some youth lads, still learning, wouldn't pay. As we arrived at Sheffield the station was full of coppers, who searched everyone and took details. Wisely, stun guns had been left at home, along with the other weapons that we had been carrying during earlier games. We thought we were getting escorted to a pub but after they searched us the OB just let us walk into the city, closely followed by a copper-chopper. Most wanted to get in boozers in the centre; the young lads tried to get everyone nearer the ground but the old lads settled into two pubs, and who were we to argue?

As we got to the Cricketers a couple of Sheffield's BBC came out but the road was full of police. Because the away stand runs alongside the road that we were being escorted along, the police couldn't contain everyone. Some needed tickets from the office at the top of the road, where the United fans were queuing to get in. Scuffles broke out all the way up the road as lads came from behind the parked coaches. When we got to the ticket office lads were waiting to get in their end and there were hardly any Old Bill so we called it on. A few older lads came running into the gap shouting, "BBC," and it went for a bit until the horses came steaming in and separated the two groups.

Inside the ground about twenty youth sat together on the bottom tier and what seemed like hundreds of BBC filled up their end block and were held back by stewards and coppers. At the time we thought it was going to be hard after the match with the numbers that seemed to pouring in but, as there were over 150 of us and probably another 100 in the ground, we were game. As this was happening, the stewards kept coming in and dragging us out, so we went into the stewards, who called for police reinforcements. This led to ten SYS being thrown out of the ground and collared by the police. This was the first time the OB let us know they were onto us and warned us we were being watched. We now realised we were having an effect on the Old Bill, and it made us more determined to make them earn their money.

After we came out we tried to lose the police for a while but were eventually collared and escorted. On the way to the station some older Sheffield lad with his name tattooed on his neck walked through the escort, which resulted in some scuffles. As the OB tried to get him out we tried to persuade them he was with us, calling him by name.

We were put on a train, which pulled into Rotherham while hundreds of Man City were waiting for their train home. We started to charge off to get over to the stairs and the Old Bill baton-charged us, trying to nick some young lads. As they grabbed one, an older lad banged the copper clean in the face. They didn't like this and let off the CS gas. As we couldn't get off the train through the doors we got some shatter hammers, smashed the windows and tried getting on to the tracks, which the Old Bill also put a stop to. Some youth were nicked for it when we arrived in Leeds, but the police got the wrong ones and didn't charge them, just kept them in. As we had some time before the Burnley train, we filed out into the Wetherspoons in the station. Some Leeds who'd arrived back from Villa early got wind and came round. Some of the lads knew each other from living near us and the England games and nothing happened. Although they were seasoned older lads, their twenty wouldn't have lived with our mob at that time. The OB shut the pub and decided it was safer to put us on coaches than to leave us in the station.

By this time the SYS was an established mob and willing to travel to call it on. We were also starting to dabble in petty fraud to finance our trips away. One such was Grimsby. We decided to make a weekend of it and seven of us set off on the Friday. We contacted Scunthorpe Youth, as they had been spouting all over the Internet. We got the train from Manchester but stopped off in Scunthorpe on the way and rang them from a boozer next to the train station. We told them there were only seven of us but we would fight any number they wanted. We felt invincible. After half an hour we rang them again and asked if they were up for playing ball and they said they were on their way. Another half hour went by and still no sign, so we sent out two spotters. Sure enough, ten minutes later we got the nod that twenty of them were thirty seconds away.

We caught them by surprise and called it on in the middle of a busy main road outside their train station. Their faces dropped. We called it on again but they said that they didn't know what it was all about. We thought that we had pulled the wrong lads, that they were just some boys on their way out on the beer, so we apologised and let them pass. Half got through when one of them said, "You Burnley bastards." That was it, batons out, "Su, su, Suicide", and we steamed them. A nearby skip was emptied and we took great pleasure in turning over twenty lads between the seven of us.

We were just about to board the train for Grimsby when another phone call came. They were calling it on again but this time they wanted us to find them and gave us directions to a local park, ten minutes away. The area we were walking into was a pretty rough council estate, but as was said earlier we felt invincible. Were we young and naive? Maybe, but we didn't give a fuck. We spotted them, jumped a wall and screamed. They thought about standing but after the first couple got slapped they were again on their toes. We set off back to the train station and were confronted by an angry looking geezer. Sensing a bit of aggro, one of our lads fronted him and asked him what was wrong. It turned out he was the father of one of the Scunthorpe youth lads, and had seen him running. We explained the situation and he made his lad apologise for wasting our time. Then he dragged him indoors for, no doubt, a good slapping for disgracing the family name.

From there we went on a major night out in Grimsby then got up early to make a call to have it on with their youth, only to be told he was getting his hair cut and, surprise, surprise, his phone was turned off for the rest of the day. But it turned out to be a very good drinking day in Sunny Scunny.

In the same season we ran small numbers of Crewe at their gaff; ten of us went in the Man City end but didn't play up when we got dicked 5–0; and we tried all day to get at the small number of Coventry youth at home, even going so far as blocking the railway lines and showering them on the train station with bottles from the milk factory behind it. Every home match turned into a game of cat and mouse with the OB as we tried every possible way to get at the away lads. We would not take no for an answer, which would end up with us getting at whatever we could around the ground or town, trying all the time to make Burnley a place you'd think twice about coming to again.

The season was coming to an end and Forest were away at Preston on the Sunday whilst we were at home. This gave the FNS their opportunity to make amends for their false promises at Turf Moor. One thing the SYS didn't do was bullshit; if we couldn't make it to a meet we would let the other firm know as soon as possible. The FNS had been making threats for the previous couple of months that they were going to "bring our skinheads up to Burnley, twat the SYS and then twat the Pakis." After their last turnout we weren't holding our breath.

We met in a boozer in Burnley on Saturday morning about eleven o'clock with the usual weapons, hoping that they would bring enough lads to match our seventeen. A youth lad from Wigan had joined us, but the others were SYS. Right on cue, FNS rang up saying they didn't feel comfortable coming to Burnley and wanted to meet halfway, in Blackburn, so it would be fairer. SYS accepted the invitation. Half an hour later they rang again and told us they didn't want to come to Blackburn, so we hung up the phone, deciding we weren't prepared to be fucked off another time by the FNS. We made the trip to Blackpool, which was dodgy as there were hundreds of Forest there for the weekend, and landed at about three o'clock. We decided not to announce our arrival too soon, but to search the boozers for them.

We had stopped for some grub at a chip shop when some youth lads with skinheads came around the corner and gave it the big one. We steamed into them and scattered them everywhere. A few were chased into their bed and breakfast accommodation and the door was smashed in but then the OB arrived and we split up. A couple of us walked around the corner, straight into a mob of more than sixty older Forest lads. They looked a real mean set of bastards and we decided not to hang about. We ended up mobbing up and ringing FNS to make sure it was them and it turned out it wasn't, but they did want a meet. We told them where to go and they duly obliged, turning up with about twenty lads, all tooled up. Taking nothing away from FNS because it was our own stupid fault, some of our lads had fucked off into an arcade which left about five of us on the front door when they came bouncing across the road waving their batons. They hesitated, gave us the time we needed to get a few more lads out and we backed them off to the tramlines with little scuffles going on. With our numbers still shy, we knew that we were going to have to stick together solidly as they outweighed us in weapons and manpower.

A tram came down the prom and split the two groups up.

This was our chance. One of our lads shouted, "When the tram goes past, we're gonna run 'em." Sure enough, thirty seconds after the Suicide cry came out, we steamed them and they scattered into the road and down the front, and by the end of the do we were about 300 yards away from where it started, in our favour. Nobody claimed a result on the day but after seeing how far we pushed them, we felt we couldn't have done any more. Old Bill turned up and we scattered, mobbing up around the corner with no injuries to write home about.

We got in touch with them and asked them if they wanted it again on Bloomfield Road but they declined the offer, so we set off home, job done. As we were waiting for our train the police searched us and nicked one of ours for possession of an offensive weapon. This wasn't going to be the last encounter with Forest that the SYS were to have.

By the 2002-03 season, the SYS had grown to its top numbers. Following on from the Blackpool incident with Forest, lads from different areas of the town had started to travel with us, as other young lads now had faith in us. They trusted us when we said something was going to happen, whereas before they didn't believe us. The first game of the season was Brighton and we didn't expect anything because of the distance, but 1,300 travelled, so we figured there had to be some lads. During the match we were getting shit from lads inside the ground so we got together after the match and walked round past the Park View pub towards the coaches. As we reached them some lads were walking out and we called it on. A Brighton lad bounced into the road saying, "Come on Burnley," but before he had finished his sentence he was on his knees with his eyes rolling in the back of his head, being kicked. His mates waded in and the police came running with horses. No matter how big or small a reputation a firm had, the SYS were out looking for them.

The following week was an away game at Wolves, another

red-hot day, so the potential for alcohol-fuelled violence was high. The older lads were travelling on coaches so some went with them, but other SYS decided to go on the train. About fifteen of us met in Burnley in the morning and travelled via Manchester and Crewe, getting off at Stafford because of line works, intending to get coaches for the last leg. We decided to have a beer at Stafford but when it was time to leave, the coach drivers at the train station, who were all women, refused to take us, claiming they feared for their safety. Eventually we got a male driver laid on and he took us to the ground. We had a wander around, announced who we were, and some older Wolves took up the offer behind the Jack Harris stand before the OB got in the middle.

As we were pushed by the police towards the subway the lads outside the Wanderer and the other pub clocked us. One of our coaches had emptied outside there five minutes earlier and been involved in some aggro, but we didn't know so didn't realise they were pissed off. There were up to 100 geezers and they took some revenge on us youth lads all the way down to the away end, kicking lumps out of us.

After the match the SS and SYS battled with the police all the way up to the dual carriageway, probably the first time the youth have fought properly, punch for punch, with police. We found out later most of the police were Specials and didn't know what to do in that situation. One of the coach drivers refused to drive the lads back so seventy of us were escorted to the train station. Coaches laid on from there were pelted with bottles from a nearby pub. We were dropped of at Stafford, where we relieved the train station shop of all its beer, free of charge. Some cheeky sods complained they'd got bitter. There are some miserable bastards about.

The next away game was at Derby and twenty of us travelled by train. When we arrived, we saw that the Burnley police spotter was outside, so we went through some fire doors at the back of the station. We rang Derby and told them we were walking through an industrial estate and about to double back to the centre. They were only a few hundred yards from us in a pub but didn't want to make a move. We tried to get to them but, as we did, we got collared by a copper on a bike and put in a pub. They were again informed of where we were and we spotted them coming towards our pub, led by a fat older lad. We tried to get out but the police stopped us and put us on a coach to the ground. During the match a few SYS got thrown out for minor offences. One of them re-entered the Derby end and called it on at the front of the Derby stand on his own. It was very funny watching the Old Bill scratching their heads, wondering how he'd been able to do it. After the match Derby said they were on their way to the England match and we said we'd travel to Villa Park for them, but they declined our offer. Some of us went back to the pubs during the match but didn't see any lads, so we watched England on TV.

On the Tuesday we were playing Blackpool in the Cup. We waited for their comically named youth squad, the "Italian Hate Squad", at Manchester Road station and, as the train arrived, we steamed down the hill. We scattered them down Manchester Road, the flyover and into the cinema. In the end it hadn't really been worth the two-hour wait, especially when they later grassed us up to the police about an imaginary bottling incident. Two of our Youth lads decided to go in the away end and collared the same youth lads, only to be thrown out. After the match it went off with small mobs of lads and one IHS team got done over, losing their phones and credit cards. They paid for all our beers that night, cheers lads!

On the Saturday, we met with the old lads on Accrington Road waiting for a convoy of Stoke arriving in mini-buses. The police eventually stopped the buses a mile away and told the local paper that we had arranged to meet up with them to attack the Asians, which was total bullshit. When we were mistaken for Stoke and searched on the walk into town, a collection of CS, batons and other weapons were found behind the wall where we were searched, which was nothing to do with us. During the match, Stoke Youth attacked the stewards, put on a show and ripped up a few seats, but nothing major. After the match the Stoke that did manage to get out of the police segregation were battered behind the Wellington by a good mob of Burnley.

Bradford away was always going to be fun for the youth lads because of the number of Asians in the town. We mobbed up and got minibuses to Shipley, about ten minutes from Bradford. We mobbed up here with other SYS until somebody in a car got lippy and one of our lads attacked him. Stupid, I know, but some youth did have a temper on them. That was it. Old Bill turned up and put us on a bus all the way to the away pub in Bradford. A good 100 Burnley lads were escorted after the match but we knew a lot more Bradford were tailing our escort trying to get at us. This day was all about over the top policing as a few SYS were arrested for racist chanting.

Next, we were drawn away against Huddersfield in the Cup on a Tuesday night. Fifteen of us travelled in cars. When we left the ground after the game, we walked in a police escort with more than twenty Huddersfield youth lads. We gave them instructions to fuck the Old Bill off and warned them what was coming, but neither of us could lose the police and we were taken to our cars where the police informed us that whatever we'd told Huddersfield had shit them up and they didn't want it.

That month was the first time we travelled together to watch England, in Slovakia. An older lad had sorted it out for us because for most of the SYS it was their first and last England away game. This was one of the best experiences that the youth have had, with a good fifty Burnley there. There was no real trouble between Burnley and other mobs, but it went off with the Slovakian OB, with us running back and forth against these big twats with thee-foot batons and balaclavas. With tanks waiting outside, this was what it was all about and the adrenalin rush was amazing. The older lads who had battled in Rome, Poland, Greece and so on, might say things are different now, but places like Slovakia are as close as we are going to get to those days. This was our experience and we lived it. After the game we made our way back to Vienna, it kicked off and a bar got totalled, resulting in five lads, including two main SYS, getting locked up for a couple of weeks. This was an amazing trip and for most of us also our last, because we were subsequently banned.

The SYS have been to many England home games since, including Turkey at the Stadium of Light, where we battled with Newcastle and Forest. We have also been to all of the games at Manchester, the most eventful being against Wales, after which five SYS were raided for their alleged involvement in a battle with a suspected Stoke mob.

Although the two key youth lads remained locked up in Slovakia, we still took thirty youth lads in a 100-strong mob to Leicester on the Saturday. The police put us in the pub before the match and we didn't see many lads before or after. Other than some scuffles outside the away end, the only trouble was with police baton-charging us during the match when racist chants were being sung. The songs had become common and the police were pissed off because it showed their inability to do their job. At half time the concourse erupted when the police prematurely shut the bar, but that was end of the trouble.

Preston away was arguably the SYS's finest hour. A good 200 boys turned up at lunchtime for a Sunday evening kick-off. We were escorted from our pub all the way to the ground. As it was pissing down, they took us the long way round, hoping to dampen our spirits, but the move had the opposite effect and riled us up. SYS were drinking under the concourse when the OB shut the bar. This didn't go down too well and the police were first pelted with beer and coins, and then it went mad. The OB gassed everyone and two different lines of police were attacked. We returned to the front of the stand and almost immediately Gareth Taylor scored and our end erupted, with 7,000 going mad. We invaded the pitch, had a bit of fun and basically wound Preston up.

After the match the SYS were waiting for the older lads to mob up with them but then decided to do it themselves. They marched around to their end and called it on. A few disgusted looks later, some lads came out and fronted the SYS but took a good slapping, one receiving a serious kick to the head before he was clean out. After that it was mayhem all the way down Deepdale Road. The SYS ran at every lad they saw and we came out well on top. The OB were confused. They had been following our older lads, who had crossed the park, and with it being pitch black they were finding it hard to contain everyone, so instead of nicking people they just got stuck in themselves. We must have been fighting all the way down that road for about twenty minutes. Preston to this day deny that their lads were there, but an SYS lad who got carried away and took a wrong turning down a street ended up in the middle of their mob. Keeping his mouth shut, he just went along with them.

Following such an explosive start to the season, the Old Bill's arses had gone. They didn't know who all these youth lads were, and the older lads enjoyed this as it took the heat off them for a while and stretched the OB's resources. They had spent years gathering information on Burnley's hooligan element, and all of a sudden the SYS had scared the shit out of them because they had no idea who they were. This led to a promise by Chief Inspector Richard Morgan to rid Burnley of hooligans within three months. "I want to hurt hooligans and to let everyone else know that we are hurting them," he said. "We also want to build intelligence so that we can hurt them in the future. There is no escape for you." Hence Operation Fixture was born. A police document explained the reasons behind the operation:

A minority of racist thugs affiliating themselves to Burnley FC were posing a threat of disorder which reached far beyond the arena of football. The so-called "Burnley Youth" were engaging in organised and spontaneous violence on match days in and around town centre pubs where the negative impact on public reassurance was often dramatic. The wider threat included their potential involvement in the ever-present risk of large-scale disorder between Asian heritage and white offenders in the Burnley area. During the riots of summer 2001 a significant proportion of the white offenders were known football hooligans.

Analysis showed that the key to breaking the mechanics of the problem lay with changing offender behaviour of the fifty or sixty individuals that were at the heart of the problem. The overarching aim of the initiative was to make the environment safer for those in the town centre and around the ground on match days by reducing the risk.

A recent Lancaster University Research project on "Racism among under 25's in Pennine Division", found alarming levels of racism were "part of the wallpaper" among young people in the town and that metaphorical glass walls divided insular and polarised communities. In June 2001 widespread disorder occurred in the town instigated by criminal acts perpetrated by both white and Asian offenders. The white offenders were bigoted, racist thugs intent on creating more widespread disorder, many of whom were Burnley football hooligans who have right wing racist tendencies.

The town has an active football hooligan element that regularly engages in disorder on match days but also presents a real and present threat of racist disorder. This problem manifests itself in the following predictable behaviour patterns. Racist chanting at the match, including verbal and even physical attacks on Asian stewards, heavy drinking following the matches, leading to attacks on Asian taxi drivers and disturbances and assaults in public houses. It is a sad indictment but we had become accustomed to levels of football disorder and it is fair to say that there was a sense of inevitability about football violence. During the latter half of last season a new, more menacing group began to emerge. This group, considerably younger, named themselves the Burnley Youth. They would associate with the older hooligan group known as the Suicide Squad, but refused to abide by the rules of the game. This group were more determined and less affected by the police tactics, than their older colleagues. The police began to receive intelligence reports from members of the Suicide Squad who were genuinely concerned that their younger brethren were "out of control" and were travelling to away matches with weapons. The level of violence and the circumstances surrounding these incidents strongly supported these concerns. Operations costing thousands of pounds were now the norm.

Burnley FC have the dubious and unfortunate honour of being the unwilling host to a group of hooligans that are larger in number and more vociferous in their behaviour than clubs of a similar position in the league. The hooligan element at Burnley proudly refer to themselves as the Burnley Suicide Squad. The self-imposed title is derived from previous behaviour at away games where the single-minded involvement in violence against overwhelming odds could be described as suicidal. The name became synonymous with the group during the early 1980s and many of the original members are now in their late thirties and early forties, many are well known to the police and have a string of convictions for violence. This group was being replaced by a new generation of hooligans called the "Burnley Youth", who were evolving into a forceful group, less influenced by police tactics. There has always been a thread of mutual respect between rival groups and, if rival groups converged to fight but were prevented by police presence, both would leave with a degree of pride. Such circumstances were relatively common and the hooligans would return to their home town describing the failure to engage as having been "policed out". Internet comments, remarks to police spotters and confidential sources confirmed this. The Burnley youth seem to have missed this subtle but important rule of combat and refused to accept that police presence was a bar to violence, indeed there was evidence at the Preston North End game in 2003 that the police were the substitute targets of the group when an incident in the concourse within the ground at half time saw a sustained attack on two sets of police officers who were lured to the assistance of bar staff by the group's action, there were numerous incidents of disorder and twenty five arrests.

Burnley Offender profile.

Analysis of those known to engage in violence led us to some common factors. Burnley hooligans are predominantly racist, male, white, aged between sixteen and thirty-five, in gainful employment, few had any criminal convictions other than football-related disorder, many had no convictions at all and were unknown to the police prior to the initiative.

The racist threat.

The hooligan element at Burnley is overtly racist and holds extreme right wing views that present an ongoing threat of disorder in the town. Evidence to support this statement includes: the key involvement of known hooligans during the riots of 2001 and intelligence that Chelsea and Burnley hooligans agreed and planned a joint attack on Asians in Burnley in September 2001 during a friendly fixture. A major policing operation involving more than 300 officers was required to prevent disorder. There was Intelligence that Stoke and Burnley hooligans agreed and planned a joint attack on Asians in Burnley in 2002. A vicious, alcohol-fuelled attack on Asian taxi drivers in Burnley followed the Sweden game during the 2002 World Cup. There are racist and inflammatory entries on the Burnley hooligan website, "burnleylads.com", and there have been numerous arrests for racist chanting and a notable arrest of a *prominent member of the Burnley Youth for Nazi saluting at Tottenham fans. On arrest the offender's bedroom was found to be a shrine to the National Front and BNP.*

This shows the Old Bill clearly knew the problem, but how to deal with it was another story. They had devised a plan, a strategy to bring us down, and we knew that we were more vulnerable than them and less likely to win against them with all the money and resources they had, which made us more intent on causing trouble in the future, and carrying on the Suicide name.

A game against Tottenham was a big draw, even if they didn't bring a mob, but the next one was definitely headache tackle for the Old Bill: Manchester Utd at home. We expected the Red Army to come early and take the piss with their numbers in the pubs before the match, but were surprised that hardly any did. We had about fifty youth lads out together. Four of us got a call saying some United were walking through the town and we ran down and asked who they were. "We're Burnley," they lied. We knew they were lying so we walked towards them as more youth lads came out of the Swan. The United lads said there were too many OB around and asked where they should go for a beer. We told them to make their way to the Walkabout and we would follow. We took seven down to call it on but they said that they didn't want it before the game and were content to wait until afterwards. We told them to go to the Litten Tree when the game was over.

Eighty of them arrived without police and ran down the main street shouting "Man Yoo". To make it worse, no SS had got there in time. They could have taken the piss. Once we got our act together we fronted what was about but the moment had gone and we have to hold our hands up, we were unprepared. Burnley's organisation was shown up for what it was against a quality outfit. No one has matched them at Turf since.

On December 7, Forest came to Turf. We had already had run-ins and we knew some of their lads, who were good youth lads, even though they had fucked us about in the past. We knew they were the same as us and we needed to be around because they'd come and probably be tooled up. Most of the day's events can only be told by someone who was there, not people who read the papers or hear shit in the boozer. They had told us they were coming, again on their own coach, so we suggested they came a different way from normal and drank in a certain place, and we'd meet them. So we faxed their top lad a detailed map and directions of a backdoor route into Burnley, which would probably take them an extra half hour, but where there was never any OB. They agreed but it went wrong again. They went a different way and claimed their coach was stopped en route, which was not surprising the route they took. We thought that part of the day was over and had a beer in town, but when we went into Yates's there were quite a few unfamiliar youth faces. It was clear they were Forest young lads and we thought they'd pulled a sly one.

We were outnumbered and we later found out they were being abusive and aggressive to anyone who looked their way. We told them where the door was and who would be leaving. They refused and a scuffle occurred in the door, which resulted in lads on both sides being punched. We chased them out but stopped at the entrance. They stopped about forty yards away and turned back. A glass was thrown on the floor, then a Bud bottle came through the air at us. They were the first ones to launch glasses so we charged at them and one of our lads caught one of theirs with a glass. He jumped up and ran off with his mates. We charged them down again, they scattered and we left it.

Their lad had apparently collapsed further down the road. We got a call saying that their coach was on its way down Todmorden Road and we went round to see it get taken past in an escort, half-full. The injured lad, Nathan Shaw, fell into a coma, and the following day, in Preston Royal Infirmary, he died. It was a sad day, as none of this was meant to happen and you never like to see anyone die. However the shit that we received from Internet cyber warriors was so strong that the youth chose to show no remorse for the incident and we defended our own to the hilt, bar a couple of little snakes who opened their mouths. This sort of thing happens everywhere in the country, every hour in every town and city in England on a night out, especially in Burnley. Any lads who can say they haven't seen a fight between two sets of lads using weapons is lying. As I said, it was a very unfortunate accident, but it could easily have been the other way around.

Oddly enough, the most understanding lads we talked to were FNS, who were sympathetic towards the situation and anybody else who was there will understand. We didn't find out till the next day the lad had died and the police investigation concluded with one of our youth lads charged with murder and later sentenced for manslaughter.

After the Forest incident, the youth scene started to die down, mainly because a lot of lads started to get nicked and banned, and the murder case was still ongoing. We were still going but in smaller numbers. The police's failings had been highlighted and they had to be seen to be doing things. The Old Bill devised a "top ten hit list" of people they wanted to hurt the most and the bans that these youth lads received were extremely harsh. They were banned from pubs in Burnley, not only on match days but every day of the week, banned from being within three miles of any ground Burnley or England play at, with that distance shortened for other clubs to a mile and a half, and banned from using a train when Burnley or England play. They received weekly home visits to disrupt their home lives, and Anti-Social Behaviour Orders (ASBOs) were enforced to stop people associating with each other. Barristers were employed by Lancashire Constabulary to compile cases against SYS lads so that bans could be secured quickly, because with the Euro Championships in Portugal fast approaching, they feared the worst. The Chief Inspector's claims in the paper earlier in the season that he'd rid Burnley of its hooligan problems within three months had been embarrassed. Despite the strict regulations put in place, the SYS was still performing.

Nothing major happened until the end of the season. Small numbers travelled to Forest but found it tame, considering what had happened. A small number went to Sheffield Wednesday but their youth never turned up. We took two minibuses to QPR for a cup match against Fulham but found no resistance. Loads of lads went to Watford in the quarter final of the FA Cup but again found no resistance.

But for the last home game of the season, Sheffield Wed came with thousands. Plenty of lads came into town and the police engineered it so that they were drinking in a pub next to the pub we were in. It was a set-up. The Old Bill wanted it to go off so they could then fuck everyone over but, apart from skirmishes, it didn't happen. After the match mobs of Burnley searched for the Yorkshire lads and some landed on two minibuses going round the roundabout at Gala Bingo. They gave the SYS shit, failing to realise that the traffic lights, recently put in 100 yards up the road, were changing to red. Burnley steamed up the road, the back doors opened and we were showered with cans and bottles. The lads were game as fuck. One came running at us with his belt wrapped round his fist, swinging the buckle. As one followed through after hitting one of our youth lads, he got banged in the face, fell and was kicked in. We were giving it to them as another minibus of their lads came running down, but more Burnley arrived and steamed into them. The drivers of the minibuses started to go without their passengers, and as the lads chased their vehicles, we chased them, showering them with anything we could find on the road, as ten police chased us. It was like a Benny Hill sketch. We were still getting into them when they got to the minibuses and the police had caught up. The police nicked no-one and told us to fuck off into town.

On the same day, another sad incident happened in the Yates's where the Forest lad had been killed. Sitting in the beer garden, a local lad threw an ashtray over the wall at the police. It hit the wall, bounced off, and hit and killed an old lady. We got shit for it because it happened when the minibus incident was going off. This just added to the Old Bill's resentment towards young white lads, especially on match days. They had probably had the busiest twelve to eighteen months in recent years, along with two deaths linked with football. Probably only Cardiff and Millwall had to put up with anything like the grief we were getting at the time.

For the first away game of the 2003/04 season, we took two minibuses of mainly youth lads from Padiham to West Brom, but got fucked off home by the police for having beer on the bus. This led to a piss-up nearby and a bit of banter with some Walsall lads until some Wolves turned up, but the Old Bill were on hand to stop any disorder. Nothing really happened in the next season until we played West Ham away in October. For the youth lads it was the first time we'd played West Ham and they wanted to see what a trip to east London was like. There were quite a lot of youth lads among the 120 that arrived by train and limo before eleven o'clock. With no OB, we moved to Whitechapel, where we knew they drank on some match days. With all the blacks around something had to happen and the lads got stuck into the stalls and Pakis. Some moved up to the ground, but most got collared by the OB and escorted through the back streets to the ground. Nothing major could have gone off with all the police and the only lads we saw were at the station after the match. We tried coming through the police but the horses and dogs pushed us into the station. Loads stayed to have a look at the strip bars and missed the train. Missing the train became a regular event for the youth lads when travelling to London, resulting in them sleeping rough in London, Liverpool, Birmingham, and Manchester or as close to home as you could get. When they came up here a group of lads were walking past the Litten Tree when West Ham came out of a kebab shop. Only one older lad noticed them, and they called it on after most of our lads had walked past. Our lad called for everyone to get into them and they didn't need to be told twice. Kebab meat was everywhere and two of their lads were knocked clean out. A few lads got nicked for it, but due to bad lighting ruining the CCTV outside the boozer, all charges were dropped.

The next time we went to Bradford there were at least 200 Burnley out but we just drank around town all day with no grief. At some point we were with one of their lads, friendly with Burnley from England trips. The away end was full to capacity as thousands of Burnley had made the short trip over the Pennines, so a couple of youth lads accompanied by an older lad entered the home end. The Bradford lot were shouting the usual banter at Burnley when the youth lads turned around and made themselves known. A gap opened up but no-one made a move and the Old Bill ended up going in and dragging the lads out. About an hour or so after the game we were escorted to the train station and put on a train. It was, however, a pretty relaxed escort and a handful of us decided to lose it and go for another beer. As we walked over the square we saw two lads being chased by about ten. We realised that they were chasing Burnley so we ran over and shouted them to turn around. There were only five of us but as we steamed into them from the back we took a couple out straight away. As they all turned we realised that they were youth we had been drinking with earlier. They ran towards us but none of them would come further forward than one big lad. They were sussed:

attack him and they would back off. It worked, but the thing was, we couldn't drop him. One lad gave him a dig and straight after another one smashed a traffic cone into the side of his head but he stayed upright. Their arses went a bit and they started muttering something about CCTV and fucked off. We walked to a taxi rank and set off home.

The 2004/05 season promised to have a couple of tasty games but, as usual nowadays, the OB have been quite on top. Looking at Division One teams you start thinking that with Wigan, Sunderland, Derby, Preston, Reading, West Ham, Sheffield Utd, Millwall, Leeds, Stoke, Wolves, Leicester, Plymouth, Cardiff, Coventry, and Forest it would be going off seriously every game of the season. Most have a youth mob and all have a decent enough set of older lads, but no-one seems to be travelling to Burnley. Like most mobs, we've not been going everywhere because of the police crackdown. We have more than seventy lads on full bans, not allowed near the ground or town, some aren't even allowed to travel on the train on match days or even be in licensed premises. Is this a police state? The country's minutes away from attack from terrorists, and the Government and police forces are spending large amounts on stopping like-minded lads fight each other. The reason: easy arrest figures and the papers that sell by spreading fear of the "English disease".

Although the OB have been on top, we have had some dancing. Apart from small groups of young lads from Stoke and Villa in the Cup who weren't up to it, and a big mob of Leeds who were heavily escorted to and from the ground, after choosing to stay on the early train to Accy instead of coming into town, there have been a couple of offs at Turf. Some Cardiff came in a minibus and bumped into five yo-yos and three SYS outside the cricket field on the way to the away end. As the yo-yos and the SYS walked round the corner, the Soul Crew steamed into them. There was a small do for a couple of minutes before the police, who were following our lads, came running in from behind. Reports by some Soul Crew claiming to have run equal numbers of mid-twenties Burnley was bollocks; there were eight Burnley, none over twenty, and nobody lost any teeth. Fair play though, we got done. A mob of SYS also did a minibus of Sunderland but, on performance, it may not have been their main lads. Our youth called it on, the lads accepted and it went off for about five minutes before the OB horses came running in.

Away from home we, like most, haven't travelled much with all the bans. We took more than 100 to Leeds for a night match. As some of the late minibuses arrived at the pub where we were drinking in Headingley, the football spotters turned up. We tried to walk to town with eighty lads, but got collared by police. About fifty got into town with the ones who came on the train and in cars, only to be put in a pub by the police. There was an off outside with a mob of mixed Burnley with a small mob of Leeds, with us fucking them off. Then we were bussed to the ground and there was some scuffling outside. The boys did us proud, beating them 2–1, and we steamed out into the road afterwards, calling it on with what was about, which wasn't a lot. Small offs were going everywhere with the OB unable to hold everyone in the dark. Some Leeds tried having a do at the top of the coach park but were small in number and got chased off by the police. Burnley steamed some lads near the McDonalds and outside the pub across from the away end, and a large mob of Burnley fronted some Leeds outside the club shop. If Leeds had got it together it could have been a quality night, but they didn't.

On February 1, the news Burnley OB least wanted was on TV: the FA Cup fifth-round draw put Burnley against Bastards at Turf. Most lads thought Bastards wouldn't turn up and the OB would have it under control. But to everyone's surprise Bastards brought a mob of 150 on the train. Not surprisingly, it contained fewer than 100 proper lads and was the last possible train they could come on, arriving in Burnley ten minutes into the game. Mobs of Burnley met up and searched for any that came in cars and minibuses. Some were given a slap inside and around the ground. Even more surprisingly, Burnley got a draw and the OB had to plan for the replay nine days later. All day, Blackburn claimed that if we could get to Accrington they would turn up. We managed to get more than 100 there a couple of hours after the game; Blackburn managed nil.

For the away match we met at lunchtime in Burnley, took hundreds over and had about 200 drinking in their town centre. More than thirty Burnley were arrested, mainly for being drunk and disorderly, however, a couple were charged with violent disorder, and a few with police assault.

Our trip to Sheffield United was cut short when we stopped for a beer in Rotherham, who were playing QPR at home. One wanker came into the pub where we were drinking and told us the boys were coming. Fair play, he started bouncing around and fucked off when someone took up the offer. But he ran out and grassed us up to the OB. Like our season, our day was over and we were escorted back to Lancashire by some very happy OB.

Although the OB have done well in controlling our mob, we're still around, and no one will come and take too many liberties, especially if we know they're coming. During the first couple of seasons we were everywhere and were regarded as one of the main youth mobs in the country, mainly because we turned out for everyone, even if we only went in small numbers. Whether you were Forest or Crewe, some of us would be looking for it. Travelling in small numbers, being cheeky bastards and usually doing the business, that was us. We made a big impression and still make an impression, recently taking over 100 to Manchester for the Wales game and performing. It is more than three years on from when Inspector Richard

Morgan decided he was going to single-handedly eradicate hooligans from Burnley's streets, and in that time there have been two deaths and football disorder is still commonplace in Burnley on a Saturday. We just can't wait for your funding to be withdrawn, then normal service will be resumed, it's only a matter of time. Do us all a favour and take note, we will not go away. It's part of our way of life, part of our culture.

The Operation Fixture file is available at http://www.popcenter.org/Library/Goldstein/2003/03-55.pdf

WHY

Why do I do it? Because I fucking love it. Some people are born to be artists. Some are born to be great footballers. Some of us are born to be football hooligans. It's in my heart and runs through my veins. I don't give a fuck about the kicking and the jail sentences, they're occupational hazards. If you're bothered about being nicked at football, you shouldn't go. The police have a job to do, it's a game of cat and mouse between us. It's up to us to evade them. Most times they are on top, but when they aren't it's brilliant, mob against mob, two sets of lads wanting to fight each other, trying to prove who's the best. The adrenalin rush, the best drug in the world, you can't beat it.

I'm proud to be a hooligan. A lot of people out there think we are scum. Well I don't give a fuck about their point of view. After the Burnley riots I was classed as a nazi who voted BNP. I've never voted in my life, and I definitely wouldn't vote for the BNP because I'm not British, I'm English. It's about time we had an English National Party; the Welsh and Scots have their own national parties so why should we be any different. Is it wrong to display our national flag? Some people in our government think it is. They don't want us to have an identity. Well, I've got a message for them: you'll never take England out of the English, and you'll never take the hooligan out of me.